To Sit on the Earth

THE FRENCH LIST

TOBIE NATHAN

To Sit on the Earth

A MEMOIR

Translated by

JOYCE ZONANA

with

JANET LEE

LONDON NEW YORK CALCUTTA

PAP
TAGORE

The work is published with the support of the
Publication Assistance Programmes of the Institut français

Seagull Books, 2024

First published in French as *Ethno-Roman* by Tobie Nathan
© Éditions Grasset & Fasquelle, 2012

First published in English translation by Seagull Books, 2024

English translation © Joyce Zonana, 2024

ISBN   978 1 8030 9 391 8

British Library Cataloguing-in-Publication Data
A catalogue record for this book is available from the British Library

Typeset at Seagull Books, Calcutta, India
Printed and bound in the USA by Integrated Books International

CONTENTS

For Lord Edwin

'And he [. . .] bowed himself to the ground seven times
until he came near to his brother.'

GENESIS 33:3

1

My Name Is Tobie Nathan

In truth, I was born after my birth. I was a little late arriving in my
country, France. It was 1958, the year De Gaulle came to power. I
was ten, already formed, so to speak. The French were just coming
out of the war; we were coming out of Egypt, having arrived
directly from Antiquity. I did not understand the atmosphere of
sorrow and recrimination prevailing then in France. My parents
had been neither deportees, nor collaborators, nor black marketeers;
and certainly not those spineless calves the General was forever
railing against. They were from elsewhere, and remained absorbed
by the concerns of that distant world. They read the papers, not to
learn the price of butter but to glean news of Khrushchev or
Bulganin, the Soviet leaders who'd threatened the French and
the British during the Suez Crisis that led to our expulsion from
Egypt.

When I arrived in France, everyone had but one thing on their
minds: to settle the war's accounts. We French, I've since learnt,
cling stubbornly to our reasons: our reasons for having been

Pétainist; our reasons for being Communist; our reasons for being pacifist. Back then, you could still find a bit of everything. My friend Jean-Loup, today a prominent reporter for a major French weekly, would point to his father's frail legs: 'It's Buchenwald,' he'd say. In all other respects, his father was fully recovered. Only his legs remained as frail as they'd been when he returned from the camp. We were eleven, maybe twelve years old; we shared our first surprises, our first stirrings of interest in girls. To me, he was France; and whenever he invited me over, I studied his family, a family of French people. They studied me too. I was the stranger they were eager to know. They were from Charente; that's what they were like. At their house, everyone asked hundreds of questions.

I encountered France the moment I arrived, at the same time as I discovered myself. I intend to give the word 'discover' a double meaning: at once to dis-robe, to show oneself, and also to learn, to recognize, one's own strangeness. I've always been strange to myself, having come to believe, over time, that our one true task as humans is to explore our hidden corners, to come to terms with our own particularity.

It was the eve of Pesach, the Jewish Passover, a beautiful day as I recall. That was another discovery, that in this country a beautiful day was remarkable. The schoolmaster, 'Mr M' (I'd use his full name, but it's best not to disturb the sleep of the dead)—crisply pleated grey smock, slicked-back hair, cynical, refined—interrupted the lesson five or ten minutes before the hour. An unscripted moment, an invitation to speak freely. Migrants should beware: there's no such thing as free speech. When it's free, your speech condemns you all the more. I raised my hand.

2

'Sir, I will be absent tomorrow. I won't be coming to school.'

'Really?' he asked. 'And why is that?'

'Sir, it's Passover. We're going to do the Haggadah!'

The class was momentarily stunned. Then the other students perked up, peering anxiously at the master to learn what to think. No one in this small fourth-grade Gennevilliers classroom had the least idea of what the Haggadah might be. Nor for that matter did Mr M, who decided to take this opportunity to make fun of me. 'You won't be coming tomorrow?' he repeated. 'Is that so? Oh, so you're going to bounce *ah-dah-dah* on your daddy's knees?' he jeered, echoing the words and melody of a common children's ditty, *Ah-dah-dah sur mon bidet.* He'd set the tone. A Lacanian before his time, he'd delivered his joke flatly, without cracking a smile; he wanted to show he could be funny. An admirer of Sacha Guitry, he was surely also a collaborator during the war. The message had been clear. The master had sounded the note of derision, and the students obeyed. They burst into laughter. During the years that followed, I've often dreamt about Mr M. I count him as among my initiators, those after whom I was never as I had been before. I often wondered—I still do—what possessed me to parade my Jewish particularity when no one had questioned me. And this despite the warning of a friend, also Jewish, oddly mature: 'You're in France now, keep your mouth shut. When you're Jewish, you hide it.' I didn't take heed. Humans are like monkeys. They cannot simply be told to beware. They need cries of pain to be convinced of danger.

Twelve years later, in the same town of Gennevilliers, on the tenth of November, my birthday, I wrote in my journal these few

3

words that I still perfectly recall: 'I'm twenty-two years old, I'm in love, and De Gaulle is dead.' I'd just become a Frenchman.

Every year, Jews celebrate Passover to commemorate the biblical Exodus from Egypt. I remember my silent perplexity as a child in Cairo during the festival. We were joyful, gathered as a family. As she did every year, my mother took out the special tableware from the cupboards: square plates and strange round spoons. Laughter, religious songs, jokes, learned discussions. 'God, blessed be He, delivered us from slavery. He led us out of Egypt.' 'That's what we commemorate this week.' If He'd led us out of Egypt, then what were we doing still there? And why were we so happy? I will always regret never having asked the questions that so tormented me back then. In 1958, in that Gennevilliers classroom, with that Mr M who reeked of the good old prewar anti-Semitism, I began to think that Egypt was not back there but right here, in France, and that God had led us not out of it but right into the lion's den. Instead of concealing my Jewishness as my friend had advised, I made matters worse by proclaiming it at every turn. Oh well, that's how I am. People call me a provocateur. In truth, it's a matter of placing too much emphasis on the facts. I display what I should hide. Later, as an insolent, unruly lycée student, I was routinely taken to task. The headmaster would grab me by the lapels: 'What's your name, young man?'

'My name is Tobie Nathan, sir. Tobie, as in the Bible, Nathan, as in the Bible.'

* * *

I turned twenty in 1968. I was a student in sociology at the Sorbonne. Mornings, I caught the train at Garges-Sarcelles Station. In winter, it was ice cold on the platform where vagrants wandered aimlessly. I wore the old coat, my pride and joy, that had belonged to my brother in Egypt, with a tweed cap pulled down to my ears and my nose buried in a long black scarf. She took the same train. She was also on her way to the Sorbonne, where she was studying English literature. She had a lively face, round eyes, a knitted wool cap with a pompom and a nose reddened by the cold. She always lugged around a huge white teddy bear—on the train, at the university, in the bistro—a teddy bear she nuzzled constantly as she read her Shakespeare. We climbed onto the same carriage. We looked at each other silently, each sensing the other's intensity. She lived in Sarcelles, the heart of the district, its core; I lived in Garges-lès-Gonesses, the housing project of the lost. One winter evening, with my nighttime philosopher-classmates, I wandered from one group of friends to the next, from one apartment to another, from glass of cheap whiskey to glass of mulled wine. We were hungry for thought and adventure. We all ended up at her place. She and I gazed at each other, smiling in recognition: the morning train, the tweed cap, the white teddy bear. We flirted, then talked. After the others had left, we were still talking. Her father was asleep in the back room. And her mother? She'd died not long before, a little more than a year, or two perhaps. Her name? Anna Langfus. Surprise. I knew her. We'd met only once, when I was thirteen or fourteen. Having just won the Prix Goncourt for her novel, *The Lost Shore*, she was already living in Sarcelles. My family had recently left the housing project in Gennevilliers, with the result

5

that in one day I'd lost my friends, that communal atmosphere and my cat, fierce tiger of the banlieues. Missing my Egyptian neighbours and community, and not especially drawn to my new environment, I'd written my first novel, typed one summer on an old Remington. I'd confided in the Sarcelles bookseller. 'You've written a novel?' he exclaimed. 'A real novel?' Indeed, I had. Two hundred pages, the tale of a lovesick adolescent, misunderstood, who ends up committing suicide—it might have been titled *The Sorrows of Young Tobie.* 'And you want people to read it, don't you?' The bookseller encouraged me to contact Anna Langfus. She arranged for us to meet at a bistro near the railway station. A small, fragile woman with huge black eyes, deep as Loch Ness, her brows furrowed by acute suffering. I spoke to her about my book. She listened, promised to read it, gave me her phone number. Of course, I had no other copy, merely a few draft pages. Abashed at my own temerity, I waited quite a while—six months or more—before calling her again. 'Yes,' she told me, she'd read it, had liked it, found it interesting and moving. 'It's a start,' she'd added, 'now you need to work, to work a great deal.' From this I drew two conclusions: first, that I would never publish this book; second, that I was a writer. Right then and there, on the first page of my little datebook, I wrote, 'Tobie Nathan, writer.' I often told myself that I would call her again to retrieve my manuscript, but I kept stalling. During those periods of hesitation, I read her novel that had won the prize. She was the first woman to write about the Shoah, in which her parents had disappeared and she had been brutally tortured by the Gestapo, forced to watch her husband's execution. I was deeply moved. I gave the book to my mother who three years earlier had been taken by André Schwarz-Bart's *The Last of the Just*—another book about the Shoah that had won the Prix Goncourt. That's when I finally stopped hesitating. I called Anna Langfus again. When no one answered, I contacted the bookseller, only to learn that she'd died suddenly of a heart attack. My novel had disappeared. I decided to let it go. And now here was her daughter, surfacing in my life by chance, and here I was in her apartment, stretched out on the sofa. Maria told me that the things in her mother's office had remained just as she'd left them. If my manuscript was in the apartment, it had to be there. But it was all such a mess, so many papers. She promised to search for it.

* * *

Stepping back:

Gennevilliers during my adolescence. At that time in France, if you had any wherewithal, you were a Communist. Gennevilliers was Communist. In the course of no more than a few decades, French villages had been emptied. Farmers' children had become factory workers, losing the almost visceral connection they'd had with both the Church and the pagan past: the feasts for the dead in November, the fires of St John at midsummer. I did not know it then, but in these working-class suburbs, nearly everyone was an immigrant: some from a province, a village in France; others from Poland, Italy, Portugal, and already quite a few from Algeria. The Communist Party offered these immigrants from the interior a substitute for the culture they'd abandoned when they left the countryside. Composite successors of priests and schoolmasters, the Party's cadres had inherited from both. In Gennevilliers, still untouched by de-Stalinization, they adhered to the Soviet system. They enrolled their school-age children in summer camps modelled on the komsomol. Teenagers were encouraged to attend Party-sponsored get-togethers on Thursdays and Sundays, where the organizers sought to enlist them in the Communist Youth. The path was laid out. Soon it would be the union, the CGT—the General Confederation of Labour—and, at the end of the road, the apotheosis: formal Party membership. I have to admit that this structure, clearly designed to entrap us, gave us something to hold on to, an armature of sorts. The art of living well consisted in frequenting the Communists while not fully submitting to them. Back then, Communists were more prudish than priests. But in the 'People's House', girls were bold and bountiful. They made it worthwhile to attend Marxist mass. I spent a good deal of time in the Gennevilliers Library, a large, well-kept building overflowing with carefully arranged books. I went through them systematically. Bertolt Brecht: I read all his theatre pieces; Anouilh: play after play; Giraudoux ('Why do you want to read Giraudoux and Montherlant?' the librarian would challenge); Sartre: especially the plays and novels. ('Do you really want to read Sartre, my boy? He's a controversial author, you know. Wouldn't you rather have a book by Aragon?') As the poor often do, I began at the end, with the most recent writers first. Céline: all they had was *Journey to the End of the Night*. What about his other books? 'You're too young for them,' the librarian assured me. I was seized by a passion for Oscar Wilde, whose caustic wit and art of paradox I adored. 'If you keep reading Wilde, I'll have to tell your parents,' the librarian warned. The people had to learn that only Communists could be good scientists or great writers. I saw this constant proselytizing as an insult. It defined those to whom it was addressed as infirm. 'You've lost God and the traditions of your ancestors. You'll accept without question our substitutes and, what's more, you'll thank us!' Communists have always thought of the people as a pack of orphans.

At the age of nine or ten, on our way to the neighbourhood school, late as always, we would recite the Shemah, the Jewish credo, as we ran, because we hadn't had time to say our prayers before leaving. I still have it by heart. Not really knowing why, I recited it again on several occasions: in Brazil, in an automobile hurtling down a mountainside at 50 miles per hour; in Burundi, in the rain, under a barrage of rockets; and most recently in Guinea, trapped in a huge riot after Dadis Cambara had been shot in the head by his aide-de-camp, 'Toumba' Diakite. I escaped each time without a scratch. I had not lost God; I still haven't.

One day, my brother came home from the library with two books he promptly hid in the back of a closet: *The Seducer's Handbook* (I no longer remember the author's name) and *Three Essays on the Theory of Sexuality* by Sigmund Freud. Naturally, I devoured them both. *The Seducer's Handbook* was not very good. It offered strategies—body language, ways to dress, things to say—to seduce girls. I immediately tried them, to no avail. Freud's book, on the other hand, proved more useful. I was fifteen, and he spoke in detail about the one subject of any interest to me, the subject that consumed every waking moment of my adolescent thought: sex. And Freud wrote of sex with authority, as a scientist and a scholar. 'We have discovered . . . thus we know'; 'Science has established,' etc. He provided answers to all the questions I hadn't even thought to ask. My friends and I were in the grips of an overweening sexuality, a fierce sexuality of resistance to the priests' ideology, our teachers' absurd morality, the Party militants. To seduce! To renew the experience, to seduce again, with a new girl, and then another, to see if what we'd felt depended on the partner; still another, with whom to go further than with the last, in a tireless quest for a liberation to come, complete, definitive. Who knew that through this systematic exploration of our sensations, our post-war generation was laying the groundwork for the Revolution of May 68? We accosted girls on the street, at the movies, so numerous back then, at parties, at dances, everywhere, whenever possible. We made it a point of pride never to miss an opportunity. The girls seemed less developed than the boys in this long march towards liberation. Many resisted our advances, others gathered in pathetic venues—the Jesus groups, afternoons at the priest's. As a result, there were fewer of them available to join our games. Privation made us democratic. We tried to seduce them all, those we found attractive as well as those we found less so. Flirtations of an afternoon or an evening, stolen moments, like those casual encounters in the darkness of the neighbourhood cinema, which hung suspended on the implicit promise of meeting there again the following Sunday. I'm certain not one of us has forgotten.

2010: a brief dialogue in a chatroom with a classmate from the lycée, re-encountered by chance on the Internet. I write: 'I don't know if you remember me, sophomore year at the lycée in Asnières.' 'I haven't forgotten a thing,' she replies. 'We fooled around one afternoon at the Comédie Française, and missed all of Claudel's *The Satin Slipper*. How could I forget?'

Some relationships were platonic, little more than an extended kiss, demure strolls hand in hand. Others were more enterprising, protected by night, in the darkness of cellars or the cinema. Truffaut, in his saga of Antoine Doinel, would later film this tireless exploration of sexuality—ours! This was the context within which I read Freud for the first time. I immediately embraced him. To me, he offered a philosophic choice—mine! I glorified sexuality, the unconquerable force within us in service of a transcendent end. I saw that without it, we would be brute beasts or egoists. And every day, life showed me that, without sexual tension, we would become exactly what our educators—the schoolmasters, the Communists, all sorts of priests assailing us from all sides—wanted us to be: blank slates. This tyrannical tension that forced you always to seek another, never satisfied with the one you had. I recognized it, as did all my friends, my fellow rovers through the neighbour-hood streets in a quest for the object's consent. We were obsessed by sex—Freud was too. He'd made it the cornerstone of his work; it imposed itself on us and completely occupied our minds. In Freud's books, I found descriptions of sexual behaviours I'd had only an inkling of, without really knowing. Homosexuality, for example. I read the promise made to homosexuals in *Three Essays on the Theory of Sexuality*, that they would become heterosexual after treatment. Today everyone knows this is bunk. What Freud called 'deviations' or 'perversions' are nothing other than variations on the expression of desire. The exhibitionism and voyeurism in Sartre's novels, also the masochism; the old-fashioned thrill of shoe fetish-ism in Buñuel's *Diary of a Chambermaid*; even Krafft-Ebing's infa-mous book, which we could find only in sex shops, frustrated that

11

the most salacious passages had to be translated from the Latin. I remain convinced that Freud is best read by adolescents. He corresponds so well to their interests. I treated his works as I had the others, Wilde, Brecht, Sartre: I read them systematically, everything I could get my hands on in the municipal libraries. (Not all of Freud's texts had been translated into French by then, far from it!)

I read Freud, reading and rereading the difficult parts. I shared this passion with my friends, to such an extent that by the age of eighteen I'd become a sort of expert. I no longer had a choice: I would become a psychoanalyst—I already was one! Not one of my friends back then was spared this wild obsession. We did not tackle the subject of sex head on; Freud enabled us to confront our adolescent desires behind the mask of science. The more we explored this crude, arrogant theory, the more we were possessed by the eagerness to experiment. I still wonder about this passion that seized these first-generation children born outside France, under pressure to adapt to a world they did not know. Fundamentally, psychoanalysis was for our little group of immigrants what boxing was for Italians in the thirties, what rap and slam poetry are today for the children of the banlieues: a way to plunge directly into the heart of society. Psychoanalysis was just taking off in France. A few philosophers, Sartre and de Beauvoir for example, embraced it. But the Communists fiercely opposed it, and theirs was the dominant voice. The discipline was not taught at university. The popular press made fun of it. You could read a few works by French psychoanalysts—Laforgue or d'Allendy—but, pale imitations of the Freudian texts, they seemed insipid to us. Everything was yet to be constructed. For we migrants, to specialize in a discipline as it was taking shape was to plunge immediately into the thick of things, to make up for, in only a few years, our millennial, existential, delay.

Sylvain was a year older than me. He too was born in Egypt, he too had landed in the cité Claude-Debussy, he too was passionate about psychoanalysis. With hair as curly as a Shetland sheep, with the big eyes of a squirrel, he would speak as if the words were coming from deep within. He'd gone from dreams of nuclear physics and building rockets like those of Werner von Braun to dreams of the demiurge of mental functioning. I was reading Freud; he always referred to a Jungian, Pierre Daco, author of *The Triumphs of Psychoanalysis*, a sort of manual for innocents of the poor banlieues. Together we'd begun to go through Freud's texts. To anyone who took the trouble to read them, they provided both the theory and the method. We didn't know then that most of Freud's 'cases' were bogus—we would only begin to discover this some twenty years later. To apply the prescribed techniques did not seem beyond our means. After all, what would it take? Two willing participants, a quiet room, some time. We began with dreams. But how would we know if our interpretations were valid? To practise psychoanalysis, you must identify a symptom, apply Freud's methods and observe the symptom's disappearance. Thus Sylvain and I decided to establish veritable sessions of psychoanalysis. He would be the patient first; and when we'd finished with him, I would take his place on the couch. And we did it! We had to find symptoms; we found them. We had to set ground rules and adhere to them. We weren't even nineteen. Armed with our youthful erudition, guided by our common passion, we invented a 'mutual psychoanalysis'. I cannot say what was the effect of this first pass. But we were left with a familiarity with psychoanalysis, like that of people who know God because they attended Mass as children. We would both go on to became psychoanalysts. We paid our dues—completing our degrees at the university, undergoing analyses with members of recognized professional societies. Our training was certified by our respective psychoanalytic institutes. Our paths diverged and we did not attend the same schools. But the experience we'd shared remained the inaugural moment, like the first cigarette smoked in secret.

We also organized a seminar. Sometimes seven or eight of us gathered, but the core group consisted of four boys, all the same age. There were of course Sylvain and I, Isaac, another immigrant from Egypt who'd ended up at the Cité Claude-Debussy, and Philippe, a tall blonde, an immigrant from Oise. Sylvain and I both became psychologists and psychoanalysts; Isaac and Philippe became psychiatrists and psychoanalysts. Most of the time, Isaac hosted us in his two-room apartment in a workers' housing project in Gennevilliers. At twenty, he was already married, a shotgun wedding, as still existed back then, imposed when he got his sweetheart of the moment pregnant. He could not abandon her, partly because his young wife, the charming Hélène of the sky-blue eyes, was also a refugee from Egypt. Her family had taken a detour through the US and Canada before settling in Gennevilliers. The child they had together, the little Michel, was as beautiful as an angel; as he grew up, he became a brilliant student. Children of free love, unfettered by rules and regulations, often prove to be gifts from God. We met every Sunday evening for sessions that rarely lasted less than six hours. Together, we made up for the poverty of university education.

I've never studied so seriously, with so much dedication and passion, as during those years of mutual apprenticeship. Patiently, week after week, we excavated the same channel. We could recite whole passages of Freud by heart. Being our own teachers, we were not subject to the professors' tyranny. What drove us was the search for a way to actualize what was brewing in our minds. We became militant. Society, we concluded, was suffering from sexual repression. Having just personally experienced the deprivation of adolescence, we were thoroughly convinced that the liberation to come would be sexual, and would produce, through a sort of mechanical necessity, the release of sexual tension. We'd been captivated by Wilhelm Reich's little book, *The Sexual Struggle of Youth*, a polemic we passed around secretly—a powerful, strange book, a sort of political manifesto grounded in psychoanalytic theory, urging young people to rebel against the sexual repression imposed by teachers, religious authorities, political organizations. Wilhelm Reich, mad scholar from the thirties, member of the German Communist Party in an era when you had to take a stand against the Nazi thugs in Berlin. A 'green' militant before his time, he would appear at meetings of the International Psychoanalytic Association in his Scout's uniform, a sword at his side. I loved the liberties he took with the priestly strictures of psychoanalysis, declaring to anyone who would listen that he did not rule out sexual relations with patients. He even went so far as to say, 'It's better to sleep with your patients, as I do, than to masturbate behind their backs, as you do.' Reich fascinated us, not because of the originality of his thought, but because of his passion for freedom. We also dove into Marx, and nearly drowned. The pamphlets, like *The Communist Manifesto*, did not pose any problems of comprehension. But when we tackled the foundational texts—*A Contribution to the Critique of Political Economy*, the first volume of *Das Kapital*—a mass of technical questions assailed us. How was it that the social revolution had never taken place in countries with developed industry and a true, unionized proletariat? It hadn't happened in Great Britain or Germany, certainly not in France. At the time, we weren't thinking about the United States. Why did revolutions flourish precisely where there was no proletariat? In Russia first, then in China, and later, throughout the sixties, in Third World countries labouring in the throes of endless decolonization. Of course I knew Marx well, having rubbed shoulders with him in Party organizations during my childhood in Gennevilliers. It wasn't until later, at the start of the seventies, that I would reconcile with him through my reading of Althusser.

Thanks to the mediation of this little spontaneous group of students, we'd cleared a path for ourselves. We were not in the least the 'heirs' described by Bourdieu. We had not been nourished from the cradle with the milk of those preciosities that open the doors to good schools and the corridors of power. As immigrants, we had access neither to the codes transmitted, here as everywhere, within families from generation to generation—nor to the guides who might elucidate them for us. Our parents had not the slightest idea how higher education in France was structured, nor of the pathways required to enter one profession or another. It was we, their children, who explained to them the world in which they were living. Yet if we were not heirs, then neither were we 'captives', creatures without names or families. Our inheritance consisted of rituals, traditions and myths; but these riches had been deactivated.

We took pleasure in the knowledge that we were studying Freud the same way our ancestors had studied Talmud, with the same fervor, quoting the same passages over and over, with endless sophistical discussions about details, phrasings, including our mental thrill at the prospect of having a breakthrough of our own. Without a doubt, our psychoanalysis took the form of Talmud, that Talmud we had barely leafed through. And we'd come together spontaneously, all of us about the same age, forming a group that didn't require memberships or rituals of initiation, within a larger society that sought to deal only with individuals—taxpayers, social-security numbers.

By the time I turned twenty in 1968, I'd become leftist to the core. Although I spent hours hunched over Marx's texts, I can't say I was Marxist. I was Freudian most certainly, saturated with psychoanalytic thought, but, as one might imagine, at a remove from institutional structures of teaching and research. True psychoanalysis, the psychoanalysis of training institutes and well-known practitioners, was a distant dream. In a journal—*Les temps modernes* perhaps—I'd discovered the Situationist International Movement, militants of metamorphosis who anticipated the revolution to come. At the lycée, my friends Gérard and Jean-Loup and I had been Situationists without the theory. We would accost passers-by in the street. One of us would step forward while the other two watched. 'Good morning sir! Hello. I'd like to ask you a question. But it's embarrassing. Perhaps you can help me. People keep telling me, and I don't understand. Why do they say a hole is always a hole?' Most everyone laughed at our jokes. France was tolerant in those days. We went into a hardware store to ask the shopkeeper if his daughter was in bed. We crossed the place Saint-Michel naked. Once a year, beginning my sophomore year, we joined the 'Monôme du bac', a carnival-like procession that caused an endless traffic jam along the big Parisian boulevards. We weren't old enough for the baccalaureate; still, we joined the procession, trying out our everyday buffooneries on a larger scale. We painted our faces with shaving cream or toothpaste. Little by little, these antics constituted our attitude towards the world, a sort of ethic of refusal. Perhaps that's why I've never been a joiner. By the time they were twenty, my friends were beginning to part ways. Franck and Pierre both ended up as members of the Communist Party. Peewee, like Gilles, was progressively being drawn to the Maoists; Colette and her friend Jankel to the Trotskyists and their workers' struggle. I was awaiting the revolution. I must say that the word 'revolution' had taken on a mystical meaning. It was that shining point in the distance which would end up as a brilliant sun. Thinking about it now, it could just as easily have been death. The awaited upheaval would, we were persuaded, transform the world. The metamorphosis of individuals was our guiding principle, we the psychoanalysts of the future, being moulded in the forges of the world to come. And when Raoul Vaneigem's *The Revolution of Everyday Life* appeared in 1967, it was a cataclysm, a mental explosion, the ripping of the veil. We'd found, traced in fiery letters, the tenets of our implicit philosophy: 'We want nothing to do with a world in which the guarantee of not dying from hunger is exchanged for the risk of dying from boredom.' They were close to what we were already feeling; the words resonated with intelligent intensity. We did not 'study' Raoul Vanenigem; we read and reread him. There was nothing to understand, only to feel, for the current that flowed through his texts was like the blood that coursed through our veins. 'Rejoice without restraint.' That's how you could summarize his political agenda. He gave us the words for our rebellion, he resolved the algorithms of our questions, no doubt too easily and without nuance, but we never cross-examined our delight.

It was in that same year, 1967, that I once again brushed up against a possible fate. In Garges-la-Gonesse, I'd made some new friends: The R's, French from France, immigrants from nowhere. Perhaps four or five generations earlier they'd been of the land, from Champagne, the Auvergne or Picardie, but they no longer possessed the memory. The Party had erased everything. There was the older brother, Richard, slender, powerful, persuasive, an auto-worker. His sister, Marie, her voice already hoarse from filtered Gauloises, a pretty girl, bursting with health and love for life, good-ness itself, was an official in the commune. She smelt good. She had the joyous sensuality of open women, women who are neither ashamed of being women nor afraid of men. They were my friends, the two eldest of six siblings. Moulded by Communism, the family was animated by a militant solidarity, receptive to others they wanted to know, with whom they wanted to speak, to speak more, always to speak. Endless politico-philosophical discussions kept us up until dawn. It was they—Richard perhaps? Or his sister?—who told me about Manitou's lecture at a youth centre in Garges-lès-Gonesse. 'Manitou' was Léon Ashkenazi, a Talmudic master, inspired leader of the Éclaireurs israélites de France, the Jewish Guides and Scouts of France, a rabbi-philosopher. He had come to impart the 'Jewish message' in this sprawling municipality criss-crossed by a vast network of public housing projects crammed with exiles. There weren't many of us at the lecture. I think Richard fell asleep. Manitou presented his philosophy at length. Young Jews today, just as in the past, were fascinated by foreign ways of thinking. If only they could see that Jewish philosophy was far richer than any other school of thought. I was enthralled by his talk. I interrupted him several times, asking detailed questions. He met me on my own terrain, debating psychoanalytic theses. The lecture concluded with a long dialogue between the two of us. It must have been close to midnight when he took me aside, asked me what I was studying. He kept nodding, as if he understood. He ended up inviting me to join one of his seminars. I said I'd think about it. I never saw him again. Much later, in 2005 or 2006, I read a selection of his recently published works. He could have been my master. In the *Pirkei Avot*, the 'Chapters of the Fathers', it is written that the student creates the master and not the other way around. I was not aware of it at the time, but I'd made other choices.

In 1966 and 1967, my university courses were deadly dull. I'd enrolled in sociology, because I was interested in a social revolution. I did not choose psychology, which seemed reserved for girls, who made up at least 80 per cent of the students. In the big amphi-theatre at the Sorbonne, more than a thousand students would assemble to listen to a professor whose silhouette we could barely glimpse in the distance, as he read haltingly from the draft of his next book. We could hardly hear him stammering into the micro-phone. There must have been some explanation for such contempt, such lack of interest in the students. The dean had been surprised by the massive influx of young people from the post-war baby boom, our generation. He must have realized it only at the last minute, when he studied the enrollment lists. The administration had primed the faculty for disaster, enrolling students by the thousands while waiting for them to grow weary and look elsewhere. Statistics showed that for each hundred students enrolled the first year, only one would obtain her doctorate. You should not let huge numbers of intelligent students grow bored at the university; they'll end up starting revolutions. Our sole consolation were the magnificent university libraries, including the sumptuous one at the Sorbonne, which I preferred to Sainte-Genevieve, too big for my taste. I spent much more time there than in my classes, sometimes just to absorb the atmosphere, falling asleep with my head on my arms, slumped over a book by Leibniz. My head against the letters, I dreamt of amorous encounters. Intellectual labour stimulates the senses. I would have so liked to meet a female student there, like that lovely Indian girl, labouring over her Civil Code.

I must have looked sad that evening, alone in the Censier Centre's cafeteria, waiting for my last class in front of a cup of cold coffee that tasted like soap. She was enrolled in psychology. She had eyes as clear as a sunlit Italian lake. I'd crossed paths with her often in the classes we had together. It was she who approached me. 'You look lost.' 'Yes, I lost my way on the road from Cairo,' I lamented. 'Don't you know any more how to go home?' 'I no longer know where my home is.' 'Do you take the Métro after class?' 'Yes, of course.' 'We can go some of the way together.' She was passionate about psychoanalysis and race cars. I was too. She lived in the western suburb, I in the northern one. We spent hours at the Châtelet interchange, unable to part. The next Sunday, we met at Montlhéry, to attend the 24 Hours of Le Mans car race. We made love for the first time under a tent, identifying the cars by the sounds of their motors. We worked together, unravelled theories, dreamt up impossible projects. She was serious and erudite. I was a rabid dog. I can't thank her enough for having given me a reason to show up day after day to university that year. During that several-month-long afffair, we mined the energy that would fuel our futures. She became a professor of psychology; I did too.

I was twenty years old in 1968, in the second year of sociology, like Daniel Cohn-Bendit. I'd run into him for the first time in March 67, at Nanterre, in the early days of the student revolts. A burly redhead, barely emerged from childhood, eyes bright with intelligence, he had an innate talent for the politics of large groups. He was of our generation's driving force, a phenomenon. He has tried to stay that way. I sometimes (though not always) recognize the spirit of our youth in what he's become today. No one has forgotten that the revolution was triggered by a sexual issue. The president of the University of Nanterre had forbidden boys from entering the girls' dorm. It was absurd. A great number of rooms in university housing, barely big enough for one, were occupied by couples. The students organized parties that brought dozens of young people togethet in rooms and hallways. These weren't orgies; they were preliminary sketches of the liberation of morals we were anticipating, a sort of communal therapy. We were ambushed. Police were summoned: the first confrontations, mad pursuits through the alleys, down to the neighbouring slum, arrests, nights at the police station. There were also thugs who chased leftists on the streets of Nanterre. Young undercover cops, casually dressed in jeans and sneakers to look like students, approached girls, thought to be more naive, to elicit information. They were looking for the leaders, to expel them from school, the way you'd try to kill a microbe that had infected a healthy body. David, one of my friends from the cité Claude-Debussy, was living in university housing at Nanterre, in the girls' dorm, in the room of a pretty blonde, a dead ringer for Mia Farrow, who was studying literature. We often gathered there, to dream of the world to come, and also to let the dead speak as we made a glass dance over a cloth inscribed with the alphabet. These first events of March 67 confirmed what we already knew: that the true revolution would be sexual, first and foremost. Sexuality, the most pressing problem, concerned everyone in the most immediate way. Deep within their fantasies, everyone—every man, every woman—was a revolutionary at heart. All you had to do was to explain that the repression of the sexual impulse produced neuroses and symptoms. Then you would show that these symptoms stifled their creativity, interfered with their happiness. They would become militant revolutionaries, on the march. We had our hands on a universal lever. At least that's what we thought. That's how the revolution of 68 got underway.

3 May 1968.

When I saw the Nanterre students who'd brought their protests to Paris after their university was closed, I thought this was another monôme. I immediately joined in, with no clue regarding the political preparation that had preceded it. Although I was fully in sync with the ideas, I was not a member of any party or political group. I didn't like crowds—I still hate them. I agreed with Brassens who'd sung, 'The moment we're more than four, we're a pack of fools.' Two days earlier, on 1 May, I'd marched with the Maoists of the UJCML, the Union of Communist Youth, Marxist– Leninist. If I were to officially join a group, it would be this one, because the Maoists spoke of a 'cultural revolution' and I was convinced the revolution couldn't help but be 'cultural'—and because they'd developed a sort of mystique of 'the people' and because I was convinced that the people 'thought'. I still believe that true ideas, the innovations that help shape the world, are invented by peoples and not by individuals—languages, for example, or traditions, ways of burying the dead or predicting the future: it was obviously peoples who invented them. I might be the last of the Maoists. Our generation had a hard time ridding itself of its illusions. To some extent, those illusions are still alive. During the march, I teased the tough CGT marshals. For them, to be militant was work; for us, it was play. With their furrowed brows and gruff manners, they called us to order and shoved us to the tail end of the march, I could see they thought of us as jokers, 'sons of the bourgeoisie'. My parents were poor, and I was even more so, but I still would never consent to join their ranks, neither for this march nor for my life. The cortèges were meant to fan out, to disperse throughout the city, to enter people's spirits, not to advance in orderly rows of four, repeating slogans shouted by Party leaders. I was knocked about; I almost got myself seriously thrashed by some CGT bruiser on that 1 May. It would happen again several more times during the 'events'.

The demonstrations of May 1968—I believe I took part in all of them. People often speak of the leaders, of Cohn-Bendit, Sauvageot, Geismar. They forget that there were up to a million people in the street. There were a million leaders. Like almost everyone, I was among the foot soldiers; I was an infantryman. My ignorance of the political objectives allowed me to move through the events as if they were some gigantic Situationist party. At the Pantheon on the night of 10 May or 11, perhaps around midnight—the CRS, the Republican Security Companies of the French National Police—were lined up, their helmets strapped on tight, their jaws clenched, their fists gripping their clubs. There were hundreds of them. We'd passed them in review. We adjusted their neckties; we dusted their jackets; we just about tugged on their moustaches. They were seething. We danced in front of them, singing, 'You won't have Alsace and Lorraine.' And there were many of us. As in the Métro at rush hour, we brushed against familiar figures. Jean-Michel, for example, a university friend, with whom I'd prepared a presentation on Durkheim's *Suicide*. He was an original too, close to the ideologies of the UJCML. 'Oh, so you're here, Tobie? Did you think to wear an egg cup?' 'An egg cup? What kind of egg cup?' He grabbed his testicles and repeated. 'You know, an egg cup, like in karate. They always go for your balls.' It was a night when anything could happen, anywhere, with anyone. 'The night of fate' in our wild kermesse, in a cloud of unknowing, a trance state with neither master nor ceremony. We'd ripped up the cobblestones to build barricades. Some overturned cars. It never occurred to me that we were destroying property people cared about. I was perched on a barricade when I had a conversation with another university friend, Alain, who was also studying sociology. He too was bored by our insipid lectures. We both wondered where we could find real professors with something worthwhile to teach us.

'You're interested in psychoanalysis, aren't you?' Alain asked me.

'Yes, absolutely. In psychoanalysis and the revolution!'

'And in ethnology too?'

'In ethnology too. I'm convinced ethnology is the future of psychoanalysis.'

'You should take Georges Devereux's course,' he advised.

It was the first I'd heard of Devereux. He held his classes in Section VI of the École pratique des hautes études. Anyone could attend.

Towards ten in the morning, fires began to erupt. I grew frightened. I left on foot down alleys leading to the place Saint-Michel. I walked for a long time, choosing narrow streets, avoiding the barricades and the CRS squadrons outfitted like Roman legionnaires. I crossed the Seine at Pont-Neuf. It took another hour to reach my moped parked at the Opéra. Once I got home, my ear glued to Europe 1 radio, I realized that I'd been Fabrice del Dongo at Waterloo, crossing a battlefield without knowing it. Explosions of anecdotes, subtle debates about strategies. Although everyone spoke during the events of May 68, it wasn't so much that speech was 'liberated' as that we were trying to arrange the unfurling events into some kind of logical order. We talked endlessly as if after a great fright, trying to come to terms with our shock by rehashing the details. De Gaulle had fled to Baden-Baden. No one was fooled by the prime minister's hypocritical airs. The Communists and the CGT pedalled breathlessly to catch up with a movement that was always one step ahead. The leftist cells, dumbstruck at their own success, indulged in endless jostling for power. The popular movement should flaunt the tinselled tatters of the old world like a banner. They called for a republic of soviets, self-determination, immediately: mad theories of blank slates, fictions of anarchist pha-lansteries that seemed like dreams or nightmares. Caught in this maelstrom of events racing faster than thought, I clung to one thread. The revolution would change people, I was sure of it. I'd thought about it for so long at the heart of my little group of psy-choanalytic freethinkers. And it would generate ideas, always more ideas. The Maoists pursued the lines of thought of the École nor-male supérieure centred on the *Cahiers pour analyse*. Surreal irony of these intellectuals of the highest calibre, nourished on Kant, Hegel and Leibniz, seriously envisioning being hired as assembly-line workers at Citroën or Renault in Flins. My friend Gilles had done it. At the lycée, he'd been so serious that he became the butt of our jokes. First he learnt everything by heart, then he became a Maoist. Magic of the dialectic that I've never understood. What became of him? I think in the end he found a way to teach philos-ophy. Praise God!

While the students occupied the Sorbonne, I discovered my passion for the night. Some people are 'of the morning', others are 'of the evening'; I am 'of the night'. At night, the university became a different world, where you would come across shady characters, those we called 'thugs' or Katangais—armed vagrants posing as Katangese mercenaries. We brought our chess sets and organized endless blitz tournaments. The taste for chess has remained with me. Along with Jean-François, who was studying maths at the time, we would meet after dinner only to conclude the last match when we saw the first glimmers of daylight. In the small hours of the morning, we would have a last cup of coffee in the bistro where workers were drinking their first coffee with cream while waiting for the bus. And we asked each other the same question: 'Are you going to the university?' And we often answered, 'Maybe not today. We'll see about tomorrow.' I've kept this taste for the night and the thrill of daybreak.

I was twenty in 68 and I confuse the events with my being twenty. At the lycée, probably in 1964 or 1965, an Alsatian maths teacher would tell us, 'You'll see, they'll be back soon. They come back every twenty years.' He was speaking of the Germans. They didn't come back, but there was May 68, a labour pang. With a huge cry of pain, French society gave birth to its modernity. No statistic is possible, but I'm convinced that the great majority of students who participated in this movement were 'non-heirs'— newcomers, children of the poor, immigrants from the countryside or just plain immigrants, foreigners, like us. Such people did not cling to the old world, which they did not know very well. They felt no real reluctance to tear down the veils with which reality had been cloaked. We'd marched shouting, 'We are all German Jews,' to protest the expulsion of Daniel Cohn-Bendit, but also to show that we were not heirs. It was the students who made the revolution of 68. All the others—the unions, the workers, the civil servants— were heirs. The revolution of 68 was not meant to seize power, but to change the world. 'Change your life,' we chanted in 68, and that's what happened: life changed. The trouble with ideas is that they always bear fruit. You can't be too careful.

This revolution, as everyone knows, was nearly co-opted by the political establishment. What's more, the Soviet Secret Services, those of East Germany, were interested—and it seems very actively—in the disorder in Western Europe. I did not yet know

Georges Devereux, but I heard that he'd participated in a huge debate, at the Theatre of the Odéon, about the relationship between psychoanalysis and the revolution. He'd been presented to the revolutionary public as the hope of a leftist psychoanalysis. Before he even opened his mouth, the two thousand people crammed into the big hall acclaimed him with a huge ovation. Yet they didn't know him. Two of his students introduced him, explaining how Devereux was the quintessence of revolutionary thought. On that day, he might have become a guru, an intellectual leader such as Lacan would soon become or as Barthes and Foucault already were. But he spoke to warn the students. 'You're young, impelled by generous thoughts. You're shocked by poverty, hunger, misery. It's your courage and your luck. Stop now. Don't go any farther. You're running a great risk. You don't realize it, but you are being manipulated. You believe you're the ones doing the thinking, but it's the Soviets pulling the strings. If you overthrow the powers that be, Russian tanks will enter Paris.' Silence at first, then cries of 'Fascist!' People started to climb onto the stage. Devereux's students feared for his life. They spirited him out through a secret door. I know he was motivated by a sincere desire to help these students—among whom he counted most of his own—to avoid the horrors of the Soviet system. Like so many intellectuals from the Eastern Bloc, he was viscerally anti-Communist. At the chess club in Gennevilliers, which I attended until at least 1972, I would often play with Boris, an elderly Russian who'd fled the Soviet Union at the end of the war. Although he lived in Gennevilliers, he was animated by this same passionate fury against the Communists. Devereux was convinced the Soviets would expand their empire into to the West. He wondered through which country the invasion would begin: Germany, France, or Italy. He believed that his stay in Europe was provisional. He expected to be chased out again by an invasion of Russian tanks whose least movements he watched closely.

2

To Sit on the Earth

As far back as I can recall, I never learnt anything in school. I'm exaggerating a bit, but only a bit. Yet I entered school quite early, at the age of three and a half, in the kindergarten at the lycée Français in Bab el-Louk, Cairo. Thanks to the high tuition, it was a sumptuous setting, with many teachers from France and hand-picked students. Everything was organized to facilitate the process of teaching. You need to know that I am reticent by nature. I learnt to read before it was taught in class; I learnt to count by myself, on my fingers. I cannot attribute my reticence to any eventual unease I might have felt in school. I was in love with my first school-mistress, the gracious Florence Sanua. People don't pay enough attention to a child's sense of beauty; my teacher's coquetry enchanted me. I remain fascinated by the magic of her scarves and their perfume. She changed them daily, so much so that it became a kind of refrain: 'What colour was Mademoiselle Florence's scarf today?' I learnt so little in my primary school in Egypt that the only memory that remains is of the Arabic class we began in the tenth grade, the year of our expulsion. I was drawn to the language like a moth to a flame, most likely because it was my grandmother's language, my grandmother who seemed to possess all the secrets of the universe. Arabic was also the language we spoke with 'the people', *el näss*, those who weren't in the family, 'real' people, in other words. We would speak Arabic with Abdou, the chauffeur for my father's factory; with Ali, the porter; and above all with the servants, Ouahiba and Baheya, two sisters, sixteen and eighteen, who were also our nursemaids. The Jews of Egypt did not, strictly speaking, have a mother tongue. If I think back to my grandfather Zaki, the pharmacist, it goes without saying that Arabic was his mother tongue. And yet he'd completed advanced studies in English at the American University in Beirut. English would remain his privileged language, the one he in which he liked to read and to inform himself, subscribed as he was to the *Sunday Telegraph* until his final days. During the 1914 war, he'd served in Italy, acquiring a penchant for Italian. It was the language of his jokes, and his off-colour military stories no doubt. And yet he raised his third child, my uncle Felix, two years older than me, in French. Felix's mother tongue, the language he first spoke, was different from his parents'. As for my parents, their mother tongue was Arabic, the language of their childhood, at least until they entered school at the ages of six or seven. They learnt French in school, and subsequently made it their 'family' tongue, as most of us Egyptian Jews had. After the exodus, our departure from Egypt, many—the majority—settled in Israel. My cousins who became Israelis still speak French, although they've typically lost their fluency in this language they use so rarely. Their children grew up speaking Hebrew, their new 'mother tongue', although French is a language they still love. Their grandchildren, on the other hand, speak only Hebrew and study English in school. It was like this for the Israelis, and also for the Australians, the Canadians and the Colombians in my family. They've all changed their mother tongue at least three times in four generations. No, the Jews of Egypt do not have a mother tongue.

Perhaps it is because they did not teach Arabic at the lycée français in Cairo, or so little, that I have the impression of having learnt nothing there—nothing that mattered to me. I don't know why people seek to infantilize children. I'm convinced they resonate with the political atmosphere. When the Jewish community of Egypt chose the French language, it was in the air. It was a time when Egypt wanted to be European, when Alexandria was one of Europe's great ports. The Jews of Egypt, with their twice-millennial presence in that land, did not realize that their choice of the French language sealed their inevitable expulsion.

October 1956, the Suez Crisis.

The adults were terrified; we, the young children, absorbed their anxiety in the silence of our wide-open eyes. At the height of the crisis, when everyone feared that Cairo was under imminent threat of bombardment, when we had to draw heavy curtains every evening to hide our lights, the moment I was alone, I tuned the radio to listen to Nasser's victory communiqués. The radio's Arabic was not that of the household; it was a refined, literary Arabic that only a few Egyptians had mastered perfectly. I remember having listened to that radio for a long time, trying to grasp the turn of events. I was eight years old. I was in love with those voices. I didn't understand everything, but what has stayed with me was a feeling for Arabic (which I still speak correctly, despite never having studied it) and the conviction that the soul of events is always political.

I learnt nothing in school, I mean nothing I did not already know. A legend in the Kabbalah relates that God bestows on each child the totality of knowledge before they are born; He then places a finger on their lips, making them immediately forget what they've just learnt. This is why, the legend continues, we bear that indentation on our upper lips, the mark of God's finger imposing that initial silence. Ever since, all apprenticeships come solely to reactivate the memories forgotten from that time before birth.

My mother was constantly teaching. Essentially, she was a professor; the entire impulse of her being was teaching. At the age of thirteen, she was teaching her cousins; at eighteen, she taught the poor children in Moise de Cattoui Pasha's charity school in Cairo; then at the Jewish community's other schools. In France, she taught youngsters in the cité Claude-Debussy, then those from elsewhere. When she grew old, families came from afar to request private lessons. She taught until her last breath. Teaching was more than a passion, it was a kind of addiction. She would wander through the apartment clutching her tattered maths textbook, crammed with slips of paper on which she'd scrawled the answers to problems she'd solved. Quite naturally, she taught her children. Edwin, my older brother, prouder than me, was also reticent. He took advantage of the torments of emigration to free himself from our mother's pedagogical pursuits. As a result, I was granted special treatment; she made up for having been pushed away by the elder by multiplying the subjects she taught the younger. She taught me maths, but also literature, the physical sciences, geography. She even taught me Latin, which she did not know. Until I was eleven or twelve, I thus had a personal tutor, so that by the time I entered school, I already knew a great deal, at least what I'd studied with my mother. She was that God of the Kabbalistic legend, the one who imparts knowledge before it is acquired. The love my mother and I gave each other consisted exclusively of the exchange of knowledge, and it was reciprocal, because later I would tell her in detail what I was learning from my books. I hope I was as generous as she. For me, to love and to know are interchangeable. It is both my good fortune, and a handicap—the good fortune to be madly interested in certain subjects, and the radical inability to study what is imposed on me. In other words, I was a miserable student during my years at the lycée. Unable to force myself, I spread myself thin seeking useless knowledge, sometimes ill-gotten. An adult, if there had been one in harmony with his world, might have promptly identified the cause of my handicap: I was lacking initiation. I had in fact succeeded in learning the rudiments of Jewish tradition in preparation for the entrance into Jewish manhood: the bar mitzvah. The classes were given by a professor from the consistory, a young rabbi from Tunisia steeped in prayer and ritual since infancy. Religion had been drilled into him, body and soul. He had the simple faith of those who have never doubted. It's true that in this domain too, I already knew everything I was being taught.

L'Étang-Salé les Hauts, 1986

On the island of Réunion, I was leading an ethno-psychiatry seminar for the staff at the psychiatric hospital. Réunion is that tiny piece of France where communities hailing from the four corners of the globe rub elbows, know one another and live together—at least that's how it was more than twenty-five years ago. There are all kinds of healers there—many of them Malabar healers of the Tamoule faith; some Malagache healers, migrants from the neighbouring island; along with Creole healers, often descendants of the poor Whites left high and dry. I discovered the island, its inhabitants and its way of life. For me, it was the reincarnation of the Egypt of my childhood, cosmopolitan and intense. After I concluded my lectures, I asked the nurses to take me to the healers. I always asked for another one, and then another. At the end of my stay, they told me about a well-known healer who practised on the heights above Saint-Pierre. He was African, they told me, a real African from Africa, not a cafre, *a descendant of slaves. On Sunday morning, I made my way to his small house perched on the heights amid the cane fields. The road ended abruptly; I had to continue on foot. The torrid heat was staggering. I arrived dripping with sweat. He must have seen me from afar as I scaled his hill.*

'You're finally here,' he exclaimed. 'I've been waiting so long for you!' A small, crooked man, with a wide smile showing white teeth.

'Because you know who I am?' I asked, taken aback.

With authority, he pointed to a tiny branch hut, set up in his yard, less than three feet high. 'Go inside,' he ordered.

I looked at him questioningly.

'Go in,' he repeated. 'You'll come out when you can recite a prayer for me.'

I entered the hut, so tiny it might have been designed for dwarves or forest sprites. Why? Of course I could have refused, announcing that I'd come solely to discuss his practice with him, to learn about his view of illness. But no, I entered the hut on all fours, I sat on the earth, searching my memory for a prayer from my childhood. I was sweating bullets. At first it was merely a melody that slowly arose, then a few words, then a few more. After some twenty minutes, a fragment of the blessings reserved for holidays was ringing in my head: 'Mo àdim hesim 'ha, hagim, ouzmanim lessasson' . . . 'gatherings for joy, feasts for the times of happiness . . .'

On the island of Réunion, I befriended one of the most celebrated healers of the day. Her name was Visnelda. I was then a very young professor just discovering this world of healing, so distant from ours. The difference is obvious: here what is required is the result, whereas for us it is competence and effort. By day, Visnelda was a secretary in the mayor's office. At night and on weekends, she was a healer. On Saturday and Sunday evenings, her husband and children led a big dancing in a large shed in l'Étang-Salé les Hauts. It was in this dance hall that she met patients on weeknights after work, and often there were so many that the hall was full. A large, biracial woman, a creole, her body exuded a studied nonchalance. But to see her from up close as she walked, dragging her slippers, you could tell that some parts of this body stayed fixed, as if in pain: her hips and her knees. She seemed to float as she walked. Her gaze, in contrast, was unusually fluid, displaying a kaleidoscope of expressions: surprise, severity, malice, and sometimes a kind of naivety.

'Where did you say you teach?' she asked me.

'At Paris 8, in other words: in Saint-Denis. Saint-Denis is a Parisian suburb, not Saint-Denis in Réunion.'

37

She frowned. 'Is it not by chance in Bobigny?' I remained silent. It was in fact in Bobigny that I'd opened the first ethnopsychiatry clinic. Perhaps she'd made inquiries. In the dance hall, photographs of Playmates with prominent breasts; and at the other extremity, a bar; a pine desk resembling a doctor's, in a corner; on the shelves, medicinal plants in industrial packets. She had me sit on one of the chairs reserved for patients. Along the wall, dozens of chairs, typically occupied by those who were there for the dancing, and otherwise used by the many sick people during the hours she was consulting. She did not ask me a single question. At our first meeting, she told me her whole story.

When she was younger, she'd suffered from extremely painful menstrual periods. Every month she would progressively enter a kind of comatose state, from which she didn't know how to emerge. When she was around thirty, in a half-sleep one morning, she heard a voice instructing her to gather a bouquet of chamomile flowers, and to make an infusion from them in order to be definitively healed from her dysmenorrhea. It was as if the voice told her the exact place where she might find the flowers. From the depths of her dream, she replied that after the night's cyclone and torrential rain had laid waste to the vegetation, she would never find them. But the next day, she found the flowers exactly where she'd been told to look. Not long afterwards, her vocation appeared. A neighbour had been suffering from a bad wound. Her leg would not heal, and it had swelled so much that the poor woman could no longer walk. Visnelda knelt by her bedside and rubbed her leg while murmuring prayers, and behold, the swelling immediately subsided! Within less than an hour, the sick woman was walking again. Visnelda realized she had a gift for healing. From that moment, she began to practise.

Over the course of my visits to Réunion, I came often to sit beside Visnelda. She induced trances by throwing salt, by making patients absorb water through their nostrils. She would abruptly ask the spirits why they had taken refuge in the hearts of her patients. 'Who are you?' she would severely ask the demon. 'A Malabar spirit? A Tamoul spirit? A troubled ghost?' The patients would fall into a trance, gesticulating, screaming, moaning. It would sometimes take two or three strong men to restrain a poor woman assailed by her spirits. A few times, Visnelda maliciously suggested that I take a turn. 'Well then, professor, will you know how to exorcize the demon? Or will you be too frightened when it moves?'

'I'm learning, Visnelda. Perhaps in a little while,' I would tell her.

As with all healers, Visnelda was praised by her patients and vilified by doctors and journalists. The last year that I visited her, she had a photographer join us; and the next day I saw myself in one of the most important local dailies: 'Renowned Parisian professor comes to learn beside Madame Visnelda.' I was not a renowned professor, but Visnelda, attacked on all sides, needed institutional validation. When I returned the following year, she was dead. I went to her grave, in the cemetery of Étang-Salé. I was expecting to find a real mausoleum, a chapel at the very least. It was a modest grave, with one or two faded bouquets of flowers. It so happens that healers, appreciated during their lifetimes, become maleficent beings after their deaths. A few people assured me that Visnelda now haunted nightmares, demanding compensation for unpaid bills. There were four or five of us visiting the cemetery, doctors and psychologists. It was a Sunday. Afterwards, we hiked up to the Cirque de Cilaos. Along the way, we drank several glasses of that wine said to render men mad. I bathed in a waterfall. It was hot out. The water was

39

cool and of a fairy-like limpidity. Suddenly I felt ill and fainted. My companions took fright. They brought me as quickly as they could to the hospital in Saint-Denis, a two-hour drive on tortuous mountain roads. I'm sure they thought I was dying. My diagnosis was 'a vagal problem', in other words, nothing. I remain convinced that Visnelda had sought to take me with her.

* * *

All food is a priori a poison, if the body is not sufficiently suffused with it to consider it a part of itself. The human body can only integrate ingredients of its own nature. A very ancient medicine, dating back to Antiquity, explains illness as a disequilibrium of absorption. Its treatments invariably consist of diets and regimens. This idea should also be applied to pedagogy. A child who does not study must be put on a diet. The transmission of knowledge should at first be suspended, in order to later identify what knowledge acts in them like a poison. One should then, little by little, accustom the child to this toxin by slowly increasing the doses.

I never learnt a thing at university, but in those days the university had nothing to offer except professors. There were in fact a handful of true masters, often well known, who'd written important reference works. They considered teaching a tedious obligation. They were paid to transmit their theories to the greatest number by publishing their work. All the students had to do was read their writings; and, if they wanted to similarly apply themselves, to take their professors' work as examples. That was all. At the university I attended, at a time that seems so distant to me now, when this system worked, it was with panache. The professor arrived like an actor coming on stage for a one-man show, greeted by an assistant who erased the blackboard. He made his preparations, cleared his throat, took an infinite amount of time to retrieve the book—the last one he'd written—from his leather satchel. He never offered a course, he delivered a lecture, in service to his theoretical preoccupations of the moment, the state of his research. At the end of the hour, he left without a word, without even glancing at his audience. The professors presented their research, nothing more. One might interpret this as a way of trusting the studens' ability to grasp the themes of these teachers parading their intellectual virtuosity. When it was a matter of Michel Foucault, or Raymond Aaron, or Vladimir Jankélevich or Gilles Deleuze, the system worked as if by magic. A current flowed from professor to student, a current charged with vitality, tensions, desires. But with the others, this system engendered, by a sort of intrinsic necessity, a handful of second-rank 'masters of thought', and a majority of functionaries of conventional, banal thinking. One should never, not for any price, offer banal thoughts to young people. It corrupts them, makes them 'fanatic', as we were called back then. In May 68, we took revenge on the simplifiers of the world. I remember one professor—I won't say his name, he was a serious, hardworking man, and I'm not proud of tormenting him:

'Sir, we cannot come to class today.'

'And why is that, gentlemen?'

'You know very well that the Vietnam Committees have declared a strike to support the counter-offensive of the Vietnamese people.'

He refused. We tied him up in a Viet Cong flag, and then left the amphitheatre after emblazoning the demonstration's slogans on the blackboard. In 1967 and 68, the sociology courses were truly surrealistic. A social movement was unfolding right before the professors' eyes, yet no one was paying any attention to it. In the streets of the Latin Quarter, a new cohort was on the move, that of the 'enraged'. Its influence was gaining ground in the provinces and spreading to the countryside. Very few sociologists were interested in either the leftist groups springing up all over, or in the ideas brewing in young people's minds, or in the sudden proliferation of new behaviours. No one was reflecting on the events stirring the people of France and much of the Western world, no one except the philosophers who were demonstrating along with the students: the Deleuzes, the Lyotards, Henri Lefebvre, François Châtelet. In what they wrote, it was impossible to distinguish between desire and analysis, between participation in the dream and the objective gaze. Sartre and de Beauvoir went even further—the Movement absorbed them completely. Meanwhile, in classes at the Sorbonne, George Gurvitch was propounding his groundless classifications. Jean Stoetzel was setting forth, week after week, gigantic tables of figures, and Yvon Belaval was once again presenting his 'What do I know?' about the history of philosophy. I'm still convinced that there should have been an inscription over the entrance: 'Sensible young people, of flesh and blood, with thoughts and emotions, ideas and feelings, do not enter this place. You will learn only rage.'

The situation in psychology was hardly better. There were only a few places where you could hear psychoanalysis discussed. There was certainly Daniel Lagache, the chair of psychopathology, whose theories were artificial and pedantic. One day, to illustrate the necessary neutrality of the psychoanalyst, he told us this parable: 'The ideal would be that the patient never sees his analyst. He would enter by one door, then lie down on the couch. The psychoanalyst would enter by another door, placed behind the couch, and sit down in his armchair—and this from session to session without the patient seeing the analyst, not even once.' I voiced my surprise out loud, 'But that already exists, sir, doesn't it? It's called a confessional.' With nothing more than experience in mutual improvised psychoanalysis, we did not let ourselves judge, but this precious discourse led to propositions that seemed out of touch with reality. Maurice Benassy, on the other hand, offered an 'introduction to psychoanalysis' at the medical faculty. His lectures were open to the public and drew crowds. It should have been called 'introduction to the introduction': the contents were so pitiful as to make one cry. Yet we ran there like starving fools. Freud's books were read aloud verbatim, without commentary or personal examples. We wanted to shout out, 'Sir, we know how to read!' I had yet to learn that when it came to psychoanalysis, as with Marxism, while there was most certainly a first level, there was no second.

In June 68, the nearly total disappearance of petrol sent us into ecstasy. Oh joy! The city belonged to us. I managed to lay my hands on one or two litres for my mobylette and I would roam through the Latin Quarter. Society had suddenly been simplified, taking on a human form. The spring of 68 was followed by a glorious summer. France was beginning to resemble my inner world. All my friends back then dreamt as I did of experimenting with new forms of existence. Jean-Loup joined the movement on the side of the

Maoists. Sylvain and I sought to deepen the connections between psychoanalysis and ethnology. We were reading Geza Róheim and still understanding nothing; Philippe was getting interested in forms of communal living, and we would discuss them for hours. *The Free Children of Summerhill: A Radical Approach to Child Rearing* by Alexander Sutherland Neil had just been published in French. It rendered us speechless. It demonstrated that one could put into effect a pedagogy of freedom—total freedom, not a supervised freedom directed by teachers, hypocritical and unhealthy, like what one sees today in schools. Anarchy was possible, Neil had done it! A freedom in which the teachers and the children treated each other as equals. And this freedom would have to begin with complete sexual freedom granted to the children, from the very start, in preschool. Such a pedagogy of freedom had already been evoked at the beginning of the Russian Revolution: in Makarenko's *Pedagogical Poems*, and in Vera Schmidt's experiments as well. We know that these ideas were never applied, even at the very beginning of the 1917 Revolution. Along with David, we were putting these ideas into practice—barely, but even so!—in the holiday camps and vacation colonies that enabled us to earn our pittance. That summer, I encountered Nietzsche for the first time. We were spending a week in the heart of France, in the country home of one of David's friends, a philosopher. The fellow was tall and wide; he never washed, and he let an enormous moustache grow, identical to Nietzsche's. He would catch spiders, which he swallowed raw, in the filthy corners of his huge family home. When I returned to Paris, I set myself to reading *Human, All Too Human*, intrigued by an author who still had such an effect, so many years after his death.

We sometimes went to stay in the country home of the parents of one or another of us. We were reading Surrealist poems while drinking litres of cheap red wine, and occasionally we ended our nights, drunk and almost comatose, out in the open. We would sing off-key at the top of our lungs, in the middle of the fields—the 'Internationale' and lewd songs from the *Breviary of Carabin*. I was writing sad poems and songs in which I expressed my nostalgia for Egypt. One evening, I no longer know who it was that suggested I meet someone who might interest me. We ended up at Moustaki's place. His guitar was no longer very fresh, and his mood even more nostalgic than mine, almost melancholic. Forty years later, in Israel where he'd come to sing, I reminded him of our impromptu visit, of the sort that took place so often in 68. Of course, he'd forgotten. When one of us had the use of a car, we would drive from Paris to Deauville and back in one night, just to dip our freezing toes into the sea. That summer of freedom was the one of every possibility. We spent it reading, talking, testing our ideas, submitting them to the critique of individuals and to lessons from history. Our loves were multiple and fleeting, often tumultuous. We men exchanged our women; our women exchanged their men. That year, spring was prolonged until the end of summer. In August 68, Russian tanks entered Prague and closed that chapter of socialism-without-barbarity. My reading, disparate and disorganized, always brought me back to Freud. This small group of young people who crossed paths and strolled through Paris as if they were pensioners, was my true university. We learnt and unlearnt. We loved a great deal and hated rarely.

At the beginning of autumn, which was quite late that year, nearly into winter, the students did not know what to make of the university. It had lost its aura, as if emptied of its substance. They had lost their illusions. From the first days of autumn, we began to feel the true effect of May 68, at first via advertisements. If the politicians had not known what to make of this movement, the publicists had recuperated the slogans. May 68 was supposed to usher in freedom and desire. It turned out to be desire for merchandise and the freedom to consume. Could it be that May 68 was invented by a demiurge of consumer society? It was a time when the professors also tried to outdo us. There's a story that at Paris 8, in Vincennes, they granted a diploma to a horse, thus demonstrating the arbitrariness of university credentials. As a result, students attended as infrequently as possible, showing up only to receive their diplomas. They wouldn't be outdone by a horse.

I made the decision to learn elsewhere. I felt like a vagrant searching for shelter. I was captivated by Jankelevitch's classes. His only notes were a few words scribbled on a Métro ticket, and we were transported into a hall of mirrors, an amalgam of ideas, music and death. I sensed a danger during these classes, that of being mesmerized by a fascinating and useless object, like my chess addiction. In 1969, I remembered my friend Alain's advice, delivered while we were on a barricade. I enrolled in the École pratique des hautes études to audit George Devereux's courses. At that time, he was holding his seminar in a small room at the College de France, rue des Écoles.

* * *

The first contact was brutal. I recall that it was a Saturday in November. The sky was low, portending snow; the wind was icy. Some fifty students were crammed into this small room furnished with old wooden furniture that seemed not to have been renovated for a century. Devereux was sixty-one at the time, but he already looked like an old man. Though rather tall, he walked hunched over his cane. Did he really need it, or was it solely to threaten importunate students by shaking it in the air, as I would see him do? He would say he'd ruined his knee in a parachute jump during the war. Even to a neophyte like me, it was obvious that there were several circles: the closest in the first row, to whom he addressed his discourse and who understood his allusions. They showered him with attention, as if he were a delicate plant. A little farther back were those who listened with a certain distance, sometimes amused, sometimes critical; and then there were the newcomers like me wondering in what sort of hyper-specialist coterie we'd landed. That year, the course was devoted to the study of dreams in Greek tragedy. Devereux had just delivered a series of lectures on that subject at Oxford. The book would appear years later, in 1976 in English, and not in French until 2006. The room was saturated with tobacco smoke. Devereux would place an ashtray on the table and proceed to light one cigarette after another, using the burning tip of one to light the next. He must have smoked a dozen per hour. He had a deep, nasal voice, pleasant enough, with a strong accent I could not manage to identify—somewhat American, somewhat German, I thought. I did not yet know that he was Hungarian. On the blackboard, he wrote four lines in Greek from Aeschylus' *The Persians*, and began to dissect each word. It had to do with the Persian queen

Atossa's dream. It's an understatement to say I felt lost. I even felt vertigo, with the sudden thought that up until now I'd wasted my time. Why had I never studied Greek? How was it that I hadn't yet read *The Persians*? I didn't even know the names of the characters whose psychology Devereux was exploring. He began with philological remarks, moved on to commentaries about syntax and the construction of the text, then offered more properly psychoanalytic insights. Atossa, Cambyse, Xerxes thus became his patients. Authoritatively, he endowed them with an inner life, with desires, hates and also dreams, of course. At one point, if you were to exclude the beginning of the course, during which he'd situated the era and had spoken of the writer and his personality, you could imagine that the queen mother of ancient Persia had been one of his analysands in New York. He described her in elaborate detail, and in a tone that forbade all critique. That widows, for example, had incestuous feelings for their sons. He believed this because one of his patients, precisely, had provoked her son to share her bed, despite the fact that he was of marriageable age. He knew that when women reached menopause, they became violently jealous of their pubescent daughters. How did he know this? Another patient, precisely, and he would describe a clinical case from New York. Did he invent these cases? Most likely they were anecdotes he'd borrowed from friends and acquaintances in America, disguised for the moment as 'patients'. Yet this would not be enough to ground his assertions. Next, he would seek a custom, a ritual or a myth from some distant culture. A mature New York woman was right to be jealous of her daughter because the Bagas of Uganda did not allow a mother and daughter to have a sex life at the same time.

Thus we travelled a torturous route, from Greek myth to American clinical case, to Indian, African or Australian ritual. For someone who joined the seminar without preparation, it was dizzying. From the text, we moved to the characters, who became creatures of flesh and blood (the moment I liked best). We were not doing a historian's work, far from it. We were not trying to reconstruct their lifestyles, their clothing, their foodways, nor even to establish their political context. We were exploring only their 'Unconscious'. Atossa, Xerxes' mother, had an incestuous desire for her son. I was astounded. And what if it were true? What then? For Devereux, it was essential. If it was impossible to know the real concerns of people who'd lived long before us, we could nevertheless infer their unconscious desires. He'd transformed the Cartesian dictum, insisting that the Unconscious was the one thing all humans truly have in common. That first encounter with Devereux struck me like lightning. It wasn't so much his conclusions as it was his means of reaching them. And also, of course, above all, his personality. Even if I set aside his conclusions—which demanded something like an act of faith—that in the fifth century BCE, Atossa had an Unconscious identical to mine, this seminar shook me to the core. I drew from it an immediate, absolute necessity: the necessity of erudition. No discussion was possible if you were not familiar with the Greek tragedies—with Sophocles, whom he did not like very much; with Euripides, whom he considered too theoretical, too 'leftist'; with Aeschylus, whom he preferred above all. Another maxim born of his discourse: psychoanalysis, as one might come to know it in books by psychoanalysts, including Freud, is a science without substance, like a motor without wheels. For anyone who wanted to explore the field, it was imperative, to find a leverage point, to become specialized in one discipline in which knowledge, as in the true sciences, is infinite. To put it another way: there was no psychoanalysis unless it was applied. The lesson stayed with me. He had been an ethnologist in Indochina and among the Indians of North America. He had studied, read, done research. He knew by heart the names of all the American Indian tribes, would recite on the fly all their cultural characteristics, the names of their chiefs. His thesis director, Alfred Kroeber, was the author of the reference text, *Handbook of the Indians of America*. When Devereux had been deprived of his ethnological terrain, when he became a professor in Paris, confined to research and teaching, he'd created for himself, at the age of fifty-five, a new leverage point. The ancient Greeks became his tribes, his Indochinese, his Indians. What's more, from our first contact, I perceived in him a sort of fierce determination never to articulate a banal thought. This could be seen not so much in what he said as in what he did not say. We'd only just lived through May 68. All his students were Marxist, the more radical to the degree that they were not actively participating in society; some were deeply engaged in political groups. Their contributions to the seminar reflected their political positions. Devereux would respond with his visceral anti-Communism. He never used arguments from authority. Instead, he drew from his own experience as a man. He recounted how his father, a militant socialist, had been bypassed and cast aside by the Communists after he'd cleared the way for them. It was ever thus: the socialists, the anarchists and today the leftists, seduced by grand ideas, made Communism palatable, even acceptable. Then the Communists would seize power and establish their dictatorship. For him, the leftists were the soft underbelly of an orderly world. They were the faultline through which terror would inexorably enter, and that terror was always red. It was not only in politics that Devereux did not think in sync with the zeitgeist. When his students mentioned the superstars of the moment—Herbert Marcuse, David Cooper, R. D. Laing, Jacques Lacan—his diatribes became even more violent. Cooper was a psychotic, Marcuse an idiot, and Lacan, whom he'd met in Paris in 46, a worldly schemer. 'He pursued me until I agreed to read his thesis on paranoia. Four hundred pages of self-satisfied thinking. It must be rotting at the bottom of my basement.' One day a student, a leftist to judge by his costume, entered the seminar room and went to sit down. Devereux did not know him. 'Who are you?' he asked.

'A student!' the other replied, without even turning around. 'This is a closed seminar, sir. You must be enrolled in order to participate,' he thundered, glaring at him severely. The other resisted: 'Culture is open to all!' Devereux drew himself up, took hold of his infamous cane and brandished it against the intruder. The student turned around. He was a good head taller than Devereux. Not one of the other students reacted. I remain convinced that they all thought just like the fellow who'd tried to enter. Devereux's determination must have impressed the student, who promptly left the room, shrugging. Brouhaha. A moment of relaxation after the sharp tension. Devereux concluded the incident by declaring: 'This young man doesn't know what it means to be Hungarian. I saw Geza Roheim challenge someone to a duel because he'd looked at his wife too intently. And this was in New York at the start of the fifties.' Devereux was not a leftist, that was obvious! He was, rather, an anarchist, fundamentally an anarchist, a right-wing anarchist.

It's true Georges Devereux did not think like the others! With respect to psychoanalysis, he had an original perspective on every concept. Psychoanalysts, starting with Freud, had knocked themselves out trying to prove that the Oedipus complex inevitably appeared at the age of four or five, the same way that children cut their first tooth at six months and walk at one year. Devereux, on the other hand, considered what Freud called counter-oedipal impulses to be the true engine. He believed that all children were necessarily seduced by one of their parents. And it was in reaction to this original seduction that children developed what Freud called the 'Oedipus complex'. For Devereux, there was no original fantasy, only a normal reaction to the necessarily abnormal behaviour of all parents. To be born from two parents was the essential tragedy of human beings. Although he was married six times, Devereux never had children. When he was asked about it, he would answer: 'It's criminal to give birth to a child in such a world!' The same for boys' parricidal impulses. According to Freudian theory, the boy would spontaneously develop the desire to murder his father. Devereux would remark: 'Come on! Let's be serious. How many parricides are there? Very few, while the cases of infanticide are legion. How many parents get rid of their children? How many would be rid of them if our society allowed it?' For him, the boy's murderous desires could be nothing other than a natural reaction to the infanticidal temptations of his parents. Above all, he liked to challenge the great theories with his commonsense observations. For example, he would speak of Melanie Klein in these terms: 'She's a madwoman!

There's no other word for it, a madwoman!' To attribute cannibalistic impulses to six-month-old babies—how in God's name could that be possible? A six-month-old infant cannot distinguish between animal and human flesh. How could it be a cannibal?' Each time Devereux took hold of a concept, it was to twist it, to squeeze out its juice, until it was impossible to consider it simply. For me, after three sessions of the seminar, it was evident that you could never be satisfied with 'ready-to-think' ideas. After the seminar, Devereux would go with his students to the Café Balzar. I can still see the group surrounding the professor in his coat and hat, carrying his cane, as they left the College, going towards the rue des Écoles. There, the discussion would go on for hours, but in a more personal vein. Not knowing anyone, I avidly watched this cluster of young people surrounding the old professor. At the sight of this escapee from Austria-Hungary so passionately surrounded by his students, I, who'd assiduously read Freud since the age of fourteen, felt as if I were in 1915 Vienna. Perhaps during the first meeting of the seminar, perhaps the second, I asked him if he'd met Freud. 'Most certainly not!' he replied with a mocking smile, 'I refused. I was presented with the opportunity several times—in Vienna, in Budapest. I always avoided Zigmund Froid! I knew perfectly well he was a tyrant!' It's vain to claim, as some do, that Devereux was a classical psychoanalyst. Having been beside him for ten years, I know that he believed in neither Freud nor the Devil. The only thing that interested him was original thought. After four sessions of the seminar, followed by even more intense debates at the cafe, I felt as if I'd been wrung out. I was not prepared, I did not know enough, I had no experience in practical application, nor did I have access to any research material. There were classes I still needed to take. I decided to return later, once I'd obtained my master's degree, with a dissertation topic to propose to him. I no longer wanted to be a 'free auditor'. I wanted to be his student, nothing else. I did not say a word to him; I did not let him know. I quit the seminar and did not return that year.

3

Weissmuller

Two years later, at the start of the school year in 1971, I was like a ticking time bomb ready to explode. I had accomplished what I thought was required of me, but only minimally. I'd obtained my master's degree while hardly setting foot in the university. By dint of all-nighters with Jean-François, I'd learnt to play chess correctly. I'd gotten married, I had a very old car that was always breaking down, a 1956 Citroën 2CV, and I was always dreaming of race cars. I felt that I was bursting with schemes I had no idea how to actualize. I'd just finished writing a novella that depicted the decay of a world that was losing both sense and nonsense, to the point that only two words remained: 'yes' and 'no', and they both meant the same thing. In hindsight, I realize I was lucky not to fall into addiction. Many of my university friends did not escape. During the year of my master's, the only class I attended regularly was Rémy Chauvin's course on animal ethology. I respected this old professor who'd devoted his life to the study of bees and termites. In homage to him, I read Jean-Henri Fabré's entomology—Fabré, poet of insects, philosopher of six-legged creatures. At the start of his course, Rémy Chauvin asked his students to tackle an unusual exercise: we were to imagine ourselves forty years into the future and to recount our career up to that point. In my essay, I'd become an old university professor known for having proved the existence of the Oedipus complex among orangutans. And because these monkeys rarely descend from the canopy, I'd had to invent a mechanism that would allow me to safely stay in the treetops. It's true that Jane Goodall's book, about her life alone with the monkeys in Gombe Stream Park in Tanzania, had just been published. Goodall described the chimpanzees one by one, like individuals, 'subjects' to whom she'd given names. In detail, she presented each one's character, their loves, their jealousies, their disputes. I was sure she was right; monkeys were almost human, since humans were absolutely monkeys. At the time, no one had published studies on the avoidance of incest among non-human primates; the first would not appear for another ten years. In my fantasy, I'd intuited the truth. Today we know that most species of monkeys avoid incest, which is infinitely more frequent among humans. After I'd passed Chauvin's oral exam, which allowed me to validate the last certificate necessary for my master's, he invited me to join him in his laboratory. 'Since you're interested in this field, why not devote your doctoral dissertation to it?' I replied that I would think about it, the same answer I'd given Manitou. I never saw Chauvin again, except on TV. I think of him often, especially something he'd said in a lecture: 'Be wary of scientific "proofs". They can be twisted like a prestidigitation. I myself had constructed a deceptive model that supposedly proved a hypothesis about termite behaviour. I'd deliberately cheated. Everyone fell for it, at least initially. I presented my hypothesis to my colleagues, who all congratulated me. Afterwards, I revealed that they'd been duped, and I explained how their "science" had been unable to catch me in my deception. From then on, I knew without a doubt that scientists lie and cheat as much as anyone else. Every thesis put forward by a researcher must be personally verified.'

At the start of the school year in 1970, I was thus like a ticking bomb. May 68 was definitively over by now. Sartre had been found guilty of defamation against the police, and Mitterrand had taken control of the Socialist Party at the congress at Épinay. I wondered why I was engaged with such studies, if you could call them that. I wondered what it would take for me to finally begin my life. As part of their beautiful NRF essay series, Gallimard had just published Devereux's *Essays on General Ethno-psychiatry*, a selection of his best articles. I bought the book, read and reread it, annotated it, dog-eared the pages. At last I decided to ask Devereux to supervise my dissertation. I called him at home and made an appointment.

October 1971. Monday morning at ten.

For once, my 2CV did not break down. He was living in Antony, in an apartment in one of the many housing projects there. The 'Musicians' Project' in Gabriel Fauré Square. Three modest rooms, designed for a family. In the living-dining room, he'd crammed a table, six chairs, an enormous grand piano and three leather armchairs. The walls were covered with shelves of books. He had thousands, in bookcases, on the piano, on the table. Also on this table, which in other times and places must have welcomed dinner guests, was an old typewriter sitting among scattered papers, dozens of precariously stacked theses. I rang at 10 a.m. on the dot. He invited me in and offered me an armchair facing him. I looked around, momentarily struck by a photograph on the piano. It pictured him, much younger, in a marine lieutenant's uniform, as handsome as a film star. 'I fought in the American Army during the war,' he told me. I didn't react. I was a leftist, but I loved America and Americans. He asked me to introduce myself. I did so in a few sentences. I was nobody and all I had to offer was a consuming desire to begin my life. I remember telling him about my emigration, my passion for chess, my political views, most notably my preoccupation with a revolution in morals. 'Where would you place yourself on the political spectrum?' he asked. 'On the far left of the left,' I replied. He burst out laughing.

'As I'm on the right of the right, we'll most likely meet in the centre.'

I went on to tell him the subject of my dissertation. After all, that was why I'd come. He immediately interrupted me, 'You must first pass a little test.'

I didn't dare say a word. After all, I'd placed myself in his hands. 'Yes, a psychological test of my own invention. You know, I'm sure, all the projective tests. You must have studied them at the university. This one, I invented. It helps me to keep psychotics out of my seminar.'

Psychotics were crazy, truly crazy, unlike the neurotics with their minor guilt complexes. That's how we thought back then. These crazies, caught up in their delusions, would destabilize a group, a class. At the time, there was even a popular theory of 'blank' psychosis, according to which some psychotics presented no symptoms—crazies without craziness, and hence undetectable. Surely this was the reason behind Devereux's test. He had to identify the latent psychotics to keep them out of his seminar. And if his test showed that I was one, would he let me know? 'Dear sir, you are psychotic. I regret to inform you that I cannot enrol you in my course.' He would never dare. Or perhaps he would, perhaps he would! He seemed so strange to me, this professor. I've never believed in tests, especially those known as 'projective', those in which the examiner, the psychologist, gives you an absurd, unreal task: for example, looking at ink blots on a card and saying what they evoke; or listening to the opening of simple stories, like those one tells children, and imagining the outcome. When my friend F. and I had studied the Rorschach test in the psych course, we'd worked in pairs. One would present the cards and the other would respond. When it was my turn, I saw penises, vulvas, couples engaged in erotic dances, couplings by campfires. It was obviously not what was expected—too many responses, far too many, above all, too much sex. The instructor said that I was not applying myself to the task, that I was mocking it instead. But she was wrong. I'd described the images one by one, just as they'd presented themselves to me. From the lively exchange we had afterwards, I came to the conclusion that tests were a kind of mental trap, requiring the ignorance and naivety of the subject. The implicit demand was: 'Be an idiot!' And here it was, starting all over again.

'You'll see,' Devereux reassured me. 'It's very simple. All you have to do is answer three questions. All right?'

Well, no, it was not all right. But since he insisted on it before enrolling me, I had no choice but to acquiesce.

59

The first question was brutal, direct, obviously designed to reveal a persecution complex—something like: 'Someone is pursuing you. Who is it?' I wanted to say, 'Sir, if I were paranoid, if I were suffering from delusions of persecution, your question is so obviously designed to have me reveal myself that I would give you the most banal answer imaginable.' But, once again, I played the game honestly. I must have told him it was a riot-squad officer or a cop—I don't know exactly any more—a natural enough answer for a student at the time. The second question was similar. As for the third, it was even more transparent than the first two: 'Someone is hiding in in the closet behind me. Who is it?' I immediately recognized the psychoanalytic theory of transference. Whatever response I gave, he would be sure the hidden person represented him and he would offer interpretations to show his real assessment of me. How could a serious professor, an erudite and original thinker, fall for such child's play? At the conclusion of the test, the degree of my psychosis must have seemed acceptable to him. He announced that I was admitted. Looking back, I now think that, despite appearances, this test had some merit, only not the one he attributed to it. Because it took place immediately after our initial greeting, before Devereux had been seduced by a candidate's words, the test forced him to reveal the first impression—brusque, fierce— the person before him had evoked. As Louis Jouvet had declared in his film, *Les amoureux sont seuls aux monde*: 'The first impression is always the right one, especially when it is negative.' In short, this test measured nothing in the student, only the level of antipathy felt by Devereux. Much later, I would observe a similar technique used by Visnelda, an indigenous healer who would accost a patient the moment he reached her office door, 'Get out, get out of here, you miserable man,' she'd shout while the patient still stood her threshold. 'Did you think I'd welcome you into my house, a completely lost addict like you?' The man hadn't yet said a word. She knew nothing about him—at least nothing that he himself might have told her. Because, naturally, as she hadn't any projective tests, Visnelda consulted her oracles in salt.

'What do you think of the responses I gave you, sir?' I ventured.

'First, now that you're admitted, I ask that you call me Georges, that you speak to me familiarly. And I'll do the same with you.'

'Yes, sir, as you wish,' I replied. From then on, I always called him Georges.

'Come with me into the kitchen, then. I'll make us two good coffees.' In lieu of a good coffee, I was entitled to a nearly translucent Nescafé. I had to add sugar cubes to make it palatable.

'See here, Tobie, you're a very intelligent young man. Of course, you have some anxieties, some uncertainty about your own worth.'

Why a test then? All he had to do was ask, I would have answered quite willingly. I would have confessed that I doubted everything, that my entire being was riddled with anxiety, that my quest was anguished. I'd chosen a thesis topic . . . He interrupted me, 'Wait, we'll have plenty of time to talk about that. Tell me about your politics instead. You were telling me a little while ago that you situate yourself to the left of the left.'

That was just it. My thesis topic was directly related to my political views. The idea had begun to germinate when, in 1969, Guy Sitbon, a journalist for the *Nouvel observateur*, had published a much-discussed article about a 'group marriage' in Sweden, where some fifteen young people had undertaken to live together in total community, including sexual. Goods were held in common, children raised in common and each could have sexual relations with whomever they chose within the community. In our little informal group of social revolutionaries, we seized the idea and discussed it nonstop. We found illustrious predecessors in Proudhon and especially Charles Fourier. This reading reassured us. Others had promulgated this idea before us. Ever since the publication of the article, every day the news brought confirmation of the existence of a veritable movement. Sexual communities were springing up throughout France, around Paris, and also in the provinces—in the Cevennes, in Larzac, in Normandy. We were tormented. Nearly all of us were married. Some already had children. Philippe had married the sweet Marie-Blanche whom he'd met in lycée; Isaac, the charming Hélene, from the avenue Claude-Debussy; Jean-Loup, Marie-France whom he'd known since childhood; Jean-François, the very beautiful Michèle who'd made him chase her, like Tex Avery's wolf; and I, David's sister, also born in Egypt, also an emigrant in the cité. Our actual circumstances seemed the opposite of our ideal. In order to take life by the horns, we'd married our likenesses, nearly our sisters. If we were serious about 'group marriage', we'd have to completely overturn our lives. Yet the idea corresponded so perfectly to the theories we kept going back to. We wanted to raise a new generation of children, the future citizens of a society of anarchists. We felt the contradiction between our communal ideals—of integral communists—and the real choices we'd made. We were not the only ones living these contradictions. The others, those who were living communally, seemed to be experiencing equally painful contradictions. We'd made the acquaintance of a sexual community in a Parisian suburb, but its reality hardly enchanted us. Its members were in in a constant state of conflict. Sexual freedom was largely theoretical. Rather than finding a joyous exercise of liberty, we witnessed, perplexed, the reign of rivalry and jealousy. I was also thinking—I'd already been thinking—that the anthropology of distant peoples was no longer for our time. Lèvi-Strauss had announced its disappearance at the conclusion of *Tristes Tropiques*. If there was to be another anthropology, it would have to be that of groups belonging to our modernity. In short, I proposed to Devereux for my doctoral research I'd study the members of sexual communes. I was imagining going off to meet them, to explore with them their visions, their theories, their references, their dreams. Imagined, of course, exploring the history of the individuals, learning by what paths they'd arrived at this novel form of personal life that put into question the very foundations of society: parenting, property, children's education, personal and familial identity. I must have spoken for two hours, describing how I would gain access to these communities, the working methods I envisaged. I told him my thoughts, my way of living. I also described my own path, the ideas I'd embraced since adolescence. He listened attentively, immediately understanding my unexpressed nuances, sometimes speaking up to rephrase a thought, to offer a personal example. Everything seemed to be going well. When my presentation was over, it must have been after 1 p.m., I rose and politely announced my departure.

'Why don't you stay for lunch?' he asked. The idea didn't exactly thrill me. I'd given all I had. For the moment, the subject of my thesis was still in a state of disarray. I would not have been able to talk about it any longer. Yet I agreed to stay.

'Let's put your thesis to the side. We'll have plenty of other occasions to return to it. Let's speak instead of life and the world, like the friends we are.'

Friends? What was he saying? I'd known him for no more than three hours and I was far from feeling at ease. He was close to three times my age; his erudition was profound. Sitting before him, with my stammering knowledge, his experience seemed infinite to me, mine purely imaginary. He'd been around the world. I'd been around my room. What's more, his political ideas seemed thousands of miles away from mine. Although, as I think about it now, this last point was the least distressing. Although his politics were downright reactionary, his apartment, his lifestyle, all expressed a gentle anarchy. In the kitchen, he took two lamb cutlets and a package of potatoes au dauphin from the freezer and started heating them in a skillet. While he worked, he began to talk about himself: 'As you can see, at my age, I have to fend for myself.'

His wife had just left him, he didn't know why. They'd got along wonderfully. She'd worked with him, helped with his research on the ancient Greeks, typed his manuscripts, reread them, corrected them with him. And then suddenly, with no explanation, she'd packed her bag and disappeared.

'How can this be?' he wondered. I feigned polite surprise.

'It was a Saturday. Like every week, I went out to conduct my seminar. She must have planned ahead, do you see? Because, around seven, when I returned, not only was she gone, she'd also taken all her stuff with her. Can you even imagine such a thing? She left nothing behind, not even a toothbrush. Do you see what that means? She must have been preparing for weeks. A person doesn't leave like that from one day to the next ...'

Our meal was spent discussing his wife's departure. I was quite uncomfortable, caught between the need to interject, to reassure him that I understood, and the need to keep a certain distance. After all, none of this had anything to do with me.

To close the chapter, he confessed with the utmost seriousness, 'I think I've been slightly depressed since she left. As friends, we can of course speak of such things.'

Binyamina, 1998

A long time afterwards, it must have been in 1998, I met a Yemenite Jewish healer near Binyamina, in the north of Israel. One of my students, Henny, was devoting her thesis to techniques of healing. When we were preparing to enter, a Fury threw herself on us spewing a stream of insults. She pointed to my student: 'You want to sleep with him, don't you, you whore?' I doubt that Henny had the least sexual desire for the old man, skinny and wizened as old Africans often are. His toothless mouth, green with the khat he chewed constantly, twisted into a rictus of impotence. He shrugged. 'What do you expect? The woman is mad. It's God who wanted it that way!' He'd never been able to help her. It was not for want of trying: prayers, amulets, baths in hidden places, buried bottles filled with names. 'One cannot heal one's own family. Can a knife cut itself?'

It was a bright day, with a brilliance you only see there. He hurled an insult at his wife in Yemeni Arabic. She ran to hide in the back of their weed-filled garden and we did not hear from her again all morning.

We went back inside with him. In his office, a young woman, also Yemeni, was weeping, her head in her hands. She'd been abandoned by her husband who'd left for Ukraine. She was waiting for him. While she wept, he pursued the narrative of his wife's illness.

'To cure her—this I learnt from my uncle's books—I poured water over myself with a large pail, then changed my clothes. I even uttered the Holy Name, with all its letters, but all in vain.'

At long last, he turned to his patient. He handed her the amulet he'd crafted and instructed her to wear it on her person for three days, 'Afterwards, fasten it with a pin to your purse and carry it with you at all times. Go now and bring me some water.'

She poured a little water from a bottle from Eïn Gedi into the earthen cup he extended, then returned to sit on a small wooden stool, facing him. Haïm whispered silently into the cup, causing the surface of the water to tremble as if by the breath of God on the first day of creation. Then he rose and abruptly commanded the abandoned wife to close her eyes. Distrustfully, she tried to glimpse him between her fingers. 'Close your eyes,' he commanded. She finally obeyed. That's when he brusquely threw the contents of the cup in her face. She remained silent for a moment, with her hands over her eyes. He gave her a towel. 'Wipe your face.'

Towards the end of that sunny morning, he went into the garden, an old devil skipping and joyously repeating, like a sort of mantra, 'ya tamanya, ya tamanya.' He was sure he he'd succeeded in reaching the husband, wherever he was.

In his office, a heterogeneous array of modernity was assembled on rusty metal shelves: Coca-Cola bottles filled with sacred ink that enables letters to exert their power over objects, humans and invisible entities;

scraps of worn parchment bearing the name of God, stored in plastic Tupperware containers; hundred-year-old books of Kabbalah, their loose pages annotated and dog-eared. I was struck by the atmosphere of truth emanating from the place. If God slips in among humans, it can only be in such places, composites. For the world is made like this, when it is alive, in disorder. I thought back to Devereux, to that day when he'd assailed me with the story of his wife's incomprehensible behaviour. I'd felt the same perplexity before the brutal paradox of the one who knows, to whom providence has given the gift of clairvoyance, who nevertheless presents himself as a victim of fate. For the old Yemeni healer Haïm, intimately accompanied, day and night, by a demon, the explanation was clear: his mad wife was proof of his power. You might even suspect that he was deliberately invoking his ched *in order to learn what lies hidden within us, to act on the invisible, without it being suspected by others. Perhaps it was the same for Devereux; perhaps his wife's departure was proof of his power.*

We left Haïm intently copying a Torah, which can only be written by hand, on a special parchment fabricated in accordance with a precise ritual, using ink consecrated by a sofer, a scribe who knows the scriptures perfectly.

With regret, I departed from the little shack in that working-class neighbourhood in the north of Israel, leaving the old Yemenite to his age-old task of repairing destinies.

* * *

Antony, 1971

After lunch, Devereux complained of being tired. He needed to rest. He invited me to follow him into his room, where he stretched out on the bed. The very small room seemed exactly like the rest of the apartment, chaotic. A bed, a night table and yet more books, books everywhere. He claimed he could find any one of them with his eyes closed. One bookcase held copies of his own works, drawn from his articles, and in numerous editions in different languages. Another displayed his complete collection of SAS, the series of German spy novels featuring the Austrian prince Malko. There were also the the complete works of Karl May. Devereux caught my eye.

'You know his Serene Highness Prince Malko Linge?'

Like everyone, I'd read SAS.

'This reading relaxes me, you see? I quiet my mind by reading popular fiction,' Devereux excused himself, 'and adventure novels like Karl May's, for example.'

Karl May is Germany's best-known novelist, the author of dozens of potboilers about the West, and about the Near and the Middle East in which his protagonists, always German, encounter Indians, Arabs and Bedouins. Simple adventure tales, they allowed Germans at the turn of the century to imagine, in the first person, these distant, quasi-mythical worlds. May wrote his Westerns without ever setting foot in America, and his Oriental tales without ever leaving Germany. He had a huge success, comparable only to that of Tintin. Noted figures publicly declared their passion for Karl May: Einstein, Fritz Lang, Helmut Kohl, Adolf Hitler. Yet May was

a mysterious, fantastical personality. Today I think that what fascinated Devereux was the ethnology of the bazaar, the multitude of
identities May assumed. The complete collection of SAS must have
disappeared in the archives, his books Devereux bequeathed to the
social anthropology laboratory at the College de France, eventually
housed in the IMEC (Institute of Memoirs of Contemporary
Editions). Today, one can no longer find a trace of SAS.

Squeezed into this tiny room at the back of the apartment,
with an erudite anarchist unfurling before me a life that seemed
more extraordinary than those in the novels, my mind went blank.
My eyes haggard, I let the uninterrupted flow of words swirl around
me. Stretched out on his bed, unkempt, his shirt open to his navel,
Devereux spoke about himself, only himself. He too identified as a
perpetual immigrant. His first emigration had been forced, an
internal one, so to speak, from one language to another. Born in
1908 in Banat, a region of Transylvania that was then part of
Hungary, he grew up with Hungarian as his mother tongue. But
after the end of the Great War, most of Banat was reattached to
Romania. From one day to the next, the administration changed,
as did as the language used in school.

'Although I had excellent grades in Romanian, I refused to
speak the language of the occupier. As soon as I had the chance,
I left the country,' he told me. 'At the age of eighteen, I went to
study in France.' This was the first version I heard of his departure
from Hungary; Later, I would hear a good many others. He
recounted the ups and downs of his studies in France. He kept
harping on the notion that there was always something working
against him, thwarting his ambitions. He'd been planning on a

musical career, was a remarkable pianist, wore his hair long like an artist. But then a fractured thumb was further complicated by muscle contractions that evolved into Dupuytren's disease—no more piano!

Next, he studied physics but abandoned it after two years. Much later I would learn that for a time he'd frequented the great families of the French aristocracy. What novel was he inventing for himself? I know that he dreamt of fortune and noble marriages. He ended up enrolling, at the age of twenty-three, in the ethnology programme that had just been created at the Ethnology Institute in Paris, with such exceptional professors as Lucien Lévy-Bruhl, Marcel Mauss and Paul Rivet. He completed his degree, and began his field research in Indochina for the Musée de l'homme, the Museum of Man. He showed me, hung on the wall behind him, a lance and a scabbard from Vietnam. 'I brought back hundreds of objects like these from my expeditions in Indochina,' he boasted. 'They must be rotting in the basements of the Musée de l'homme.' But the atmosphere in France was becoming increasingly xeno-phobic. And when the Stavisky Affair broke in December 1933, he felt he was in danger. Time for a second emigration. He seized the first opportunity to leave for the United States in order to attend the University of California at Berkeley, and to prepare his dissertation.

'I've always been poor, never recognized for my work. The day of my thesis defence, I was literally dying of hunger. A secretary took pity and offered me a sandwich, so I could survive the ordeal.'

The man was suffering; he seemed old—was he playacting? Since our first meeting two years earlier, he seemed to have decided to reduce his smoking. Now he was slipping his cigarettes into a filtered holder to reduce the nicotine. As a result, he sucked like a madman, consuming twice as much as before. The atmosphere had become suffocating. He was full of recriminations—against his wife who'd left him, against his teachers who'd failed to acknowledge him, against his colleagues, against life, against fate. Suspended, not knowing what to think or to say, I kept my mouth shut. There were moments when I wondered if this wasn't a variation on his infamous test. Night had fallen long ago. He suddenly rose.

'Why don't you stay for dinner? You'll leave with your stomach full.'

I didn't have it in me to protest. He took more cutlets and potatoes from the freezer, and continued to talk about his studies, his doctorate, his thesis director, Alfred Kroeber, who'd mistreated him.

'Kroeber was a little obtuse. And then professors are sometimes the victims of their own ideology. I once pointed out to him that what he'd written on the subject of purification rituals among the Hopi Indians was impossible. Obsessed by the symbolism of the number '40' for Native Americans, he'd written that women purified themselves every forty days. Do you realize the absurdity of that? How could they have purified themselves every forty days when they had their menstrual periods every twenty-eight days, like all women?'

After the meal, we sat down again in the armchairs in the living room. I tried to bring the conversation back to what interested me, psychoanalysis, ethnopsychiatry, my thesis. He continued to talk about himself, to complain. 'During my psychoanalytic training, I worked in Dr Karl Menninger's clinic in Topeka. I was working as a researcher, producing reports and funding proposals. In exchange,

Menninger had accepted me as a psychoanalytic trainee. In those days, in the United States, a non-medical doctor could not enter a psychoanalytic training programme, unless he were enrolled in one or two known research centres. Menninger had entrusted me with a patient for analytic supervision. Even though the patient was doing perfectly well, he made the supervision drag on so that I couldn't be given a second patient. He didn't want to see me finish my programme, He feared that as soon as my training was over, I would leave him behind. I was there for almost eight years. There's nothing in Topeka, you see, there's nothing. It's at the end of the world, in the desert, and there's nothing, nothing but this psychiatric clinic in the middle of nowhere. When you go into town, you meet only psychiatrists, nurses and patients. That's it! Come, let me show you some photos.'

From a shoebox sandwiched between two books, he drew out two faded photographs. A young man, holding a magnificent collie by a leash. He had brown hair and sported a little moustache. The fellow was certainly handsome. And what style! Clark Gable in *Gone with the Wind*.

'You're so handsome,' I observed.

'I was handsome, yes,' he lamented again, 'but poor, very poor. With the pittance I earned at the clinic, I bought myself a used car, a 1932 Cadillac 452.'

I was beside myself.

'A 16-cylinder!' I gushed.

'Yes!' Devereux confirmed. 'Do you want to see it?' And he left to look for another photograph in his shoebox. I could make out the Cadillac, a pre-war roadster, which must have been a beauty when it was new. At the date of the photo (around 1955), the car was at least twenty years old. He was standing, one hand on the door, beside a woman whose head was missing. He'd cut it out. It dawned on me that this must not be the first time his wife had disappeared.

'I only started to earn some money,' he continued, 'when I set myself up as a psychoanalyst in New York City.' The chairs on which we were sitting dated from that period, as well as some of the other furniture in the apartment. 'It's always like that for people who think.' (One might have suspected that he was warning me.)

He continued to describe his psychoanalytic training at length. None of his mentors in the field found grace in his eyes. Menninger thought only of growing rich. Jökl, his psychoanalyst, was an ordinary man ('nice enough, but uninteresting'). As for Roheim, who'd taken him on as a patient at the beginning, for six years, maybe more, he was no doubt a genius, but everything he wrote was so confused that he himself couldn't make heads or tails of it.

It must have been 11 p.m. when he finally gave me leave to go. I was standing, putting on my coat, when he held me back again: 'Wait, sit down for a minute, I have something important to tell you.'

I sat down, facing him.

'Tobie, listen to me carefully. It should be clear to you that I don't speak at random . . . and so, I can announce to you, Tobie, that you will be my successor.'

I had no idea what to say. I opened my eyes wide, astonished.

'Come, Georges, you're joking . . .'

He looked at me severely.

'I'm not joking, nor am I trying to flatter you. I'm simply announcing what will be the case. You will continue my work. You'll be my successor.'

He walked me to the door and shook my hand, with the anarchist salutation: 'Farewell, and fraternity!'

It was cold and damp out. My old clunker didn't like this weather. I had to start it with the hand crank. During the good hour it took me to return home, I had plenty of time to reflect. This thesis advisor's manner was certainly surprising. I did not tell myself that he was crazy, or motivated by some mysterious, perverse intention. I didn't understand, that was all. If he'd wanted to make me lose my bearings, to cloud my judgement, he would not have behaved any differently. What he'd imparted pertained largely to advisor–student relationships. He obviously had not known how to 'find a master', as the Talmud advises. He'd wandered from music to physics, from ethnology to psychoanalysis, from literature to Greek studies. I was coming to him under the illusion that in him I would find a master; he spent hours explaining to me that not one of those he'd known had been able to fill that role. Why had he announced that I would be his successor, if not to break the spell, to banish the illusion? One thing was certain: I would never forget what he'd taught me that day. And yet, he'd told me nothing new. Some of his anecdotes had appeared in the book of his that I'd just read: *Essays on General Ethnopsychiatry.* As for the rest, once I came to know the totality of his work, I would find them all, in the same words, and with the same delivery. Even what might have seemed to be confidences—his wife's departure, for example, or the discord between him and the institution of psychoanalysis—all this was was public knowledge. Once I was regularly attending the seminar, I would discover that he served up the same discourse to each of us. So what was it that I would never forget? His stories had become mine; they'd metamorphosed into my own experience. That is what I will never forget. He'd performed a kind of magic trick. I'd gone to him with a request (that he take me on as his thesis student), with a question that concerned me (my thesis topic), and plenty of other questions regarding my future. I left with my head full of questions about him. He'd achieved a sort of transposition of my mental universe—focused on myself when I entered, magnetized by him when I departed

My friend Abdelhamid, who also knew Devereux quite well, once related to me the Sufi parable about a student in search of a master. He is told about one to be found living alone in a hovel, in a lost valley. The student climbs the mountain for several days before he reaches the old man's door. 'Who is it?' the old man inquires. 'It is I,' the student replies. Silence. He knocks again. No one answers; no one opens the door. The student goes back the way he came. Ten years later, he has grown, gained experience and feels ready to find his master. The student once again climbs the same mountain. He reaches the door of the same hovel, lost in the distant valley. He knocks. The same voice asks from inside, 'Who is it?' 'It is I,' the student replies again. And again, the same silence, the same absence. Twenty years go by, and once more the same man, now approaching old age, undertakes the ascent of the mountain. He reaches the hidden valley, finds the old shack again, knocks at the same door. 'Who is it?' asks the voice again. 'It is you!' the student replies. And this time, the door opens at last.

This parable is a perfect description of my first encounter with Devereaux: When I arrived, I was myself; when I left, I was him. And I no longer felt like a ticking time bomb ready to explode.

Winter 1973.

On my behalf, David had tracked down a sexual community in a London suburb. To add to my research material, we decided to spend a week there. We climbed into his 2CV, more reliable than mine, and off we went. The information we had was not precise. No one was living at the address we'd been given. We ended up spending the entire night wandering across the London suburbs from one contact to another, from pub to cafe. Finally, we obtained the correct address. We rang. A sleepy young woman opened the door for us. The English back then didn't usually heat their homes. Inside, the windows were covered in frost. It must have been around zero degrees that morning. We explained the reason for our visit. Pamela was the leader of this community. We could wake her if we wished. We entered her room and found several beds in the half-dark. We approached the first. A tuft of red hair was poking out of the covers. The young woman thrust out her head. A few moments later, a young lad emerged in turn, from under the same cover where he'd been completely hidden.

'Hello!' I said to the boy, 'What's your name?'

'Hello! My name is Tobias!' replied the little imp, no more than four years old, 'And you?'

'Me? I'm Tobias too!'

Tobie, Tobias in English, Tobías in Spanish, Tevieh in Yiddish, Toviah in the Bible, which means, 'God has done well.' It was a name that came from afar . . .

4

Feast Day

It was a big, old-fashioned house at the far end of a winding alley in old Cairo. The side facing the street seemed nearly blind, with just a few windows hiding their eyes behind delicately carved olive-wood mashrabiyas. In such houses, the world opened up from within. There was a garden and, unheard of luxury, a small fountain that flowed continuously into a stone basin. The short man with the serene face was dressed in Turkish style, wearing a caftan made from sumptuous fabrics. On his head, a turban gave him the look of a fifteenth-century Arab merchant. A long, silky white beard flowed down his chest. When you looked at him, your eyes were drawn by sparkles. On his slightly rounded belly an eight-pointed gold star, pierced by a large ruby, dangled at the end of a long chain. He was imposing. A man of power to be sure, and, most certainly, tradition. It was five-thirty in the morning. He adjusted his clothing in front of the mirror at the entrance and left the living quarters. Skirting the garden, he took a detour along the paved alley, then entered a small office on the other side of the courtyard. In the sky above Egypt, kites, fierce birds of prey, are as common as pigeons in Paris. It was the 15th of September, 1866, a Saturday. An unusual mood was hovering over the city. On that day, Ferdinand de Lesseps was unveiling the plans for the construction of the Suez Canal to several visiting heads of state, and from the very early morning, you could hear the bustle of the preparations. The rabbi, as was his wont, had risen an hour before daybreak. He savoured these moments when the city was disturbed only by the cocks crowing in imitation of the muezzins' calls to prayer. It was a moment of silence and solitude, when he could consult the books, he would not for any price have entrusted into anyone else's hands. Some existed in only a single manuscript copy, like the one he was perusing just then. It had been penned in Saragossa in 1485, by Ya'akov Ibn Habib, the renowned author of 'eïn Ya'akov, (The Source of Jacob), a kind of 'best of the Talmud' every pious Jew should own. The rabbi was slowly reading the section entitled 'The beauty of the sapphire'. The author, Ya'akov Ibn Habib, was his great-great-great-grandfather, his most celebrated ancestor, one of the past masters from the era of Arab splendour in Spain. It was said that Ya'akov Ibn Habib was Maimonides' equal, that none of the three languages—Hebrew, Arabic and Aramaic—withheld any secrets from him. The rabbi was examining the text traced in chameleon's blood, the mere sight of which made the hand holding it tremble. He kept looking at the same page, going over it, reading it again. He was aware that the next day the sultan would be announcing whether he would be named Grand Rabbi of Egypt. He was scrutinizing the Scriptures, trying to divine their hidden meaning, yearning for both their prescience and protection. His mind was lost in contemplation of the letters, unable to determine what they augured. The horizon was reddening, the sun just beginning to appear. The rabbi adjusted his prayer shawl over his shoulders and spoke the first blessing aloud. His wife, the robissa Marième, entered the office, carrying the breakfast tray laden with coffee, rounds of Arabic bread, a few black olives. She placed it on the window ledge near where he liked to sit alone every morning, savouring the silence. She withdrew without a sound, leaving the old man to his prayers. At that moment, a great noise in the sky could be heard, a piercing scream, like an infant's cry. The rabbi did not react, standing unmoved as he faced the first rays of the rising sun, reciting the *Shema Israël*, the words of love for his God. A second cry made the cats' hairs stand on end before they scurried into the walls' crevices. Next, the powerful beating of wings could be heard. From high above, as swift as a ray of sunlight, a kite swooped down and snatched some rounds of bread. For a moment, there was silence. You could not even hear the mumbled credo. His prayer complete, Yom-Tov approached the window and gazed up at the sky, searching for the vanished bird. All he could see was a black feather drifting slowly down to the tray. He took hold of the kanaka, the small, still-steaming brass coffee pot, and poured his coffee, *sokar zyada*, with plenty of sugar. He uttered another blessing before bringing the cup to his lips. Then he studied the claw marks left on the stone sill. They formed a sort of writing, a grimoire. Delicately, he grasped the feather dropped by the bird, dipped it into a dark ink made from a mixture of clays, and on a scrap of paper wrote the word that had caught his eye: *dan* in Hebrew, 'the judge'. He carefully folded the paper and slipped it against his chest, under the flannel of his small body shawl. Then he sat down, closing his eyes for a long moment. Thinking he was asleep, his close aides entered without knocking.

The men engaged in a heated debate that day. Given that it was forbidden to carry anything on Shabbat, was it permissible to carry one's handkerchief to the synagogue? Levi Tantaoui, the rabbi's aide, argued that yes, it was permissible to carry your handkerchief, since a handkerchief could be considered part of your clothing. The rabbi, on the other hand, insisted that no, a handkerchief was not clothing but baggage; hence to carry it was tantamount to work. The debate lasted a long time. Afterwards, the rabbi rushed to the synagogue, followed by his two assistants, the beadle and several students. At the synagogue, the faithful had been growing impatient. While waiting for the master, the other rabbis had begun to chant some psalms.

'Rabbi, what happened? Did you forget to wake up?' asked Yehezquel Pardo, a community leader who never missed an opportunity to criticize the rabbi.

They were impertinent, these Jews of Egypt, as impertinent as during the time of the Exodus when they'd questioned Moses. Could it be that these Jews had never left Egypt? The rabbi stayed silent, opening big surprised eyes, as if he did not understand the question he'd just been asked.

'But rabbi, we've been waiting for the Shabbat prayer for at least thirty minutes,' Pardo insisted.

'Thirty minutes? What are you saying?' Yom-Tov exclaimed. 'The sun is barely visible. Did you get up in the middle of the night?'

'It's true,' admitted the surprised beadle, still standing by the large entrance. 'It's not yet day.'

The faithful rushed to the windows and the door. They had to yield to the evidence. Day was barely breaking. Yet time does not go backwards. Half an hour ago, the sun had been shining like a lantern, and they'd felt its heat on the back of their necks. Yom-Tov was smiling slyly.

'It's a little early for the prayer,' he announced. 'Let's begin with a psalm.'

Later, the faithful who'd attended the service on this Shabbat, the 15th of Elul in the Hebrew year 5647, swore to whoever would listen that, just to avoid admitting he was late, the old man had reversed the sun's course. They likened him to Moses or Joseph— Joseph, who'd stopped time to win the war. It may be that Rabbi Yom-Tov did not know how to reverse the sun's course; perhaps he simply knew how to cloud the eyes of his flock. The next day, Sunday, 16 September 1866, the sultan signed the decree naming Yom-Tov Israël-Sherezli the Grand Rabbi of Egypt. He succeeded his father Eliahou Israël Sherezli, the Grand Rabbi of Alexandria and then of Egypt. As it is said, Rabbi Yom-Tov Israël Sherezli judged Israel in Egypt from 1867 to 1891. I bear the first name of this man who came to visit my mother during her pregnancy to taste her preserves and drink her coffee. He was me, living one hundred and twenty years earlier; I am him, arriving fifty-seven years after his death. I would like to be him still.

I'm called Tobie because my name is Yom-Tov, after the Grand Rabbi. I was born in Cairo, Egypt, in 1948, the year the state of Israel was created. I was the second child, the second son. My brother bore the first name of my father's father, and I, according to tradition, ought to have been given the name of my mother's father. I should have been called Isaac, or perhaps Zaki, a more ambiguous first name with the advantage, during those troubled times, of passing for Arab. But my mother had quarrelled with her father and would not, under any circumstances, agree to give his name to her son. It was a quarrel that would mark the family, scarring us for generations. She'd recently lost her mother, and her father Zaki had decided to remarry less than six months after, abrogating the traditional year of mourning.

'What do you expect?' he'd said to justify his behaviour. 'I eat meat. I can hardly remain a widower.'

My grandfather had studied science for many years, and thus felt he was an authority on such matters. He presented his theory to his friends: meat provoked sexual desire. Didn't flesh call to flesh? And there was nothing worse than spilling your seed in your sleep. Your energy would be sapped and you would sink into nervous exhaustion. But as my mother saw it, what he did next was even worse. Not content with subjecting her to this remarriage, he then went to her home to retrieve the smoking-jacket he'd worn for his first marriage. He wanted to have it altered for the second! This was too much! My mother sought advice from her aunt Engela, who didn't waste a minute before insisting: 'Make a scene! You need to make a scene!'

'Make a scene?' my mother echoed dubiously, 'How?'

'Fling yourself onto the floor, cry, rip your clothes, slap your face, tear your skin.'

So that's what she did. One afternoon, when her father invited himself over for some *ful oué ta'meya*, the traditional meal of favas and fritters, she flung herself to the ground just as he opened the door. Right there on the floor, in the entrance of their Abasseya apartment, she tore her dress. She shrieked, beat herself with her hands, she wept, she gasped with rage, she nearly fainted. My grandfather, Zaki al-agzagui, Zaki the pharmacist, looked heavenward and muttered a Latin phrase, *globus hystericu*, in which one word—'hysteria'—could be made out. My mother heard the word as it was intended—an insult. She rose up like a Fury, hurled herself at her father, shoved him, beat his chest with her two fists and drove him out of the door. Ever since that day, she had not exchanged a word with him. Now, two years later, she was pregnant; was she going to glorify him by giving her little one his name? To this child she could feel stirring in her womb, who, she was sure of it, was a boy? That's how my first few months in the world were spent, in the belly of a mother who did not know how to avoid passing down her father's name to her child. Fortunately, during the fifth month of her pregnancy, she had a dream. Her father's grandfather, the Rabbi Yom-Tov Israël Sherezli, the celebrated Grand Rabbi of Egypt, her ancestor, stood before her, dressed in a long white galabeya. First, like any visitor, he asked for a cup of coffee. She served him his coffee, but it did not seem to satisfy him. 'What else would you like, *ya geddi*, O Grandfather? What is your pleasure?' He asked if he could sample her preserves. And when she offered him the last three she'd made—her date jam, her coconut jelly, her bitter orange marmalade—the ancestor added: 'For I'm coming to live in your home.' After my mother woke up, this dream continued to occupy her mind. She repeated it again and again to her aunts Engela and Sarina.

'Don't you see, Ranou my dear,' (Ranou was my mother's name) 'Don't you see, Ranou, there can be no doubt.'

'No doubt?'

'One hundred per cent, my dear.'

'No doubt,' echoed the other.

The elderly women had no trouble interpreting the dream: the rabbi had appeared in order to announce his plan to move in with our family. That was why he'd first taken coffee—coffee, that quasi-sacred substance in an Egyptian household, the elixir of life. The first blessing you confer on a host who offers you coffee, *ah'oua daymone*, means: 'May there always be coffee in this house!' And then he'd asked for preserves. This was to announce that he would be bringing sweetness and pleasure to the home. This was how my mother learnt, well before the delivery, that the son she was expecting would be a reincarnation of Rabbi Yom-Tov Israël Sherezli. And when I was born a few months later, there was no question what my first name would be. They would give me his: Yom-Tov would be my name.

Still, I doubt the truth of this tale. Did my mother invent it? Or, more likely, had she simply had a version of the dream that had announced the birth of Rabbi Yom-Tov Lev Tantaoui, for many years a secretary to Rabbi Yom-Tov Israël?

Family lore has it that when my father carried my older brother on his shoulders on his way to record my birth in the civil registry, he was caught up in a riot in an inflamed Cairo, chased by a crowd shouting *dabba'h al yahoud*, 'slaughter the Jew'. It was 1948. The Middle East was born that year, with a scar right at its centre: Israel. Unless it be a festering wound, sucking in the phantasms of generations. Given the prevailing mood, my father did not have the courage to utter a Jewish name before a government official. How could he have spoken that name, my name, Yom-Tov? He might as well have committed suicide right then and there. 'Tobie', its abbreviation, was worse, sounding both Jewish and European. He decided to translate my name into Arabic. Yom-Tov, 'feast day' in Hebrew implies 'Jewish holiday', a religious feast like Yom Kippur or Passover. (Actually, if one had to translate, I should have been named 'Pascal'.) In Arabic, Yom-Tov becomes Eïd, short for 'Eïd el Kébir, literally the 'great feast', 'the feast of the lamb'. It was settled. For the state, my name would be not Yom-Tov but 'Eïd. Thanks to politics, I'd been transformed from the slaughtered goat of Yom Kippur into the sacrificial lamb of 'Eïd al Kébir. On my official papers, I was thus named 'Eïd, which is of course unpronounceable in French. At home, everyone called me Tobie. It was my name, the name to which I answered. It remains my name. Yet I've never been able to use it on my identity papers. Twenty years later, in Paris in 1969, at my naturalization, I asked to change my first name. I was hoping to regularize my identity.

'Tobie?' the police commissioner exclaimed. 'What kind of a name is that? Come on now . . .'

I insisted. 'Tobie, for heaven's sake, Tobie—it's in the Bible.'

'Who cares about the Bible?' he brusquely dismissed me. 'You need to choose a name from the Saints' Calendar.' (At the time, Tobie was not in the Calendar.)

'Why can't you choose a name like everyone else,' official scowled, 'a name like Maurice or Marcel?'

I searched for a week. I wanted to at least keep the initial T.—Théophile! That's the name I chose. I would be Théophile.

The commissioner sighed. 'Clearly, you don't want to be like everyone else.'

I bear the name Yom-Tov so as not to bear my grandfather's name, Isaac or Zaki. My name is Tobie, in the place of Yom-Tov, perhaps so that a saint's name not be taken in vain. For a long time, I was called 'Eïd, so as not to have a Jewish name in a country at war against the Jews. My name is now Théophile because a French police commissioner, a touch too identified with the Republic, did not know his Bible. 'Théophile'. I like this name I've chosen, a name I translate as 'lover of God', which is true of me. I would have preferred being 'God's beloved', but one cannot have everything.

Rabbi Yom-Tov Israël Sherezli, grandfather of my grandfather, was Grand Rabbi of Egypt during the best, the final, days of the Ottoman Empire. He was the last in a long line of rabbis who'd fled Spain at the end of the fifteenth century. At first refugees not far from Salonika in Serres, whence they derived their surname, 'Sherezli', they'd attempted Jerusalem before ending up in Egypt. Why were the Jews in Egypt despite the Talmudic injunction not to dwell there? Among Maimonides' prohibitions, one, the most fundamental, recurs again and again: 'It is permissible to live anywhere in the world, with the exception of Egypt.' And yet, not long after he formulated this rule, after an abortive attempt in Jerusalem, Maimonides himself settled in Egypt, in Cairo, where he spent a large part of his life and where he eventually died. Like him, my ancestors tried several times to live in Jerusalem, but the poverty of that desert land always drove them back to Egypt. Such were the descendants of the Talmudist Ya'akov Ibn Habib. Eliahou Israël Sherezli was born in Serres. He emigrated to Jerusalem where he lived for part of his childhood and where he studied. But he also lived in Alexandria and then in Cairo. Yom-Tov, his son, was born in Jerusalem, lived and worked in Egypt and died in Jerusalem. He was buried on the Mount of Olives, as befitted a man who'd spent a lifetime attending to his God.

Jerusalem, 2005

I search everywhere through the cemetery for the tomb of Yom-Tov, my grandfather's grandfather. An unlikely guard locates an old register. Yes, he was definitely buried here but the grave was precisely where the road was built after 1967, the road separating West Jerusalem from East Jerusalem. 'The grave must be underneath. Perhaps you walked on it.' I and the friend accompanying me that day sit on a boulder to rest. The sun is rapidly setting, and a cool breeze, of the kind there is so often here, causes us to shiver. Suddenly, my friend cries out. Emerging from the graves are earthworms, thick as a finger, like little snakes. Assuredly, when you invoke the dead, they will appear. It's time to leave.

* * *

The Israël-Sherezlis have been rabbis since the dawn of time. One branch of the family had been in Spain before 1492, the other was from here, 'around here', that is, this part of the Ottoman Empire— Jerusalem, Salonika, Cairo, Alexandria, the islands of Corfu and

Rhodes. Witness to the Jews' journeys and wanderings, they carried the memory of a people. This must be why we had the sense of having been contemporaries of the Jews' millennial history. I recall weeping as a child when I heard how the Jews had suffered during the Inquisition. I don't know from whence came this deep sorrow as I was told about persecutions, the mad flight of Marranos accused of 'Judaizing', the practice of holding religious rituals while hiding in cellars and attics. And the delight I took in stories of secret alliances, especially—my favourite!—the one about a young Marrano boy falling deeply in love with a young Marrano girl, each unaware that the other was a Jew. My family remembered the Jews of Spain, their story engraved within us in bitter letters. Our expulsion from Spain was yesterday, the memory of this Exodus more vivid perhaps than that of the Shoah, even though members of the family who had remained in Greece were among the 55,000 Jews slaughtered in 1944 by the Germans in Sherez.

Yom-Tov was the last of our family's great rabbis. The dynasty died out with him, a little before the end of the Ottoman Empire. His sister Bida married a wealthy banker, the Pacha Yaakov Cattaoui, a Jew ennobled in the Turkish manner, granted the title of 'bey' by the Sultan. You could even say that the rabbi held sway over the community from both its ends: by way of the spirit, thanks to the religious aura that radiated from him; and by way of money, thanks to the place he held among the rich and powerful as a consequence of his sister's marriage. He was the last in a long line of multifaceted men: at once patriarch, head of the family, religious guide, political leader and mage. After him, his three sons, with varying degrees of success, went into business: banking, the stock market and cotton. They made loads of money and lost even more. Mayer, my grandfather's father, built a huge fortune by introducing the steam-powered cotton-gin to Egypt. His oldest son, Samuel, squandered most of it. Only a small portion was saved, enabling my mother's father, my grandfather Zaki, to study medicine at the American University in Beirut. My mother had an encyclopedic memory. She knew the genealogy of every member of this immense traditional family. Whoever wanted to learn a grandfather's name, to ascertain a degree of cousinship, or inquire after a family member's fate, turned to her—a sort of Egyptian griot. But even more than this knowledge of the living, she was steeped in the family's history. She had the sense of belonging to a noble lineage, which is why she kept my brother and me at a remove from the community during our childhood in Egypt. She thought of herself as an heiress. Yet she knew only fragments of Rabbi Tom-Yov's life story.

When the rabbi walked down the street, everyone made way: vendors disappeared; women ran and hid in their courtyards—not because he was harsh, but rather because a sort of troubling power emanated from him. His face was gentle, almost feminine, and he never raised his voice. He worked within people; he knew he could never have an impact through the use of violence. In those years, there was once a couple who fought constantly. One day, Yom-Tov came upon them quarrelling in the street. He walked quickly towards them, and upon reaching them, he literally took the man in his arms, exclaiming, 'Oh my friend! My dear friend. God has sent you here.'

Dumbstruck, the couple immediately ceased their quarrel.

'For so long, I've been hoping to meet you,' the rabbi added. 'Truly, God has sent you to me.'

'But rabbi,' the man stammered, 'aren't you mistaking me for someone else? Of course I know you, as does everyone around here, but why would you so ardently wish to meet me? '

'I do! What day is it? Thursday, no?' the rabbi replied. 'Why don't you have me to dinner tomorrow, for Shabbat. I'm sure your wife will make us an excellent meal.'

Of course the couple had to reconcile as they prepared to welcome the Grand Rabbi. Thus they came together, if only to make a good impression on the great man—certainly the most important man in their community. Yom-Tov, for his part, saw nothing dishonest in his plan. For why else do men and women, so different from each other, come together, if not to welcome God on the eve of Shabbat? The God of the Jews, like Baal, the God of their Canaanite cousins, also mated with adoring humans. But for this God, a single man or a single woman could never be a partner. Only a man and woman together, intertwined as a couple, forming a perfect bond, could interest our God. There is no question that the Jews invented romantic love, and for strictly religious reasons at that. Yom-Tov knew that God, his God, was drawn to this type of hybrid. And so Yom-Tov appeared at the couple's home the following evening, recited the blessings, discussed religion, politics and life, and thanked them when he left: 'I'm blessed by God, my friends, my God who has allowed me to spend this wonderful Shabbat with you. I hope you'll invite me again. But why do I say "hope"? No! I'll ask you now. Please, invite me again. Or better yet, no need to invite me, I'll be back for dinner again next Friday.'

He left the couple speechless on their doorstep. They made love that very night. And it was good. The rabbi returned the following week and again the week after. And each Shabbat night, after his visit, the couple made love. But, despite the rabbi's presence, despite his prayers and the songs he joyously sang with them, God did not visit the couple: the woman did not conceive. The rabbi visited less and less often, and soon he no longer came to spend Shabbat evening at the couple's home. Their harmony lasted for two years. And then they began to quarrel again. The wife had taken to insulting her husband. One night, beside himself, he beat her. She spat in his face. Incensed, he kicked her out. Egyptian law, in conformance to Islamic custom, held that if a man repudiated his wife three times, the couple would then be divorced. The husband had spoken the dreadful words, *Netal 'gki,* 'I repudiate you,' and then repeated the formula of repudiation.

'Say it once more,' the wife threatened, 'and you'll lose me. It will be useless to come and cry to my parents. I won't return. This time we'll be divorced for good, do you understand? Di-vor-ced!'

'Get out of my sight, you whore, I never want to see you again,' shouted the husband. And for a third time he said, 'I repudiate you.'

But the next day, as his anger dissipated, the man was distraught, wondering how he could get his wife back. She'd already returned to her parents. He requested an audience with the rabbi.

'You are divorced,' Yom-Tov confirmed. 'I'll draw up the official document. It's over. We need to find you another wife.'

The man wept, mourned, begged the rabbi for a solution.

'There's nothing to be done,' the rabbi repeated. 'There is no solution. You must formally liberate her. You must grant her the *get*.'

The man grew quiet, sinking into the chair the rabbi offered and beginning to weep.

'My poor friend,' the rabbi said. 'We live in Egypt. You know very well we must respect the laws of those who've welcomed us. Three times you said "I repudiate you." You said it in front of two witnesses. You can no longer go back. You've lost her.'

The man remained prostrate for a long time, then slowly raised his head. He'd just thought of something. If he had to divorce her, so be it. But why couldn't he marry her again? He would accept divorce if the rabbi agreed to remarry him immediately to the same woman, his wife.

'Our law states that you cannot marry the woman you've divorced,' Yom-Tov answered severely. 'If you want to have her again as your wife, she must first take another husband. She cannot return to you unless she has divorced her new husband. To put it simply, your wife is forbidden to you, as are, for example, your sister or your mother.'

The man again dissolved in tears. He wept for a long time— one, two hours. He refused to leave the synagogue. He was so overcome that the rabbi finally took pity on him.

'I might have a solution,' he offered.

'Really?' exclaimed the unfortunate man. 'Tell me, rabbi. I beg you. I promise that in the future I will be the most devoted husband. I will never again raise my voice against her. She will be the light of my eyes, my breath, my soul.'

The rabbi continued: 'I have a solution, but if I do this for you, you will never be able to part from this woman again, not in any way.'

93

'Yes, I agree,' the man acquiesced, nodding.

'You have perhaps not understood me,' Yom-Tov replied. 'I said, "Not in any way."'

'I do not wish to be separated from her, rabbi, I want to live with her for the rest of my days, in this world and in the world to come.'

'And in the world to come?' Yom-Tov repeated.

'In the world to come, as I said!'

'At home and abroad?' the rabbi insisted.

'To the grave, and even as our bones are returned to dust.'

'And in the two Egypts?'

'In Upper Egypt and as far as the meanders of the Delta.'

'Very well then,' said the rabbi, 'come back to see me tomorrow with a doll made of breadcrumbs.'

'What are you saying, rabbi? A doll?'

'As I said! Must I repeat myself?'

'A doll made of what?'

'A doll,' the rabbi repeated, 'made of bread, which you will dress with a scrap of your wife's clothing.'

The man left the rabbi with his head hanging, feeling as if he'd stepped into forbidden territory. The next day the two men went to the Kasr el Nil Bridge, where the rabbi conducted a ceremony, marrying the wife, represented by the bread doll, to the Nile, the most powerful of Egyptian beings. He addressed the river, introducing it to its new wife, identifying her by her father's name, and asking the river to welcome her.

'O Nile,' the rabbi intoned slowly in Arabic, 'you, most fertile of beings, you who nourish men through their labour on the earth, you who enrich the earth through men's labour, I present to you your new wife. Her name is Henriette, but everyone here calls her Richetta. Take her unto yourself as her husband.'

He instructed the man to toss the doll over the parapet. How could it be that this man of God, who delivered long sermons explaining that the Jews had abandoned idolatry for thousands of years in order to devote themselves only to God, the One God, how could it be that this man was engaging in some sort of barbaric sorcery? The husband hesitated.

'Do you really think so, rabbi? Do you think I can do it?'

'You'll do it because I've said so! Do it!' the rabbi commanded.

The man tossed the doll into the river. They stood there for a moment, watching the little bread person spin around in a whirl-pool before disintegrating. And then the rabbi said, 'Richetta's new husband treats her even more poorly than the last. See how he made her spin, how violent he already is with her, barely wed. This is unacceptable. You see it as I do, my son. I call on you as witness.'

The man stood speechless.

'Did you see it?' Yom-Tov again asked the petrified man, who had no idea how to respond. Yom-Tov insisted again.

'I saw it, yes, I saw it,' the man finally acknowledged.

'I saw it too,' the rabbi confirmed. 'Just like you, I saw the violence of Richetta's new husband. Here we are, then, two witnesses.'

'Two witnesses in fact,' stammered the man, scratching his beard.

'I will declare the divorce,' the rabbi concluded.

A group of onlookers had gathered on the Kasr el Nil Bridge. Not too many Jews had accompanied the rabbi this morning, but a crowd was beginning to form. As always in Egypt, the jokes pro- liferated. 'You're right, old man. This river harbours only devils. You wanted to give it a wife? The river deserves only crocodiles.'

And Yom-Tov divorced the new bride from her husband the Nile. Before the crowd, he conducted the ceremony. And the man could once again marry the woman he'd repudiated.

Yom-Tov was known for his interest in the common people of the community, but also for his frank talk, especially with the elite. He spent the better part of his time soliciting money from the rich to give to the poor. During the years when the Suez Canal was under construction and the cotton industry was developing, a good number of wealthy Jews began to frequent Europeans, forgetting their obligations to the less fortunate and neglecting the demands of their faith. Yom-Tov threatened them again and again: if they continued to take themselves for *khawagat*, fine gentlemen, despite having come directly from the Jewish alley, haret al-Yahud, then he would leave them here and go to live out his days at home, in Jerusalem. He predicted disappointment and distress if they thought that in this way they would become masters in Egypt. First they would again become slaves, then they would be chased out by the grace of God, as it was written. But nothing changed. As always, the wealthy at the head of the community wasted their time in power struggles, and the poor were left with nothing but to sift through dust and stones. Yom-Tov demanded, stormed, resorted to a thousand ruses to force the rich to give. And then, having had enough of begging, without warning, one fine morning in 1884, he mounted his snow-white donkey and vanished from Cairo. That morning the community awakened to discover that they had lost their guide. A while later, they learnt he was in Jerusalem, settled in his house in Mahane Yehuda. He continued, however, as the Grand Rabbi of Egypt. The community leaders moved quickly to find a substitute who could manage their affairs in his absence. They sent emissaries to the far corners of the East, to Iraq and Iran, finally convincing Rabbi Mercado Tarragan to come from Shiraz to attend to Egypt's Jewish community. But for important civil matters—marriages, divorces—they still needed Rabbi Yom-Tov's seal. Something had to be done. They were forced to make the pilgrimage to Jerusalem if they wanted to obtain the documents. Rabbi Tarragan retired seven years later, and Rabbi Yom-Tov, although still absent from Cairo, remained Grand Rabbi of Egypt. It was not until the spring of 1891 that he returned to Egypt for a few months to resume his duties. He died on 17 August 1891 in Jerusalem, four days after the festival of Tish'a B'av, the commemoration of the destruction of the Temple. This period has always been a sad one for us—the destruction of the two Temples and the death of my grandfather's grandfather.

Jurist and mage, learned scholar and man of the people, at once ingenuous and mysterious, his name was Yom-Tov, 'feast day'. I am named like him, Yom-Tov in Hebrew and 'Eïd in Arabic, doubly 'feast day'. Feast day? Perhaps because my birth heralded a time of tumult.

5

Dobó and Ayató

What the students had left behind in the wake of May 68 was now, in the 1970s, something everyone was trying to recapture. Mitterrand had the intuition that the ideas of May 68 would end up being actualized, taking shape in the society at large. He was right, even when it came to the wildest ideas. I remember seeing someone during one of our demonstrations, on a balcony over Magenta Boulevard, saluting the cortèges of students as if he were greeting his own army, like a chief of state saluting the military as they filed by during a parade. In the exhilaration of the moment, Serge July was scheming with Sartre to launch a daily that would revive the name of an underground journal that had resonated during the war like a call to arms: *Liberation*! Bingo! It was exactly what we were expecting from the revolution: liberation. But liberation from what?

May 1968 gave birth to the social sciences; book sales skyrocketed. *Les Mots et Les Choses* (*The Order of Things*) by Foucault, *Pour Marx* (*For Marx*) by Louis Althusser, Lacan's writings. Difficult works, incomprehensible at times, became true bestsellers. Collections of psychoanalysis proliferated like poppies; the works of Freud were now being systematically translated into French. We impatiently awaited the release of titles announced in the publishers' catalogues. Any analyst of the society of the time could predict that these ideas, now dispersing through a multitude of channels, would eventually converge to become the mainstream. I remember those years as an instance of Brownian motion, as if we were a colony of ants stirred up by a giant, scattering in all directions, seeking to reconstitute our world. Some of us were in more of a hurry to induce the labour, to give birth to the revolution. My Maoist friends started moving in a radical direction, soon skirting disaster. They discussed (and I sometimes participated in such discussions) attacking government offices, kidnapping government officials or industry magnates, or even robbing banks to finance the revolution. Anarchist bandits illuminated our movie screens. In 1969, Faye Dunaway and Warren Beatty were *Bonnie and Clyde*. Paul Newman and Robert Redford incarnated *Butch Cassidy and the Sundance Kid* in George Roy's film. It's no accident that in the film they end up being beaten by a Bolivian army, the same army that had killed Ché. And in 1972, the apotheosis, Steve McQueen and Ali McGraw burst onto the screen as intelligent, human and effective gangsters in Sam Peckinpah's *The Getaway*. Towering, charismatic actors in refined screenplays, showing images never before seen. In the end, it all eventuated in the renaissance of belief in a sort of necessary violence, the contours of which had long been drawn by the masters, the philosophers, the Sartres and Althussers. Extreme leftist movements had culminated in terrorism in Germany, Italy and

Japan. France was not far behind: some French Trotskyists left to support the revolutionary guerrillas in South America and elsewhere in Africa. The Maoists of the UJCML, those from the proletarian left, started to form groups like those in Italy and Germany. Benny Levy, the leader of the proletarian left, an erudite young man with a smouldering gaze, surely played a huge role in tempering the Maoist movement in France. He'd been Althusser's student at the École Normale Supérieure, and learnt from him that the perfect theory—one that would account for all of social complexity at every point—was possible. His disciples were first the Maoists of the UJCML, and then the proletarian left. His speech was precise, philosophy at the tip of his tongue, quoting from memory Plato, Spinoza and Leibnitz. When he spoke, everyone was still, as if the essence of things were being revealed. His thoughts aligned with the proletarian left right up to their theories of revolution. The next step was forcibly taking action, or 'actualization' as we might say. He stopped himself before he crossed that line. I encountered him again in Israel on two separate occasions: in 1998 when I was attending a social psychiatry conference in Jerusalem, and again in 2004, after he'd become a devout Jew, dressed entirely in black, his head covered by a wide-brimmed hat. The only things he discussed were points of doctrine. He prayed, respected the letter of the law, the *mitzvot*, and studied the Scriptures—the Talmud, the Kabbalah. He was just as intelligent as he'd been before, but now his erudition was applied to Jewish thought, which he analyzed incessantly. Nevertheless, I recognized the same preoccupations as in the times of the proletarian left: the legislation of daily life, and the ever-exacting reasoning for why this and not that, and why not nothing at all. In

1968, he'd managed to justify every action, every thought, in reference to revolutionary values; after his 'turning'—his own word, which also suggests '*re*-turning' and 'turning around'—after that sudden and radical metamorphosis, he did the same with respect to Jewish ritual. As for me, I found him more convincing in this new posture. His thinking as a religious man was more grounded and more precise. The Maoists of the École Normale wanted to make an exact science of Marxism, allowing for rationalization— something always easily done—as well as predictability—essentially constructing a theory just as scientific as particle physics. During his Orthodox Jewish phase, Benny Levy was expecting something else—the arrival of the Messiah, not the Revolution. Born in 1945 in Egypt, he was among the 'Jews of the Nile', as my cousin Jacques Hassoun liked to call us, but he was not like any other other Jew from Egypt that I knew. There was something Ashkenazy about him—I don't know from where he got that veritable passion to persuade. Whenever we met, he provoked an intellectual excitement in me, the desire to go further, to not remain where I was. I always left him with a need for debate. I never dreamt, however, of embarking on the same religious journey. He was always seeking the absolute, flirting with the extreme, like a bungee jumper, or those daredevils who walk on the rooftop ledges of skyscrapers. I've always suffered from vertigo myself. Moreover, it has long been my understanding that, for a Jew, belief in God is a result, certainly not a starting point. Which is why I never wanted to force my belief. I have loved God—I love God still—as my father gave me the example, by way of family tradition you might say. I enjoy praying, I'm interested in the study of Scripture, but I do not force myself to believe. Every day I tell myself, it's too soon to believe! I acknowledge that this has been the challenge of every Kabbalist since the beginning, that one endeavours to force God to reveal Himself. I know that this endeavour can completely take over one's life, one's thoughts, one's waking hours, one's days and nights. With Benny, there was something more, something held over from university philosophy, a kind of renunciation of the world. In 2004, the last time we met, he told me about an incredible event, which to this day I remember vividly, as if it resists the ever-changing form of thought: it cannot be dissolved in the flux of thought. The day he returned to the religion of his ancestors—it was in 1978. He'd been accompanying Sartre on a journey to Israel and Egypt. That day, Benny had gone to the Kotel, the Wailing Wall in Jerusalem. At the entrance to the section reserved for men, he was approached by the Lubavitchers, orthodox Jews who worked towards the 'return' of 'lapsed' Jews, were proposing to those who seemed distanced from God that they wear the *tefillin*. The tefillin is worn each day for the morning's prayer, except on Shabbat, and is traditionally wound around the left arm and the forehead, the phylacteries containing several Torah verses. For the Lubavitchers, the scattering of Jews throughout the world had fragmented God's light into a myriad of sparks, and they had taken on the task of bringing each of these sparks back to the central flame. The brilliance of the divine message grew brighter every time a Jew returned to the fold, and thus they seek out the lost throughout the world. They began this work after the war, recovering those to whom the Shoah had signified the absence of God, and had thus abandoned Judaism. Wouldn't it stand to reason that the Shoah was proof that God had abandoned us? In which case, the effort made should be to force Him to return. Why don't we think instead that the Shoah demonstrates His presence? In that case, we should redouble our devotion. I have never understood why one would put God on trial in this way. As time went on, the Lubavitchers extended their efforts towards Jews who'd turned to foreign gods, the gods of India, for example, or artificial paradises—and, evidently, those seduced by Greek philosophy. What happened on that day that led to Benny Levy agreeing to let the Lubavitchers impose the tefillin? He didn't say. He only said that he'd wrapped the straps according to custom and echoed his holy initiator in prayer. From then on, he swore, he never let a single day go by without observing the custom. Élie Ben Gal, who was with him that day, told me that Benny hadn't even had his bar mitzvah. Upon learning that this was his first time, the Lubavitchers rejoiced, shouting, 'Bar mitzva, bar mitzva,' gathering a group overjoyed to be converting a Jew to his own faith. All this seemed unbelievable to me . . . not that such a thing had happened; this would not be the first time I'd seen such a 'volte-face'. But that this should happen to Benny . . . I've come across the Lubavitchers so many times, at the entrance to the Wailing Wall, and elsewhere in Jerusalem, in Tel Aviv, in Paris. I too was invited to wear the tefillin. I never accepted, was never even tempted. For me, it would have confirmed that I had strayed, it would be to admit that I was lost, that I no longer knew my own name. I neither condemn nor deride; simply surprised that Benny had found himself in that moment so far from God that he was vulnerable to the solicitation of a proselytizer. Each of us follows a path determined by fate, as chance presents us with new people, new experiences. The path is so tenuous that we don't see it for what it is until the very end. After May 68, I imagine that Benny too was a ticking time bomb.

I avoided the extreme fallouts post-May 68—political violence, addiction—because Devereux had captured me, kidnapped me, removed me from the contemporary dialogue. During my years at school, I've known many who had the function of transmitting knowledge—professors, educators of all stripes . . . I'd already felt admiration, such as for Louis Vincent Thomas, a man of great intelligence who taught anthropology at the Sorbonne, who knew Africa so well, and the literature of science fiction so perfectly. Gentle, joyful, affectionate, competent, he was one of those professors who took their work seriously, without pretention or spectacle. I remember his first words at the opening of his course, in October 1969: 'Some roll for you . . .'—it was, I believe the advertising slogan for a brand of trucks—'Me, I read for you!' And it was true! Each week he told us about books he'd read for his weekly course. It also happened that I felt anger, as I had towards a psychologist who told me that all my theoretical proposals were destined to fail. Usually, however, I was indifferent. My professors dwelt on another plane; they were not part of my world. What's more, their preoccupations often pointed to the autobiography they didn't dare write. Sometimes teachers rewarded me; often they scolded me. I was always a troublemaker; they could have simply laughed. Instead, they sometimes humiliated me—it was a time when that was not forbidden by law. But I must acknowledge that most of them ignored me, and I preferred it that way. It's not good for professors to interfere with their students' lives, just as I'm convinced that it's not good for parents to interfere with their children's lives. What I felt for Georges Devereux was of another order. I neither loved him nor hated him, neither idolized nor despised him. He had become for me an inner function, a container, the implicit grammar of my words. This no doubt is what one experiences in the presence of one's master. During all my years at his side, I felt suspended, as if every thought of my own was frozen in place. A comfortable position, a position of little ambiguity, infantile, in fact. I felt small, a child for the first time, I who'd been born a grandfather. This experience somewhat resembled the entrance into a convent or a seminary. I was indeed, for a long time, cloistered in the vicinity of his thought. I'd forbidden myself nothing. I drifted through spaces, theories, attended the courses and seminars he recommended and avoided those he abhorred. I encountered people, rituals, beings. Everything brought me back to the perimeter of his thought. It took me a long time to admit that this was a kind of mechanism. What was happening was mechanical, set in motion during our first meeting, which would only reach its conclusion on the day of my thesis defense. I was reluctant to meet with him. My discomfort was persistent, as if it were improper to watch him live, as if I were uncovering a parent's nakedness. Yet I enjoyed participating in his courses, which I attended with a perfect assiduity, an assiduousness I'd never displayed before. But I dreaded the private meetings he required of his students. Whenever possible, I avoided time spent one on one, as he unconcernedly continued to expose who he was by remembering this or that, by making statements he thought were profound and definitive, the advice he dispensed freely and the endless condemnations—of Communists, of his colleagues, his former students. The seminar was regularly disrupted by a crisis. This person here, for example, had betrayed his work. He was heretofore to be excluded, placed in isolation, with the intent that he leave of his own accord. A while later it would be someone else who'd taken to contradicting him at every turn. 'But Georges, why in the world would he want to challenge you?' He would reply seriously, 'The murder of the father, you know, many are too fragile to cope with our difference in age.' I told myself I would end up like the others, disavowed, rejected in turn. Because here too, as with so many matters, psychoanalysis has got it backwards. It's very rare for a student to reject the thinking of his master, but very often the master becomes jealous of his student's creativity. Devereux was aware of this; he pointedly drew our attention to Daedalus, the first engineer, who assassinated Talos, his too-brilliant disciple. Our work meetings, when I of course had to present my research, lasted a long time, four hours, twelve sometimes. I emerged ground down, dazed. What I wrote of course bore his mark; reading it, you would not be able to say who the author was, him or me. It's an understatement to say he was brilliant. His mind sparkled like fireworks, it was sharp, avid, leaving to the listener the difficult task of following his meandering explanations. He had an intelligence that lifted the lid, that uncovers, that dis-covers, not one that parrots, proclaims or paraphrases. When he took hold of a problem, a sort of intuition led him straight to where no one had gone before. He was a discoverer, a synthesizer, a mad prospector. Though he held my mind captive for quite some time, he also (in exchange?) pacified the fire in my soul. His words, his thoughts, his theory, worked in me like a balm. Today I tell myself that our encounter so perfectly corresponded to my preoccupations of that time, my history and the history of my family, to the extent that it could not have been by chance. At the time, I must acknowledge, I was not aware of it. And yet, he spoke of psychoanalysis, the discipline I had longed to enter at any price, ever since my adolescence. Moreover, much of what he asked us to consider pertained to identity, affiliation, language, culture. I had lived three cultures, without knowing how to identify which was mine. To this day I remain convinced that it was neither his psychoanalytic study nor the themes of his lectures that kept me there: it was Devereux himself, nothing other than him.

His teaching was not of a very high calibre. He was neither a lecturer nor truly a professor. He did not have the brio of a Deleuze or a Foucault; he did not have the cockiness nor the intensity of a Lacan or a Sollers, he did not have the affected seduction of a Barthes, nor even the good-naturedness that makes learning enjoyable, that of a Rémy Chauvin, for example. Instead, he had something that transcended all these qualities: he *was*! He thought out loud, in our presence, he took a risk with everything he said— always against the grain, expecting to be contradicted. I never heard him utter a commonplace. You had the feeling he staked his life on each new thought. There was also a certain beauty that emanated from him. If he had been a film actor, one would have said that he 'catches the light'. The weekly seminars, three hours every Saturday afternoon from two to five, were basically dedicated to reading and commenting on his own work. It was a sort of infinite regress—Devereux commenting on Devereux, who, in his text, commented on Devereux ... an endless kaleidoscope from which he drew out the imperative to integrate, to take in his knowledge until it became an integral part of ourselves. I can only compare this apprenticeship to that of scripture, where it is not necessary to understand, at least at first, only to recite, over and over. A day comes when one knows that it is there, engraved forever. I never learnt anything at university, excepting those first two years in Devereux's seminar, when I did nothing but learn. In two years, I made up the five years of the university's vacuousness. It is thanks to these two years, no doubt, that I developed the conviction that, in order to educate students, there is no need for a programme, a plan, a course of study—only professors, true ones, those who were once called 'masters'. But dammit, hell! I'm well aware that the time of the masters is over. I remain convinced, nevertheless, that this is not a good state of affairs. In lieu of providing them with masters, we have condemned our young people to shape themselves through trial and error, to get caught on life's snags until the accumulation of experience approximates that of a master's instruction.

Nor was it necessary to spend hours and hours in class in order to learn. The seminar occupied our Saturday afternoons, nothing more—to which were added an infinite number of intense telephone conversations. Georges had writen all our names on tiny slips of paper the size of calling cards, arranged in alphabetical order. Whenever he was bored or anxious, which was almost daily, he would leaf through these slips of paper and call one or another of us to talk. He would catch us right in the midst of an activity, at work, with friends, late at night. He would talk about everything, about nothing, a theoretical point, a dispute in the seminar, the psychological peculiarities of some student. I had the sense of something rather improper. This relationship was too close to be pedagogic, almost incestuous, too distant for friendship. In a word, it was maladaptive, and it reeked of artifice. I protected myself by thinking that none of it was very serious, that the truth of Georges Devereux lay elsewhere. I've always been convinced, from the very start, that he was hiding the essential from us.

During those years, I was seeking only to inhabit myself completely, to live what I was living, to think what I was thinking. I had not yet dwelt in myself. I was skinny, I wore velvet suits, narrow at the waist, with bellbottom pants. Naive and unknown, I dreamt of my contribution to the making of the world to come. After the upheaval of May 68, the world had been thrown wide open. But I had even more difficulty than before in finding my place within it. I scoured the Latin Quarter searching for inexpensive books and jazz records. I watched the girls, hoping for a smile. I was obsessed with women. I'd married at twenty, no doubt to be free, yet I felt like a prisoner in my own life. I fell in love at every opportunity, sometimes twice in one week. There was rendezvous after rendezvous, no doubt to make up for lost time. I liked mature women, those around forty years old, I liked how free they were; for example, the library director I'd spent the night with once, whose memory rocked me to sleep for years afterward. I liked wild young girls, but also strait-laced older women, like the maths teacher with the severe eyeglasses who turned out to be as passionate as a dance-hall girl. I liked liberated women, like Mirabelle, my pet name for her because she lived near the Mirabeau Bridge. She'd stunned me the first time we met when she asked me, after five minutes of conversation, to sleep with her. I wanted to sleep with her, right there, right then, right on the rug. And what was I waiting for? I liked refined intellectuals, like the 'Duchess of Guise', 'Guise' in reference to the street where she lived; or 'Madame de Staël', so called because she wrote to me endlessly. This Madame de Staël was so intelligent, so free, that I felt a sort of mystical energy at the thought of being with her. We spent several nights together, dividing our time between love and literature. I left early in the morning, without having slept, celebrating my freedom as I walked against the flow of morning pedestrians. I also sought to recapture so many lost opportunities, girls with whom I'd crossed paths at the lycée, or even in primary school, back when I hadn't dared to confess my attraction, girls like Jeanine, a magnificent dancer who'd blossomed in the shade of our Gennevilliers slum. I besieged her for weeks until she accepted my advances. Whatever I wrote described her, was dedicated to her, was for her. She haunted every word I set down on paper. My time with her was wildly passionate.

During my first two years in Devereux's seminar, all my energy went into experiencing the extremes of human emotion. I wrote romantic poetry in adulation of women, and I fervently read the foundational literature I should have taken the time to read during my years at the lycée. I discovered Flaubert, and read all of Stendhal, the perfect writer, in one go, Céline, who invented everything, and Homer, Homer above all. I was always rereading *The Iliad*—in the metro, on the bus, in bed . . . I shared my life with the Greek divinities who'd become my daily companions. I was captivated by *The Odyssey*, that mystical tale about the visceral attachment to one's mother country. I was fascinated by this text, without wondering why I was so drawn to it. Like Odysseus, I'd left my native land. Also like him, I did not know whether I would ever return. Surely the Greek hero was an example for me: he'd been able to resist every temptation, bound as he was to his island, to Ithaka. I too was exiled, but although I did not know my Ithaka, I was like Odysseus in his tormented wandering.

In the first year, I'd been given the task of discussing 'Normal and Abnormal', the principal article in Devereux's *Essays on General Ethnopsychiatry*. As a novice, it was difficult for me to understand the nuances of this patchwork text, crammed with contradictions. I latched onto the most surprising concept: the idea that some psychic disorders were provided, 'ready to wear', by culture. The Malay people, for example, 'run amok' when they go mad; the Algonquins see spectres they call Windigo; the Southern Chinese have a strange illness called Koro, said to cause their genitals to disappear into their abdomens. In other words, the expression of certain mental illnesses conforms to an ambient model, and has nothing to do with the personality of the subject. Devereux could have added to the list—and we did so during our discussions: the French become alcoholic; Maghrebian women are possessed by djinns; the Indians of the Cordillera in the Andes develop a strange depression, the Susto, in which their soul is captured by the earth; the Congolese are victims of a sorcerer's curse, whereas for those of us who have been nurtured on psychoanalysis from the cradle, a symptom can only be a 'complex', a development of a subconscious impulse, developed in line with defence mechanisms formed over the course our history, in other words: our 'character'. Psychoanalysis has convinced us that the makeup of the symptoms *is* the person. Hadn't Lacan emphatically reaffirmed this, taking up Buffon's dictum that

'the style is the man'. And here was Devereux turning everything
upside down, and, what's more, providing a myriad of examples.
He taught us that the *style* of the symptoms could be something
exterior to the person; it might even be the element that belongs to
them the least. Not one of us, (we were hearing these words for the
first time!) had ever met someone *running amok*, we had never seen
an Indian, a Malayan or Indonesian shaman, we had no idea of what
it was to be possessed, or to be put under a spell. I fervently defended
Devereux's ideas, even though I was hardly more informed than my
fellow students. The oldest members of our group, Richard, Edith
or Jean-Claude, fiercely opposed this hypothesis, for it flew in the
face of their convictions. The Lacanians in the seminar launched
into long diatribes, explaining pedantically that it was impossible,
and that there was not a single example that disproved the dominant
theory. There seemed to be a misunderstanding between Devereux
and his students—it was almost as if it were a question of translation, as if he were speaking another language. Besides the fact
that his long experience constituted a universe of facts we knew
nothing about, we were working from different traditions of
thought. When he spoke of psychoanalysis, he was thinking of what
he had encountered in the United States, a psychoanalysis of 'adaptation', highly criticized in France. He appreciated (with good reason) the sophisticated psychological theories of Hartmann and
Kriss, both of whom he knew personally. We, however, were familiar
only with the French corpus. Our touchstones were Serge Leclaire,
the two Mannonis, Didier Anzieu or François Perrier. If we were
to cite foreign authors who'd been translated into French, they
were mostly British: Winnicott, Masud Khan or Balint. Moreover,

Devereux's 'others', his foreigners, the populations he'd encountered and sometimes studied, were all of the 'Orient': the peoples of Indochina, where he'd lived for three years; the Indonesians and Malays, whose language he'd studied and still knew perfectly; the Indians of North America, whom he'd met under the direction of his mentor, Kroeber; the Mojave of Arizona, whom he left to visit for short weekend stays, or during holidays spent editing his thesis. He had a deep knowledge of these cultures—personal, empirical. It was their thoughts, their customs, their songs, the atmosphere of their world, that composed his points of reference. He sometimes amused himself by chanting the songs of Mojave shamans, a music so unlike anything else. Our 'others' were of a completely different geography and culture. We were familiar with the populations of Southern Europe, the Italians and the Portuguese(there was a sizeable population in France); the Maghrebis, especially the Algerians, with whom we shared the banlieues, and the Africans from Senegal and Mali who were just beginning to arrive as migrants. Devereux was certainly not an African. The earliest impressions I have, that I carry still on the surface of my skin, is the touch of my Arab nursemaids and the fragrances of the Sudanese servants who'd taken care of me as a child. Despite all this, we all pretended to be speaking of the same thing. The mutual misunderstanding was especially apparent whenever we encountered a doctrinal problem. Unfortunately, we took these conflicts to be a question of theory, when in fact it was a question of culture.

Devereux had passionate relationships with all his students. Many did not stay with him for more than a few months at the most, continuing their studies elsewhere. A few stayed for a long time—two years, three, or longer still. There were perhaps some fifteen of us, at most twenty, who regularly attended the seminar, in short: those who could be called his 'students', who were marked as with a branding iron, each one certain he possessed the truth about the master, knowing him intimately. No one knew him! He kept himself hidden. He lied about everything regarding his personal life, as if he were a gangster on the run. He lied about his name, about the number of his successive wives, about his religion, about the places he'd lived. If he could have, he would have applied greasepaint or undergone plastic surgery to change his features. We constantly wondered why he would hide who he was, why he would create a persona for himself, why, despite the evidence to the contrary, he would continue to maintain his lies. Nothing was forcing him to do this. He might have, like most professors, kept himself at a remove from his students, revealing nothing about himself. Why did he feel the need to tell us these tall tales? Over time, we thought of many ways to justify it. Perhaps, like so many immigrants from Eastern Europe, he'd developed a sort of persecution complex—a feeling which, one must admit, would not have been entirely groundless. The secret police of the Eastern Bloc sometimes pursued members of the opposition who'd taken refuge in the West. The attacks committed by the Soviet, Romanian or Bulgarian secret services were regularly reported in the press. Did he suspect that he was being pursued by Communist agencies? But a much simpler explanation came to me one day by way of Michel Sapir, a psychoanalyst of Russian origin who was instructing me in psychoanalytic relaxation techniques. Sapir was a wonderful therapist, a refined, elegant man, with a strong Russian accent that

only added to his charm. He had a sharp eye and a mocking intelligence. One day he asked me point blank: 'So, your mentor, is he
still in hiding? In the US, everyone says he took refuge in France
to escape his alimony payments . . .'

Sapir would regularly meet with Balint, another immigrant
Hungarian Jew, who was surely his source of information. My ears
perked up.

'Do you mean Georges Devereux?' I asked

'Of course I mean Georges Devereux, who else? But of course
Devereux's name is obviously not really Devereux, am I right? And
he doesn't even want to admit that he's Jewish.'

'He's a Jew?' I didn't hide my surprise.

'You don't know? What does he claim to be then? Buddhist?
In America, he frequented the Hungarian Jewish community. Over
there, everyone knows he's a Jew.'

When I saw Devereux again, I asked the question, as naturally
as possible, during a lull in the conversation.

'Georges, do you know that people are saying you're Jewish?'

He got a little angry.

'Jewish? And then what? If I were Jewish, why in the world
would I hide it?'

Gathered together at a cafe with an Israeli psychoanalyst originally from Hungary, who'd finally settled in France, we asked each
other, 'How could he not be Jewish? He talked endlessly about his
first cousin Edward Teller, the son of his mother's sister. Everyone
knows that Teller is Jewish . . . if Teller is Jewish, Georges's mother

must also be Jewish. Thus he is Jewish. Apparently, his name is not Devereux ... Really? If his name is not Devereux, then what is it?'

One day, when Devereux and I were talking about this and that, I posed the question: 'Devereux is a French name, isn't it?'

'Yes,' he replied, 'my ancestor was a soldier in the Napoleonic army who settled in Hungary after the conquest of Europe.'

I interrupted him. It wasn't very elegant to let him get entangled in his lies. Ever since Sapir's revelation, my mind had been made up. Devereux was Jewish. But I did not understand the reasons for the fables with which he regaled us. There was something strange about this attitude. The truth hit me with full force in October 1973, during the first days of the Yom Kippur War, when the Israeli defences had been breached and the Egyptian and Syrian armies were advancing on two fronts. Just when we were beginning to think an Israeli military defeat was possible, Devereux had grown frantic with anxiety. He telephoned me at all hours to compare the news he'd heard on the radio with what I had. He telephoned each of us, asking the same questions over and over. I firmly believe he spent two entire weeks glued to the phone, incessantly gathering information about the conflict. Later I would learn that he'd been deathly afraid for his sister and nephew—his only living kin—who both lived in Tel Aviv. As is so often the case, as in Edgar Allan Poe's celebrated 'The Purloined Letter', what Devereux was concealing so vigorously was hiding in plain sight, precisely where no one thought to look. The false name he'd invented for himself, 'Devereux' could be broken up into D + evreu. *Evreu* in Romanian simply means 'Jew'. In 1967, he published an article in the *French Psychoanalytic Review*, entitled, 'The

Renunciation of Identity, a Defence Against Annihilation'. From the title alone, we should have understood it to be a confession. Devereux had one day renounced his identity to escape the death he thought was imminent. The first example presented in the article is Odysseus declaring to the giant Polyphemus who is readying to devour him that his name is 'Nobody'. Yes, to escape death, Odysseus claims to be 'Nobody'. Once safely back in his boat, when he knows he has escaped the cannibal Kyklops, he shouts, 'I am Odysseus, son of Laertes, king of Ithaka.' Odysseus, too, could not keep himself from proclaiming his identity in the end. Naming himself D-*evreu* was Georges's way of shouting out his true identity. I'm convinced that this article is the most autobiographical of his writings, a sort of proclamation of identity, but in his own fashion, also bizarre, encoded.

Our mentor was an odd man with many secrets. I wonder to what extent his behaviour was typical of this generation of Hungarian Jews. There was at least a historical explanation. During the 1890s, the Hungarian government, in preparing the festivities for the founding of Hungary in 1896, had indeed implemented the 'Magyarization' of minorities. Jews, caught in a process of more or less compulsory assimilation, had changed their names by the hundreds. Weiss became Feher, Klein was changed to Kis, Ferenczi was originally Frankel, Bergsmann became Balint. No one knows with any certainty the original name of Devereux's paternal family—some told me they were named Weissmuller, like the actor who immortalized Tarzan, and who was also from the Banat region. What we do know is that Eugene, his father, traded the family name for Dobó, the name of a Hungarian horseman who'd fought valiantly against the Turks in the sixteenth century. Devereux's name at birth was thus Georghe Dobó. It was he himself who requested it be changed to to Devereux, no doubt at the time of his conversion to Christianity in 1933 or 34. He he'd been living in Paris, frequenting the aristocracy, imagining a grand destiny for himself, when news of the Stavisky Affair burst out. Stavisky's orchestration of bond fraud through Bayonne Municipal Credit was a huge scandal, shaking the Third Republic down to its foundations. A xenophobic and anti-parliamentarian fever had swept France in the wake of this affair, culminating in the vicious riots of 6 February 1934. Leon Daudet, a journalist of the far right, had been calling for the lynching of the 'Stavisky-esque'. And among the false certificates of deposit produced by Stavitsky were Hungarian letters of credit. Stavisky was a Ukrainian Jew who'd emigrated to France following the terrible pogroms at the end of the nineteenth century. He'd taken to calling himself 'Mr Alexandre'. Devereux must have been frightened by this affair. It was around this time that he converted and changed his name. One day he confided in me that it was the Stavisky scandal that had impelled him to leave France and complete his doctoral studies in the United States.

I've since met many Hungarians who'd similarly concealed their identity—out of the fear of being annihilated. Some have been among my friends, people I encountered in my practice and during my university days. I've also read several accounts. The most unusual is surely that of Imre Kovács, as told in his posthumous book, *The Avenger*. Kovacs was a Hungarian Jew who enlisted in the Waffen-SS to skirt detection during the war. He was then captured by the

Soviets, escaped Russia, reached Palestine, took part in the Israeli war of independence, then became a member of the French Foreign Legion until they were demobilized after the wars in Indochina and Algeria, at which point he settled in Paris and worked as a waiter at the Lip Brasserie for thirty years. He did not assume his identity again until after his retirement, which he took in Hungary, where he died in 2003.

But, after all, what did it matter to me, to us, that Devereux was Jewish? In truth, not at all! Except that during his lectures, he spent hours analysing literary characters, patients and others—his colleagues, his students—in terms of their connections with a community. He would forcefully insist that an individual's cultural background was the determining factor in understanding them . . . and here he was lying about his own! And these lies bespoke a kind of troubling oddity. We knew that in the United States, and especially in New York, he would have had no problem living openly as a Jew. In France, at the beginning of the 1970s, anti-Semitism, extirpated after the war, had not yet reappeared. What then had led him to hide his Jewishness? I spent years, long after his death, trying to elucidate the enigmas he'd bequeathed us. But isn't it the essence of a mentor to be opaque in the eyes of his students? I neither criticized him nor called him out. I had adopted an inner rule: I knew nothing, and he knew everything. Later I would learn the reasons for his behaviour. I'd designated him as my mentor, and therefore I had no choice but to accept everything from him as an aspect of my apprenticeship. His reasons were Reason; it fell to me to decipher them, if only for my own use. In addition, I had to grasp the questions. The first was about his Jewishness, the second regarded his practice of psychoanalysis, the third his relationships with women. He spoke so much of psychoanalysis, and in such an original way, that we were all eager to learn the specifics of his practice. Had he completed his psychoanalytic training? Had he really practised psychoanalysis in New York? And if so, for how long? After rapid calculations, we concluded it could not have been for very long, a few years at the most. Several suggested that he'd encountered numerous problems with the Psychoanalytic Institute, which appreciated neither his too-novel theories nor his personality, eccentric to say the least. In short, although he practised in New York, he was only admitted into an out-of-state, provincial psychoanalytical society in Pennsylvania, which enabled him to be admitted by the Psychoanalytic Society in Paris, but not until 1965. He never practised psychoanalysis in France.

During the fifteen years he spent in the United States, between 1947 and 1962, Devereux was married six times. He had only recently married the last one, Jane, the woman who would abruptly leave him in 1971 when he returned to France. He said again and again to anyone who would listen that, in order to sleep with an American woman, you first had to marry her. Surely it was his way of explaining to himself why he'd married so many times. But there was perhaps another reason. Devereux loved women passionately; he loved them compulsively. He could not keep himself from proposing sex to a new woman. There was a fierce youthfulness in this elderly man, clearly marked by life, a kind of perpetual hope, as if he were ready to start over again, at every moment, with another, at his place, in the café, on the street, no matter where, no matter when. He kept his eyes wide open, taking in everything around him—people, women in particular, like a starving infant. What he liked especially about the Mojave people, who'd adopted him as one of their own, was precisely this sexual freedom. Mojave couples, he said, were married without a ceremony. Once a woman became pregnant with her husband, she would fall in love with another man and go to live with him. The man would become the father of her child. To account for how frequently this occurred, the Mojave had developed a theory: They claimed that the new man who would become the father helped the foetus to grow, for his sperm would continue to nourish it. By having sex with the woman throughout her pregnancy and nourishing the child in the womb, her new companion was thus considered to be the father. This inconstancy among the Mojave thrilled Devereux, their ribaldry as well. He was not suffering from a 'sexual addiction', as we might say today. He was a compulsive lover; a lover in waiting also, always on the lookout for *the one* who would, once more, transform his life. You could see why his wives did not stand for it. It's also clear why he was immediately interested in the doctoral subject I was proposing, on sexual communities that meant to abolish jealousy. No doubt he considered himself the victim of the jealousy of the women who'd abandoned him again and again.

In 1972, I conducted dozens of interviews for my research. I met with several sexual communities, spoke with them, had a dialogue. My thesis was progressing by leaps and bounds. That is the whole advantage of having a mentor. He opens doors, provides the means by which to enter; he supports the first steps, tentative, in the dark. Until this point, I'd been an amateur. In the space of just a few months, I'd become a specialist. One can study, accumulate knowledge from here and there, but a moment comes when one must radically modify the content. This is where a mentor comes in. He was obviously greedy for the reports I brought him from what is conventionally called my 'field'. He was chomping at the bit, wanting to know more, offering to accompany me on my visits to the communal living groups. That was the year that Nicole, one of Devereux's students, and also a professor in a school of social work, proposed that I deliver a lecture to her students on my initial findings. I must have spent three months, full-time, preparing for this lecture. I weighed each word, verified each fact, redefined each concept. The teachings of the mentor had entered my veins. If Devereux was a mentor, if his function was that of an instructor, I know that he did it unconsciously, without really realizing what he was producing.

Cotonou, 1996

In 1996, I travelled to Benin with Lucien Hounkpatin, who was working on his doctoral thesis on traditional systems for treating madness. Together we visited healers in villages hidden in the bush conducting their abundant research sheltered from scrutiny and criticism. We met the people that in Yoruba are called babalawos, *masters of the secrets. There, initiation is never accidental but always a deliberate choice. By the time we arrived at Ayató's place, night had fallen two hours earlier. Ayató, a bokonon, lived in a tiny cob hut in a tiny village of no more than three hundred inhabitants. After we crossed the threshold, he offered us a vessel of that clear water that soothes the spirit and allows one to share existence. Lucien swallowed a mouthful, and then I did. We sat on the earth.*

Ayató was stretched out above us, on a canvas deck chair from another era. He looked like a king, and we his captives. On the walls, two or three lopsided photos: his grandfather; the president of the republic; a young girl, gracious and smiling. The hut was faintly lit by an ancient oil lamp that distorted our silhouettes and made our shadows dance. Ayató's simple shorts covered a large, perfectly round belly, from which his deep voice resounded. He punctuated his sentences with great slaps on his belly, attacking a prowling mosquito. He exchanged greetings in Fon or Nagô with Lucien. Every now and then, Lucien translated.

'He says he is honoured that we've come so far just to see him.'

Every fifteen minutes or so, he served us a goblet of sodabi, *the palm wine of the region, a sort of artisanal gin, stronger and more aromatic. We gulped it down together, in unison. Regularly, he poured a bit onto the little statue we could glimpse in the shadows behind him, his* legba. *Towards 10 p.m., he took out flasks of powdered roots and plants and sprinkled a trail in the palms of our hands. He served himself, then filled our goblets to the brim. We licked the powder and swallowed it with the help of the* sodabi. *By midnight, we were completely plastered.*

'You've come to cleanse yourselves. Let's go,' he commanded.

We followed him in the darkness along an earthen path that snaked through the countryside. A faint light was filtering down from the stars. We slipped on the mud of the bank. I had not even seen the backwater. He asked us to disrobe. I wasn't thinking about a thing, not about the animals that might have found us there, nor the mosquitoes nor, even less, of the bacteria. Naked as a worm, I immersed myself, repeating after him, three times over, words in Nago that I did not understand. Then he gave us each a bottle containing water drawn from the swamp and recommended that we not wash until the the next morning.

123

'And the bottle?' Lucien asked.

'It's for your shampoo,' Ayató replied.

We returned to Cotonou, soaked through and jubilant. That night, I slept soundly, dreamlessly. The next day, when I was taking my shower, I examined the bottle. The water's surface was black. I shook it, only to discover dozens of mosquito larvae dancing about—black, red, green. Mosquitoes spend the better part of their lives under water, from which they emerge after a metamorphosis. This is what is also meant for us. Without a doubt, the village backwater was brimming with beings.

* * *

In these worlds, to learn is to come into contact with things from the beginning, to be initiated to oneself. Lucien came from there, was from there. His grandfather was also a *bablawo*, like Ayató. During his childhood, he'd shown him objects, had taken him along, right before dawn, when the wind rises to chase the moon, to gather the plants that open at the first dewdrop. He'd sat him on the earth, in his hut, while he interrogated fate with the help of walnut roasaries. Black soap shavings, bottles, 'passports', amulets were set out before him. To learn is to take in the objects, substances, the words, the places that witnessed our birth, to absorb one by one the elements of our being.

6

Tyrone Power

My name was the one thing I could count on during those many moments of immigration that were especially sad for me. No matter what I suffered or how overwhelmed I felt, no matter how beset by the world's forces, I resolved never to renounce my name.

My father, he was Tyrone Power. First of all, there was a real physical resemblance. And then, there were other coincidences, such as the fact that Tyrone Power died of heart failure in 1958, in Madrid during the filming of his last movie, *Solomon and the Queen of Sheba*. There can be no doubt that my father died for the first time in 1958, upon our arrival in France.

I don't truly know my own name, I mean my father's name. I don't understand all its implications. I know of course that I am preceded by a long line of ancestors. But my father's surname 'Nathan' is a first name, not a last name. His family must have hailed from one of those countries where people had only first names: Abraham, son of Isaac; Daoud, son of Benjamin. I recall how in Egypt people teased him by reminding him that his family once ate locusts. What they meant was that the Nathans were from Yemen. These remarks deeply affected me, laying the groundwork for my future emotions: for example, the beauty of Noa, an Israeli singer of Yemenite extraction, encountered one evening at a hotel bar in Sicily, and that sudden feeling of love, as if ancient, surging from deep within. I did not say a word to her, except that her voice made me dream. We often pass like this, unaware, before our ancestors. In Hebrew, 'Nathan', which should be pronounced 'Naatan', means 'He has given', as in the biblical phrase: *natane lanou et hatorah.* 'He (God) has given us the Torah.' In our family, we called ourselves Dieu a donné, 'God has given' (the Torah?), *Dieudonné*, given by God if you will, so long as it does not mean 'give to God'. My father's first name was Joseph; his father was David. This grandfather, whom I never knew, who died before his son reached puberty, left his mark on our family's history. My father was sixteen. One day, he did not go to school, most likely so that he could help his overburdened mother. My grandfather, a severe man with a Garibaldi moustache, demanded that he give an account of himself. He raised his voice. No one raised their voice to my father. He could not bear it, he could never bear it—he who never raised his voice to anyone, especially not his father. He escaped out the window. In Egypt, we all had nicknames: Joseph, my father, *Youssef* in Arabic, was 'Sousou'. My grandfather David, like most Davids, was 'Doudou'. Doudou Nathan had married one of the two Cohen sisters, my grandmother Bertha, whom we called Bonna, 'the well-named'. Bonna and her sister Esther lived in the heart of *haret el Yahud*, 'the Alley of the Jews', in a grand house with several dozen rooms that everyone called *Beit el Cohen*, 'The Cohen House'. It was a huge traditional dwelling with a patio on one side and a garden on the other. Decorative animals wandered freely on its lawns: a pony, a peacock, a monkey and several cats—not those emaciated, yowling cats you encountered on the streets of Cairo but long-haired, purring cats the Cohens claimed were angoras. It was in this family home that the two sisters, Bertha and Esther, had lived since childhood, and it was there that they continued to live after their marriages. They were inseparable, like twins. They'd insisted that their two husbands move into the Cohen House, where there must have been some fifteen families, nearly a hundred individuals, tribal, almost a 'concession', as it would have been called in Africa. My grandfather, a taciturn and reserved modest bank employee, who cherished petty-bourgeois aspirations, wanted to free himself from the constraints of this traditional family, especially since it wasn't even his. He found an apartment outside the *hara*, and eventually persuaded his wife to move. They already had six children and could hardly benefit from this new arrangement. Two weeks later, Doudou Nathan returned from work one day, collapsed into an armchair and lost consciousness. A heart attack. They called the doctor, who arrived too late. The next day, the two sisters returned to the Cohen House, where life resumed its eternal course, as in the time of Maimonides, as in the time of Rabbi Yom-Tov. From what did my grandfather David die? From having unjustly berated my father? From having sought to separate the twins, joined together by an indissoluble, ancient bond? From having inserted himself, a nameless Yemenite, into a family of owners of the earth?

The two sisters were from the Cohen family, known as the 'elevated' Cohens, *Cohen Mé'éli*. In this family, piety was not an acquired virtue. God was a natural partner. Prophets, kings and masters of the Talmud were not relegated to the past. They were daily companions. Maimonides was an intimate; Joseph Caro, a member of the family. For the most part, the Jews of Egypt, were like this, contemporaries of the founding fathers. They had that natural piety, far from the mystical, that I will never again find. They had nothing in common with those Ashkenazi Jews, men you sometimes came across in the alleys of old Cairo, dressed all in black, faces obscured by filthy beards, with those big, wild eyes, scrutinizing your face. You could say that, having once put too much distance between themselves and God, they now drew too close, as if to reassure themselves that His face was not definitively turned away from them. Very few Jews of Egypt shared the illusions of those Ashkenazis who'd become Communist and sought to enlist others in their mania for liberation. There were a few, for example my cousin Jacques Hassoun, Léon Castro, Joseph Hazan, or the Curiels, but it was whispered that they had abandoned their God. Furthermore, Egyptian Jews were not like the Algerian and Moroccan Jews I would meet years later, people who believed in God but whose simple faith seemed to me the faith of those we called coal-mongers. Egyptian Jews knew that you cannot begin by believing in God. No! I'm one of them, I'm like them. I know that belief in the existence of God is the product of long reflection that can occupy a lifetime.

From generation to generation, the *Cohen Mé'éli* were rabbis and jewellers—jewellers to feed the rabbis, rabbis to justify the jewellers who fashioned silver *reimonim* shaped like pomegranates, filled with jewels and little bells, to adorn the Torah scrolls. Bertha Cohen's father, my father's maternal grandfather, was named

Mess'oud Cohen-Mé'éli. He was a jeweller who kept a tiny stall in the goldsmith's souk in old Cairo. Every now and then, I dream of being his apprentice, accompanying him in that tiny stall, no bigger than three square metres. I love to pronounce his name, which rings in my memory like a protective mantra: 'Mess'oud Cohen-Mé'éli'. His brother Élie, known as Lieto, blind since the age of five, was a born rabbi. Not having had the time to learn to read, he memorized all the useful scriptures, the prayers and verses of the Torah. If anyone had a question about the order of the ritual, he always could provide the answer. He too had a daughter named Bertha. They were both named after the same grandmother. The second Bertha Cohen married in 1914 or 15. Her first child, a girl, was born in 1917, on the 18th of April. That girl became my mother. My two parents each had a mother named Bertha Cohen. These two mothers were cousins, namesakes, because they were both named after the same ancestor, to the consternation of the French officials charged with producing an extract of my birth certificate or perhaps issuing my identity card during the 1970s in Paris:

'Joseph Nathan, son of David Nathan and his wife, Bertha Cohen; Rena Israel, wife of Nathan, daughter of Zaki Israel and Bertha Cohen, his wife. It's impossible. Your parents can't be brother and sister. There must be a mistake somewhere.'

There was no mistake. My parents were second cousins once removed and, in a certain sense, brother and sister, like Abraham and Sarah, as recommended by the Scriptures.

My father lost his father as he was leaving adolescence. He never lamented this loss. He described his father as honest and upright, respectful of religion, but distant and severe. My father inherited two principles from his father: one positive, that of daily prayer at sunrise and sundown, which he never neglected up until his final days; the other, contempt for the pedestrian. Already the son of a foreigner back in Egypt, he'd concluded that no law merited his obedience. But my father's insubordination was not solely due to his father's example; it was more personal, inscribed in his flesh, so to speak. For my father was uncircumcised. David and Bertha's first male child had died from complications of circumcision; the second as well. According to the law, when one has lost two male children, one is authorized not to circumcise the third or the fourth. The fourth arrived in 1912 on the day of Rosh Hashanah, the Jewish New Year, which fell on the 16th of September that year. It was my father, my grandmother's second surviving child. He remained this way, uncut, until he reached marriageable age. One might say that, like Abraham, my father circumcised himself, on the eve of his marriage at the age of thirty. Not that he actually performed the operation. I mean to say that his circumcision was an act of his own volition. My father did not submit to the law— he he went beyond of it: his circumcision was not arbitrary but chosen. That's how he was, for his entire life, insubordinate, beholden only to his own will which applied to him alone.

But another story, more sensual, explains the survival of my grandmother's third and fourth children. After losing her first two, my grandmother, the beautiful Bonna, fed up with the rabbis' ineffective prayers, allowed herself to be persuaded to consult an Arab healer. I can readily imagine what the matron said her: 'Poor woman. Your children have gone to rejoin their father.' Wasn't their father her husband, my grandfather? 'I'm not speaking to you of their father in this world, but in the other world, the invisible one.' No one dared utter his name, they didn't dare describe his nature, but everyone knew it was a spirit, an '*afrit*. The explanation was that this beautiful woman, with her too-green eyes, had drawn to herself the love of a demon, one of those made from the primal substance, the mud drawn from the great river. The demon who'd visited and impregnated her during her sleep had come to reclaim his children at their birth. Her two eldest were not dead—they'd simply gone to rejoin their father in the depths of the river. The healer smudged the grieving young mother to cleanse her orifices, and prescribed rituals of separation, designating certain days for her to be with the legitimate husband. She also imprisoned her ankle in a copper anklet, a *kholkal*, sealed for life. For as long as I knew her, my grandmother's foot was heavy from this union.

I come from that, from that strange amalgam, one part biblical reasoning—'if you've lost two male children after circumcision, do not circumcise the third'—and the other the search for the unknown. 'There is an intention behind every event. Seek tirelessly for what influences you without your awareness.'

My grandmother Bonna, whom we children called Nonna, or 'Grandma', lived with us in our home until her death in 1955. Thus she was spared our exile to France. How many such Egyptian grandmothers have I seen, slowly wasting away in the housing projects of the banlieues, isolated in their language, collapsed in the back bedroom? Like them, my grandmother spoke only Arabic. We answered her in French, which she sometimes understood. From her commerce with the spirits, she'd retained large vacant eyes and a nighttime anxiety. The scent of her Eau de Cologne and her incense wafted through the apartment. She dressed in the old style, draping her knees and keeping her forearms covered, her head enveloped in pretty *mandils* adorned with gold charms. I saw her hair only once, glimpsed after her bath, completely white and long, descending like an avalanche to her lower back, a quasi-divine eroticism, I would understand only ages later through my reading of Ovid or Klossowski—Diana surprised at her bath. My grandmother Bonna had a kind of intuitive knowledge of the unseen, which she kept to herself. At times she went up to the terrace, where the women and the servants gathered to hang the laundry and discuss women's affairs. Occasionally I managed to slip in beside her. I did not understand all that they were saying; I only knew that they were discussing the comings and goings of 'beings'.

My mother liked to tell me one story in particular, a story I never grew tired of hearing, a story fundamentally similar to my grandmother's.

There was once a young woman, Salwa, the heir to an enormous house. She loved her father so much that she never tired of gazing upon him. One day, the father died. Suddenly orphaned, Salwa was entrusted to the care of a preceptor, a *fe'ih*, a tutor of the Qur'an. When the family was present, the holy man taught her the Qur'an. But as soon as he was alone with her, he would show her his magic tricks, like his ability to disappear into the wall and reappear at will, thanks to the power of a secret prayer. That was how she grew up, instructed in religion and in pagan secrets, literally 'ravished'. When she turned sixteen, she was married to the son of the house's new owner. She did not love him. In one blow, she'd lost the *fe'ih* and her memories of her father. She spent her days crying and her nights thinking. To console her, the *fe'ih*, who appeared every Thursday night without fail, and sometimes on Monday nights, gave her a patience stone, the kind you place under embroidery and which also allows you to forget your sorrows. After her first child, when she was hardly recovered from her labour pains, the *fe'ih* suddenly appeared, seized the infant, and disappeared into a fissure in the wall. The husband then arrived, asking for his son. Unable to describe her secret liaison with the *fe'ih*, she didn't dare explain how the infant had vanished. Instead, she told her husband that she'd had a miscarriage. Everyone was astonished; they discussed what had happened, they argued, and then they forgot all about it. A year later, she gave birth to another son, and again, on the very day he was born, the *fe'ih* emerged from a fissure in the wall, seized the child and disappeared the same way he'd come. Then the mother-in-law arrived, wild with rage, accusing the young woman of robbing her of her descendants. This time, after much deliberation, it was decided to confine the young woman to a hidden place up on the terrace where the servants went to do the laundry, her foot chained and her tears as her only companion. No joke. When my mother told this story, she made no connection between it and my grandmother's story. In those days, the world was in order. Tales and legends were an integral part of people's lives. The mother-in-law seized Salwa's third child the moment it emerged from her womb. She raised it herself, far away. This child grew up with only one ambition: to reestablish his mother as the head of the household. Once he reached adulthood, he returned. They tried to bar his way. He brandished his sword, shouting, '*El beit beit abouna oué nass yetrodouna*?' 'This house is my father's house and these people want to send me away?' This was the key phrase, my mother's philosophy, she who'd rebelled against her father's matrimonial choices; it's a phrase that comes back to me whenever I think of returning to Egypt someday, to revisit my childhood home. I've never returned to Egypt.

As children, whenever we caught cold or got too much sun, my mother administered drugs from the pharmacy while my grandmother practised magic—with the result that no one could tell which remedy had worked. When an infant cried, my grandmother would go about massaging him. "*Han issou*,' she would say decidedly, 'I'll measure him.' Then she would place him on her knees, buttocks in the air. And she would bring one leg towards one arm, diagonally, the right to the left, the left to the right. She would compare, frown, start over again and conclude by saying, '*Ma 'woug*,' 'He's all twisted.' The other elderly women would smile knowingly. Sarina, my mother's aunt, or Rachel, her cousin, would nod their heads. "*Han delou*'—'I'll straighten him out. Bring me some sesame oil,' my grandmother would order and my mother would make a face as she brought her a little oil in a saucer. Then my grandmother would vigorously massage the child. After a good half hour, she would measure him again, bringing the right leg to the left arm and the left to the right. '*Et 'adal oualad*'—'I've set the child straight.' 'Look,' she would add, 'they're now the same length. They're just right.'

After such a treatment, the baby would fall asleep and my grandmother would go on her way, proud, and with a bit of scorn for these modern types who didn't know how to care for their children.

My father, he was Tyrone Power ... attractive, naturally elegant, a slightly wild beauty with strangely clear eyes, honey-coloured, which grew almost translucent with age. I was fascinated by my father's eyes, ever since an elderly woman in the family, a grandmother or a great aunt, casually said, 'Do you have any idea what I would do for your father's beautiful eyes?' I'd taken her at her word. He walked swinging his arms freely, a newspaper folded in his right hand. He made fun of everyone and everything. To him, nothing was commonplace, nothing was serious, everything lent itself to mockery. I never knew what really interested my father. Beyond pleasantries, banalities of the moment, I would be unable to say what occupied his mind. The family bored him. He understood nothing about money, children were women's business, politics were not worthy of attention. He existed only in and for himself. Basically, he was of another world. He was always of another world. And yet he was the guarantor of the essential.

Nanterre, 1983

1 October 1983: in a large, sinister hall at the University of Nanterre, I was defending my doctoral thesis entitled 'Relations between Ethnopsychiatry and the Theory and Practice of Clinical Psychoanalysis'. The jury consisted of renowned psychoanalysts and psychiatrists: Didier Anzieu, Serge Lebovici, Colette Chiland, Claude Veil and the spiritual Luis Vincent Thomas. The old-fashioned defence included an especially rigorous textual analysis, engaging with important theoretical debates of the day, It lasted five and a half hours. An announcement had appeared in Le Monde—*at that time, the newspapers would routinely announce thesis defences. As a result, the hall was full, 150, maybe 200 people—colleagues, friends, fellow students and those just there out of curiosity. I was dead with fear. I didn't know then that all I had to do was to keep quiet. A thesis defence is the opposite of what it claims to be. It is certainly not an assessment of the candidate's knowledge; rather, it is dedicated solely to the professors' speech, to what they have imparted, as if to impress upon the candidate once and for all that his professors are the ones with the knowledge. After three hours, during a sort of inter-mission, we were wandering through the corridors, looking for the toilets. An unlikely encounter between Serge Lebovici, president of the International Society of Psychoanalysts, an advisor to princes, who was at that time restructuring the study of psychiatry in France, and my father, the little emigrant with an accent that betrayed his Egyptian origin. My father called out to Lebovici, pronouncing his name as if it were Italian: 'Vous êtes Lebovitchi?' Lebovici raised an astonished eyebrow. My father announced, 'I'm his father.' Silent, I anxiously watched the two of them, my eyes wide open, as when one knows that the significance of what is happening is not yet clear. Two worlds were colliding, creating a mutual misunderstanding. Lebovici replied, 'You can be proud.' Then, in response to my father's perplexed look, he added, 'Of your son, I mean. You can be proud of your son.' Lebovici had straightaway attributed to my father the psychology of a common petty bourgeois who wished to bask in his son's glory. If Soussou Hantoussou (one of my father's nicknames, which could be translated as 'Soussou the joker') was feeling proud, which I doubt, it would not have been because his son was receiving his doctorate. He'd simply wanted to inform the educated Jew, which Lebovici clearly was, that he was the father of the initiate. I'm sure he considered it his duty, just as in the religious initiation of bar mitzvah, when a boy goes up to the Torah and takes hold of the sacred text for the first time. It would be unheard of not to name the father. Something obvious, a sort of atavistic impulse, had impelled him to react, to recall the ancient laws. What was this world in which a young man was initiated before his community, and the proceedings never mentioned the name of his father? A world of monkeys or of dogs?*

* * *

My father had that serene knowledge—not erudition, but a knowledge that comes of itself, like the prayers he knew by heart without knowing what they meant but which he read nonetheless, going over the same pages day after day, right up until his death at the age of ninety-three. I have kept his prayer book. I have it still. All the pages are loose, having been turned and manipulated thousands of times. But a man made like that, without the least pretension, deeply confident in his own nature, sometimes makes obscure pronouncements that go beyond him. I've preserved a few of them, like unopened letters, awaiting the day when their meaning would unfold.

At my home in Montmorency during Passover, after my mother's death, while we were reading the Haggadah, that extraordinary text composed of selections from the Bible and the Talmud, my father was sitting, staring into space. My two children were also there, and I'd invited some friends. There were some twenty of us gathered around the table to once again celebrate, the 'exodus from Egypt'. He must have been ninety-one or ninety-two years old. The text, read every year since childhood, rose easily from his memory. All we had to do was to say the first word, and the rest followed. I felt that this was one of the last Passovers I would share with him; I nestled close to him, taking every opportunity to touch him, to caress his hands. At one point, he turned to me and said: 'The essential thing is to be together.' It was not merely a platitude. My father did not speak so often as to utter some banality. It had to be decoded; it was up to whomever heard him to restore the context. Here is the sentence, as I've come to understand it: 'You can leave to discover the world, things, beings, and men, but you cannot leave your people behind. The essential thing is to be together.' It reminds me of an African proverb I heard in Mali, in Benin: 'See the bird fly. You see it come and go. You think it goes where it will. But watch it closely, it will always return to perch on the same branch.'

My father, he was Johnny Weissmuller.

He would enter the water like a torpedo, crossing the pool from one end to the other like a lightning bolt, without disturbing the order of the elements. I will never be able to swim as he did. Summer rendered him joyous. Photographs of Tarzan in a swimsuit at the beginning of the century, striking athletic poses on the beaches—at Ras El Bar, in Alexandria, where he would drop us off for the summer before running back to Cairo to live his life. I know that over there he joined his friends, played cards. I imagine he also went there to see women, his lovers. I know he had many. Mademoiselle Leonie, for example, who worked for a while at his factory. Just as I did, my father liked to explore the world, even if most often it was between the sheets.

The 'factory' was the Nessler Perfumery, which my father had taken over and managed with an associate. He, who had no advanced degree, only a quasi-autistic passion for numbers that allowed him to calculate infinite multiplications in his head, had thrown himself into the manufacture of perfumes. Sudan, the land of fragrance, was his principal client. He himself blended the scents in enormous flasks. Did he write down the formulas for his creations? I only know that it was difficult for him to recreate the perfumes whose names he'd popularized. As recently as 2000, people still spoke of *Bett el Soudan,* 'The Girl from Sudan'. I mentioned it to an international Sudanese official I met in Bujumbura in 2004. He remembered the label, which explicitly depicted a sensuality currently forbidden in Sudan. He recalled the magical insistence of its imprint on a woman's body. It remained for him the scent of voluptuousness.

Years later, I would write a book about the use of perfumes by the masters of the *zars* in Sudan, in Ethiopia. Each *zar* has a scent, *is* a scent. (With spirits it's difficult to distinguish having from being.) The principal task of a *zar* master is to identify the spirit, not in order to define it, as has sometimes naively been claimed, but in order to find a way to constrain it. One identifies a spirit not by an act of knowing, but through a process—through the blending of essences until the presence is revealed. When the specialist has finally found the scent, once he has succeeded in mingling it with the blood of a sacrificed animal, and once he has made the designated human absorb the mixture, that's when the *zar*, the spirit, appears. Did it ever occur to my father that his day-to-day work, in which he took genuine pleasure, was exactly what might have one day liberated his mother from her '*afrit*, her demon, freeing her ankle from its copper *kholkhal*? I do not know. It was impossible to seriously bring up such matters with my father.

My father, who knew neither the world in which he was living, nor whether other worlds existed elsewhere, had begun to earn some money with his perfume factory. According to my mother, it was very much against his nature, for he had the tendency to give it away as soon as it was in his pockets, first to his parents, then to his friends, to his lovers of course, and, so people said, to whoever asked him. Two of his brothers, who hadn't found employment, were on the factory's payroll, as were plenty of others no doubt. Still, some money remained for the household. He'd purchased a 1948 Morris, in English green with black mudguards and green leather seats. Even now, I still love its steering wheel with the three metal spokes and a black bakelite horn encircled in silver at the center. To this day, such a steering wheel in an atmosphere of worn leather has the capacity to fill me with joy. One can still find its like mounted on the dashboard of a refurbished Austin Healey. The 1948 Morris was his car. For my mother he found a used car, less dashing but with a certain flair, a 46 Hillman in midnight blue, whose seats he had upholstered in blue leather. But the most beautiful to me was the gigantic 49 grey Ford Mercury, a service car for the factory, which he sometimes borrowed for our long summer trips from Cairo to Alexandria by the desert road, a journey of 200 kilometres that took us a full day. I loved cars; I still love cars. One day my father confided in me: 'We will never be poor. I've put some money aside . . . 5,000 pounds.' It was a veritable fortune. I was eight then. Perhaps it would have been better if he'd kept quiet. The following year we found ourselves poorer than we'd ever been, expelled, migrants in a strange land, without work, without family, without prospects—at the mercy of the elements. From then on, a kind of implicit rule silently guides my life—never defy the gods.

I was a rich child, then a poor child, then an adolescent who was neither rich nor poor, and so, I know full well that money comes and goes. Always a proletarian. I've only ever earned enough to restore my strength to work from month to month.

Around the time of my political awakening, I reproached my father one evening as we sat around a pot of linden tea, 'But, after all, you must have read the papers. You must have listened to the radio. Your friends must have spoken to you about it, no? The Egyptian Revolution lasted a good three years. How could you possibly be taken by surprise? How did you manage to let yourself be dispossessed? Why had you not already left?' Raising his eyes heavenwards, he answered me, 'In those days, I was an idiot.' Absurd question, absurd answer. He most certainly was not an idiot. He lived in another world, a world in which men do not determine their own fates, where what happens to them is not of their own volition, but rather constitutes a message from elsewhere, a sibylline text that must be deciphered. Events happen through the workings of external forces. Events are an occasion to identify those forces, to reveal their intentions, but the forces themselves are not at the disposal of men.

October 1956. Once again, Jews were being chased through the streets of Cairo, as in 1948 and 49. Our maid Ouahiba returned from her errands, her ears ringing with the words of the revolutionary order. The Russians were in the streets, as were the Chinese and the Germans, Nazis who had taken refuge in Cairo after the war. I was a child, but I clearly remember everyone's anxiety in anticipation of the apocalypse. I would listen to the radio, which was broadcasting in classical Arabic. I could not understand one word out of two, but I knew that I needed to know. I tried to hear what there was to hear—we were living through an extraordinary moment. Moreover, we already knew how the story would end. It was the same story we'd been telling from time immemorial. The words were in the biblical text: 'A new pharaoh arose in Egypt, who had not known Joseph.' Joseph was my father. The pharaoh: Gamal Abdel Nasser. Jews were imprisoned, humiliated, pursued. Some were assassinated; all were despoiled. The new pharaoh, a nationalist and socialist, placed a sequester in every Jewish factory, in every Jewish business, in every Jewish shop every Jewish home. Ours was a military man, a captain I believe. He entered the factory, approached my father, took out his revolver and placed it on the desk, then ordered my father to open the safe. My father complied. The safe was empty. His partner had absconded to the Sudan. The Egyptian military man could not believe his eyes, convinced that the truth was being hidden from him. He moved into the factory, determined to live there while waiting for the money to return. As far as I know, he's still there, still waiting perhaps. Three months later we embarked in Alexandria, destination: Italy. On our passports the stamp: 'Departure without Return.' We Jews of Egypt, a small community of seventy thousand souls who'd lived there for a thousand years, would be chased out, to the very last one. Today there is not a single Jew left in Egypt. I may be exaggerating a bit.

There remains a handful of elderly women—perhaps some twenty of them, huddled in old-age homes.

Tel Aviv, 2006

A conversation with the chief-of-staff at the Egyptian embassy. Surprised by my Arabic, he asks: 'You speak our Arabic perfectly. Have you lived in Egypt?' 'I'm Egyptian,' I tell him, 'I'm a very old Egyptian in fact.' 'You can't be,' the diplomat replies. 'There have never been any Jews in Egypt.' This young man in his early forties, educated, speaking impeccable English, otherwise quite amiable, could not for a moment imagine that a Jewish community had lived for a time in Egypt. We were the first victims of what was not yet called 'ethnic cleansing'. The Egypt of my childhood was diverse—Muslims to be sure, a small majority; Copts, a large minority; and all the others: Jews, Greeks, Armenians, Turks . . . today the country is almost entirely Muslim. By what miracle? By whose political will? Or, rather, to what obscure will was the political realm forced to submit?

* * *

My father never imposed on me the rule of law—not any law! Nor was he himself the law. He readily assumed his non-participation in the law. He prayed to God, not out of duty but because God was right there beside him. Twice daily for some twenty minutes, he whispered to Him in Hebrew, words he barely understood, about which he never reflected, words that were a music of the heart. Twice daily, unfailingly, upon rising up and before lying down, framing those fecund, treacherous moments of the night, he stood erect, in the morning wearing his prayer shawl and the phylacteries around his arm and forehead, and in the evening with the yellowed prayer book that is now in my possession. This is all that was conveyed to us. There was no proselytizing, not one injunction. My father never reproached me for not praying, my brother even less. He never explained prayer or its necessity to us. He neither justified nor glorified himself. He simply demonstrated his personal love for God through his twice-daily rendezvous, conducted in complete humility, hidden in a corner of the house. He neither shared it nor boasted of it. He neither bemoaned it nor rejoiced in it. It was as if it were the air he breathed. Outside those two moments when it was impossible to disturb him, when he never responded to our pleas, no matter how insistent, he was joyful, always ready to enjoy himself with this one or that. He was not a religious man, not a believer in the ordinary sense of the word. The sages say we should adopt two attitudes towards God: we should love Him and fear Him. My father only loved Him. I am like my father. His two sons never prayed. My brother, it seems to me, has shown no interest in it. As for me, prayer remains a mystery. All I learnt from my father is that prayer cannot be forced, that God is only a presence and that prayer, from time to time, is the opportunity for a visit.

I do not know from where my father derived this knowledge of beings and things. He knew that one transmits to children for their entire lives, not for the five or ten years to come. To explain things would necessarily lead to discussion, to opposition perhaps, There were things—very few things, it's true—one does not discuss. Having grown up free as a bird, on the streets, so to speak, he'd studied very little. He'd emerged from the *hara*, Cairo's Jewish ghetto, hoisting himself up to the position of a comfortable petty bourgeois by the sheer strength of his intelligence. In 1956, he was forty-four years old. He was good-looking, elegant, athletic, attractive. He was famously successful with women and in business. He was a guide and a support for his family, appreciated by his Egyptian friends for his gentleness and humour. And then, from one day to the next, he found himself tossed onto the port of Naples with a wife and two children to support, without credentials, without references, without prospects. He did not cry, did not curse God or man. Little by little, he built a life for himself. Whenever I think of him, I am inexorably overcome with sorrow. He never again found the splendours of Egypt. His time spent there would remain his loss. I've met many elderly persons. As the hour of departure approaches, the more intently they bury themselves in their past. This was never the case with my father. During the last years of his life, I would try to speak with him in Arabic, his mother tongue. He would always answer me in French. He refused to look back at what was now behind him.

I constantly think that what happened to him could very well happen to me in turn. I think about it daily. Forced to start over in a new country, to learn a new language and profession. I think this might even be the meaning of the recurring dream I have several times a year. And I think back to my father, my throat tight. How did he manage to keep up his spirits, to withstand whatever came his way, without being hardened by it? But I think I've guessed his secret: small pleasures. Even when things were at their worse, he knew how to steal away, to find his fellow Egyptian exiles in the backroom of the Monte Carlo, a tiny bistro on rue Cadet, where he would while away the time between 5 and 7 p.m.

My father, he was Humphrey Bogart! He thought like no one else—no one knew what he was thinking actually. He did what he wanted to do, with ease, as if he were playing. But he left the impression that real life existed elsewhere, that this world was merely one of appearances. My father was never like the others. Some were already Zionists. His brother-in-law, Chababo, his sister Adele's husband, had decided to go to Israel with his five sons in 1949, just after the creation of the state. For my father, Zionism was a given. Why insist upon it? He loved Israelis the way he loved his family, and that was the extent of it. He did not speak Hebrew, except with his God. His Hebrew was spoken with an Arabic accent, most likely close to the Hebrew of Antiquity, in which the consonants roar and the gutturals weep. He spoke and wrote Arabic like an educated man. He also knew the gods of other peoples. He could recite suras from the Qur'an by heart and 'Our Father' in French without any errors. He laughed about it. He'd absorbed it, along with the blows of a ruler, while attending the LaSalle Brothers' school in Cairo. Other people were nationalist or Communist. These affiliations made him laugh. He saw them as addictions, like hashish or alcohol. He felt sorry for them, these *hashashins*, these addicts, derelicts on the pavements of old Cairo. There were also the orthodox, dressed all in black, their heads covered with wide-brimmed hats, passing like shadows, grazing the walls. He didn't spit behind their backs as some did; he simply turned away. He thought that this heightened relig-iosity did not belong in Cairo's burning heat. In any event, these were mostly Ashkenazis, in other words, foreigners, *schlekht*, who had not grasped the subtleties of this religion particular to the Jews of Cairo, a certain moderation in the adoration of God—a love that minimally disrupts daily life. What's more, one could not be Jewish without that bit of self-deprecation, that propensity to laugh at oneself. The devout did not have this quality. They seemed to have shuttered their eyes.

My father never travelled to Israel. Today it seems incredible to me that a faithful Jew who lived during the second half of the twentieth century never set foot in Israel. He left Egypt in February 1958, then lived briefly in Rome before coming to Paris, where he remained until his death. Why did my parents not go to Israel when they left Egypt? For my mother, raised on classical French literature, Victor Hugo, Musset, Barbey d'Aurevilly, France was a dream of youth. Because it was necessary to leave, it could become an opportunity to learn other things, to learn more. One had to make up for the misfortune with a throw of the dice. Perhaps it was for the best? France? The France of Mr Moline, her French teacher at the lycée, that of the universities, the France of the chateaus on the Loire. Surprisingly, my father did not oppose this plan. In Israel, he would have found his brothers, his sisters, his cousins . . . no doubt he had no desire to assume once more the role of supporting the extended family. If he were to consent to the rupture, it had to be radically. For the Jews of Egypt, to emigrate to Israel was not really an emigration—it was barely more than moving from one apartment to another. In Egypt, before the great departure, they discussed it: Tel Aviv, beside the sea, with its long beach and corniche, it was essentially Alexandria. And Haifa? Perhaps it was more like Cairo? Except for the fact that my mother hated the heat. When it would start to get hot, during the first days of May, she would lie down half-naked on the kitchen tiles, moaning, 'I'm suffocating. It wasn't hot like this in France.' In her geography books, it was written that 'France is a temperate country.' 'Temperate', a word I've had such difficulty understanding, as in 'measured', 'reasonable'. We gave up Israel because my mother was too hot in summer, for Victor Hugo and a temperate country. We shivered during that first winter in Paris. We'd never imagined one could be so cold. And then the years went by. Every year we returned to that famous question: Would we go to Israel this summer? But it's so hot over there. In winter, we had no desire to move. In the spring? There are no holidays. We never went on holiday ... In truth, something had been broken. Neither one nor the other knew what attitude to adopt towards the cousins, once so close but now so distant. More years went by. The Israelis came, despite the economic difficulties. My cousin Yossi came, my father's nephew, his sister Adele's eldest. Yossi was a nickname for Joseph; he bore my father's name in homage. He was perhaps twenty-eight, a lieutenant colonel in the Israeli army. He brought with him images, stories and a sense of humour reminiscent of my aunt Adele. Cousin Edith came, my mother's alter-ego, and even her mother, whom we called Mama Nina, my mother's elderly aunt. Albert Heifetz came, an engineer in the Israeli aeronautics industry. He sojourned in France for some time, at Sud-Aviation. Almost all of them came to Paris. Each time, we promised a visit in return. It never took place. My parents never made the trip. Why did they never reach the Promised Land? When they'd first arrived in France, it wasn't yet time. A few years later, they didn't feel like it.

In their old age, it was too late. My father, God's intimate, never set foot there. Upon leaving Egypt, he wandered for forty years in the Parisian desert. Forty years? I count, from 1956 to 1996, after which time stopped. Forty years during which he looked at the Promised Land from afar. As for me, I held off until the year I turned fifty. It's a mystery, about which I ponder and continue to ruminate.

God counselled the Jews to always choose life over death. Through an act of personal will, my father had chosen life. He lived for ninety-three years, and it was his own doing. I have the impression that he could still be living, eternally. Age had no hold on him, affecting only the clarity of his gaze which became more translucent over time. He passed away quietly in Paris, without making a fuss, without letting anyone know, one Sabbath, as befits a man close to God. I like to think that he departed just as the patriarchs had, simply because one night he found he'd had his fill of days. Time got to him only once, in 1996, at the death of his sister Adele, who'd been living in Israel and whom he had not seen since 1949. Aunt Adele's death left him the sole survivor among his siblings. He loved this sister, so beautiful, who bore an uncanny resemblance to a portrait from Fayum. She was his favourite. She'd been a close friend of my mother's before my parents married; my father was most likely allying himself with her when he chose his wife. He mourned her for a very long time, much longer than the mandated mourning period. He kept his feelings to himself, except that when I asked him what year we were in, he invariably answered 1996. 1996? In 2000, we were in 1996; in 2003, too, and in 2005, the year he died. We were always in 1996. Time had stopped in 1996, at the moment when he found himself unjustly alone in the world, he who was the second child, almost the eldest; he who should have gone before the others.

I sometimes see my father in the mirror; his face appears behind my features. We have been deeply familiar, from our very DNA to our appearance—from our words to our experiences. And yet we were so different. He was as secretive as I am transparent, as sure of himself as I am hesitant. When we arrived in Italy, he didn't speak a word of Italian. I was nine years old. I was enrolled in the neighbourhood school and speaking the language within a matter of weeks. This time spent in Italy, where he was suspended for a year, not yet detached from Egypt, unsure whether he would stay here, gazing over the sea to a distant shore that he would never reach, hoping that the world would miraculously right itself, remained a parenthesis in my father's life; he never wanted to speak of it.

As for me, I liked Italy—Rome, with its communal school, relaxed, joyful, with its fountains and our games in the post-war streets. In Egypt, I'd been a protected child who never left home without the driver, the maid, the servants, and, more often than not, the entire family. In Italy, the door was suddenly thrown wide open. I played in the street with the other children. Italy was struggling to recover from the war's devastation. In the open areas of the city, you could still find immense craters. We rummaged through the garbage dumps looking for weapons the soldiers had left behind. Antonio, a chubby, angry little boy lived at the top of Via Sorrate. We lived at the bottom. I would pass in front of his house and call out, 'Antonio!' He would appear at the window.

'*Cicione, Cicia Bomba . . .*' (fat pig), and out he would come, racing down the street, pursuing me. I'd become a wild little Italian, an expert in Italianness. I served as a guide for my father. Such is often the fate of children in migrant families: they become guides for their parents whose clouded souls remain hypnotized by a too-new world.

While still in Egypt, we were already Italian. That is, we'd had Italian nationality for two or three generations. Our ancestors had purchased Italian nationality in order to enjoy the privileges granted to foreigners by the Ottoman administration. It was certainly not entirely honest, but it was possible. Before the world wars, European nationalities had not been imbued with that sacred mysticism that would give them fire, blood, and tears. The French conferred French nationality on select minorities in their colonies; the British did the same, in order to make inroads into the heart of indigenous communities—in short, to divide and conquer. The Italians, who did not have the means to found such colonies, sold nationality to individuals. In this way the European powers with their materialistic appetites benefitted from the presence of foreigners, and could, at little expense, increase their representation in those distant, promising countries. When Livorno's city hall burnt down in 1873, the administration vanished, and the Egyptian Jews, from one day to the next, suddenly found themselves to be Italian, originally from Livorno. There was a certain logic to this: during the sixteenth and seventeenth centuries, Livorno had harboured a large Jewish community. During the time of my grandfather's grandfather, Jews who had the means to purchase Italian nationality became foreigners in a land that had been their home for a millennium. The small privileges they enjoyed as 'foreigners'—in arbitrating minor offences, settling the little day-to-day problems— laid the groundwork for the problems to come. In this way, the European powers created 'foreigners' by adopting native peoples. In this instance, the Jews, accustomed to being foreigners, multi- lingual by tradition, had dug in their heels, pursuing a mirage of prosperity. They assumed positions in the banks and corporations that operated the Suez Canal, or in the new companies supporting the cotton industry. They extricated themselves from the ghetto, dazzled by the lights of the West, by the opportunity to establish themselves in a foreign land about which they knew nothing. Meanwhile, Egypt, the ancient land of the Christianity of the Orient, was drifting towards a Muslim identity. Soon, it would no longer be possible to be Egyptian without also being Muslim. That is where we come from, that hundred-year-old faultline that con- tinued to widen, eventually fracturing the nation into irreconcilable communities. Today most Egyptians have no idea that there were once in their country indigenous Egyptians who were also Jewish. As for my father, all he knew was that we had bought our nation- ality. He measured the peculiarity of our identity by the bewilder- ment of the Italian officials who could not understand these Italians who knew nothing about Italy and spoke not a word of Italian. Egyptian (though not administratively so), Italian (with true-false papers), Israeli (despite never having set foot in Israel), we were becoming solely what we'd always been—Jews, simply Jews.

My father was Marcello Mastroianni—the same recalcitrant lock of hair that no amount of brilliantine could control. He had the same ease in his walk. In Arabic, people said of him: *bi hantache.*

Untranslatable! You could say: 'Tall and thin, he walks onwards, sure of his place in the world, happy with his life and capable of everything.'

October 1956.

French parachutists invade Port Said. People talk about the bombing of Cairo. In the evening, watchmen patrol the streets. Calling for lights to be extinguished. *Tafou l'nour ged 'an.* 'Turn out your lights!' Throughout the city, a mood of insurrection. It's not good to be a Jew during such troubled times. We are anxious, most certainly. My mother comes up with a plan to travel south to Minieh, a city in Middle Egypt, 250 kilometres from Cairo. It's war! The Egyptians are fighting on two fronts: in the north, against the Europeans, French and British, whose forces are landing there; in the south, against the Israelis, invading the Sinai. In complete innocence, we arrive in Minieh, a garrison city, looking very Western with our cameras slung across our chests. We are immediately noticed by the Moukhabarat, the intelligence agency, and whisked off to the police station. We claim to be tourists, wanting to visit the city. The police are sure we are spies, hoping to photograph military installations. My father negotiates, explains . . . we are released, on condition that we catch the next train back to the capital. The night train is crammed with exhausted young soldiers returning from the front. Before we leave the station, an entire battalion pours into the overheated carriages, collapses on the floors, flings their rifles across the central aisle. They've just suffered a humiliating defeat at the hands of the Israelis. If they were to learn that we are Jews, we're done for. My father orders the women to be silent. I sit beside him. He fobids me to utter a word of French. And I listen to him for hours, as he explains in Arabic that his name is Mr Georges, that he is a Copt and a professor at the university. He announces to the young soldiers that to remunerate them for their valiant service, the government has decided to advance them their salary for the year, without an exam. Within an hour, the entire carriage is gathered around him, listening as he expounds on things he never studied—the Qur'an, history, politics—creating, through the magic of his words, a humane Egypt, aware of its soldiers' suffering, an Egypt of light, which did not exist. My father, he was Marcello Mastroianni! The cinema, it knew him!

I became a professor although my father never set foot in a university. The false name he gave himself, 'Mr Georges', would be the first name of my mentor twenty years later, Georges Devereux. I have always thought there are no lies, only premonitions!

7

Natacha and Louisa

In an astonishing essay, 'Analysis Terminable and Interminable', where he explains, once and for all, that psychoanalysis is ineffective, Freud writes that there are three impossible professions: governing, healing and educating. I've practised only two of them. I've never governed, have never taken part in power in any way. But I did not find the two other professions, healing and educating, to be impossible, merely anxiety-provoking.

To foster the maturation of a being, to dig the channel that will irrigate them for a lifetime perhaps, seems to me an almost unbearable responsibility. I was never able to contain this fundamental anxiety . . . What if I lost my way, if I led the innocent, the patient, the student into a dead end from which they would never be able to emerge? Who am I to lead a living creature in a direction they would not have chosen had they not crossed paths with me? I experienced this anxiety during a patient's treatment, while directing a doctoral thesis, even while delivering a lecture or teaching a course. But in 1972, with the illusions of my age and my era, I was

155

aspiring with all my being to become a psychoanalyst and a professor. My entrance into active life presented itself under the best auspices, as it should be. In those days, to become a psychologist, it was sufficient to have only a Master's degree. Barely six months after earning mine, I enrolled in a doctoral programme under the direction of Georges Devereux. My friend Isaac, who'd actively participated in our wild seminars on psychoanalysis, had completed his medical degree and begun his specialization. He was then an intern in psychiatry. He informed me that a position of psychologist had just opened up in the public clinic where he worked. Why didn't I go to meet the head doctor to propose my candidacy?

His name was Georges Ostaptzeff. He was nearly six feet tall, with Mongolian eyes, folded behind the thick glasses of a myopic, a pipe perpetually dangling from the corner of his lips and the most nonchalant manner I've ever encountered. He must have weighed 120 kilogrammes, but seemed as frail as he was large. He bent down mechanically as he passed through his office door. I followed him, catching my feet on the rug.

I was not yet twenty-four, my head full of theories, chomping at the bit, burning to get down to work. He spoke little, every now and then stringing out a sibylline phrase that plunged me into perplexed insecurity. 'What do you want to do in my clinic?' he asked me right off. 'Wait! What do I want to do? I will do whatever you want, isn't that right?' I thought, but didn't have the nerve to say. I played the game. I answered him; I delivered the result of years of thought. 'Psychoanalysis! That's what I want to do. Psychoanalysis in a clinic, free psychoanalysis for anyone who shows up.' I no longer recall the exact phrases I used, something like, 'To bring the most advanced psychoanalysis to the least privileged populations, to the residents of the poorest neighbourhoods, to the destitute hospitalized for psychiatric problems.' Ultimately, that's what I dedicated my career to, although at the time it was little more than a pipe dream. He did not react, did not look doubtful. I went on; I explained that I was preparing a thesis, that I was interested in the pathologies of people who came from afar, from another country, another culture, another world. It seemed to me that in the neighbourhood where the clinic was located, there might be a need for my competencies and for those I was in the process of acquiring in ethno-psychiatry. The interview lasted barely half an hour.

'Very well!' Ostaptzeff concluded.

'Very well?' I asked.

He rose.

Again I asked, 'So, do you mean ...'

Abruptly, he said, 'For me, it's good. If you can work things out with the prefecture for the administrative papers.'

'When do I begin?'

'Next Monday. But if you'd like, you can come on Friday, to meet the team.'

It was Wednesday. Up until then, I'd led the life of a student. I worked odd jobs, earning just enough to cover room and board. The rest of the time, I found occasions to think. to speak, to discuss. I wrote, I attended courses and lectures. And here it was that within a few minutes my life had been transformed.

At the Friday meeting, Ostaptzeff mentioned an alert that had just come from the police station. A man had locked himself with his mother into a room on the top floor. He was armed with a rifle and threatening to kill her and shoot anyone who tried to enter. The head of the clinic began with his little dictum: 'We're the district psychiatric team, are we not? If we don't know how to intervene before hospitalization, we shouldn't be surprised when very ill people arrive here in a catastrophic state.' He looked at us one by one before continuing. 'Would you rather have Mr Vladimir come to us after having been officially placed? Would you rather spend a month treating him for the trauma of police intervention, for being transferred to the special infirmary?' He looked at us once more and asked again, 'Who will go to Mr Vladimir's home?' There were not very many of us: two interns, four psychiatric nurses, the social worker, and the latest arrival, brand new, me. We were all staring at the floor.

'I want to go!' I ended up stammering, 'I'll go.'

'I'll come with you,' my friend Isaac offered. He was attending the meeting in his capacity as an intern.

Six floors without a lift! A dim corridor smelling of mildew. On the door, a Russian name. Isaac was behind me. We did not have much to go on. If someone had come to consult us in our office, we would have been prepared, but to arrive like this to propose psychiatric care to an unknown person . . . I could hear us thinking: 'At least we're not cops!' We were applying the very young politics of the district. We felt we were some kind of pioneers. But we hadn't imagined that this idea would lead us here. Out of breath from having climbed the six flights, we stood in front of the door, feeling a little foolish. I knocked. Nothing. I knocked again. We waited a few minutes. The door finally opened a crack. A young man, short, obese, in knit underwear, a large, hairy head.

'Who are you? What do you want?'

We explained that we'd been sent by the local clinic. (We didn't dare specify it was the mental hygiene clinic.) We introduced ourselves: Dr Isaac, a psychiatrist, and I, a psychologist,

'Do you have any proof?' the man queried us.

'Proof?'

'Something that identifies you, a business card, I don't know . . .'

We looked at each other. No. We had nothing of the sort.

'Well then, I won't allow you to enter my home . . .'

He had a point, after all. I slipped a foot into the doorway. We negotiated . . . We'd heard he was having problems. Could he perhaps speak with us about them? He ended up inviting us in. A tiny room, paint peeling off the walls; all four corners of the faded linoleum coming up. At the centre of the room, a coal stove, burning. The heat was stifling. An old woman: his mother, just as dishevelled and obese, stretched out on the only bed. Just one chair. They didn't offer it to us. We began to talk, the three men standing, the mother still on the bed, punctuating our conversation with words in Russian. Mr Vladimir explained. He was twenty-five years old. His problems dated back several years, to when he was still at the lycée. He'd frequented a group of neo-Nazis, attended their meetings, watched war movies with them. Nothing more. Then one day he'd noticed he was being followed on the street. At first men, then automobiles, a black Citroën DS. He finally understood. He'd been discovered by a commando of Jewish avengers who, ever since, had never let him be. As soon as he stepped into the street, they were upon him. Sliding notes under the door. Occasionally calling out to him on the street. He would hear, 'Vladimir! Vladimir! Vladimir!' The mother nodded in assent. She too would hear his name called from the street. The commando's strategy was clear. They wanted to drive him to the edge, to render him insane, so that he would commit suicide or something like that. 'It's a perfect crime,' he said, nodding. 'Neither seen nor heard'. . . . 'Neither seen nor heard,' He kept repeating, like a leitmotif, 'No one was guilty, no one would be concerned. A madman had killed himself, that's all there is to it!' That was why he'd armed himself. He showed us the weapon, a loaded 22 LR. He held it with the barrel forward, his finger on the trigger. He felt ready. More than that, he was waiting for them. He wanted it to be over. If this story had to end in a bloodbath, then so be it. Sometimes he heard them talking behind the door, 'in Jewish'. (No doubt he meant 'Yiddish'.). Sometimes he heard them walking on the roof. He pointed to the filthy skylight, almost opaque. . . We should now understand why he hadn't wanted to open the door. We discussed his problems; it's true he had some. We contemplated the scene, dumbfounded. My name is Nathan; my friend Isaac's name sounds even more Jewish. If Mr Vladimir were to suspect we were part of the commando, our hopes for earning his confidence would go up in smoke. We suggested that he come to consult us at the clinic. We could probably help him.

'Could you convince the police to protect me?' he asked.

'Come see us, on Belfort Street,' Isaac replied. 'We'll find a way to help you.'

'You've understood the kind of help I need,' Mr Vladimir insisted—'bodyguards, intermediaries too who will explain to the commando that I've changed my mind, I'm no longer a neo-Nazi.'

Later, I would often observe that seriously disturbed patients, those we used to call 'psychotics' or 'schizophrenics', actually foresaw what was about to happen to them. In his delirium, Mr Vladimir had believed that Jews were pursuing him and in a way, that's what was happening. One day, without warning, two Jews had entered his home.

In the end, our intervention was unsuccessful. Vladimir did not come to the clinic. He continued to hear voices calling and threatening him. One day, he saw the avengers on the roof trying to get in. He ended up firing his rifle at the smoking chimneys. The neighbours were frightened and called for help. The police arrived, subdued him, put him in a straitjacket, and he ended up at the psychiatric hospital, shackled.

Several months later, during a meeting at the clinic, a discussion with the head doctor about Vladimir's hospitalization: 'He's delirious, it's obvious,' Isaac claimed. 'He still hears those voices which, to put it mildly, worries him a great deal. He is literally terrorized.'

The medical team was perplexed. The patient had received heavy doses of psychotropic drugs that had proved ineffective. The voices were calling him, ever-more insistent. He kept saying that his final hour was at hand. He went from a state of prostration to a state of frenzy.

'An entrance into schizophrenia,' Isaac observed quite seriously, 'further complicated by the fact that his mother confirms the delirium. It's what's called a *folie à deux*, isn't it?'

'But no,' interjected the head doctor, Ostaptzeff, in a low voice. 'He's Russian, that's all there is to it.'

Isaac, interrupted, was speechless.

'Russian?' he asked, truly astonished.

'Yes, Russian,' Ostaptzeff continued. 'His delirium is not madness. He's Russian.'

Isaac did not know how to react to his boss's comments. He remained silent.

'It's normal for a Russian to hear voices, even without drinking vodka,' Ostaptzeff added. It can even happen that a Russian has conversations with the moon, the clouds, the stars.

Isaac shrugged. All this went completely against his training. 'What are these Russian matters doing here?'

This was my first time, my first experience at the clinic, my entry into the world of psychiatry. There was work to be done. If I wanted to realize my dreams of psychoanalysis in a public clinic, I would have to create the right conditions. My encounter with Ostaptzeff was a piece of remarkable luck. A man of wide experience, with a profound and original personality, he'd been trained some twenty years before us. He'd known the post-war insane asylums, madmen before modern medication, the great imprisonment, as Michel Foucault called it. Before 68, hospital psychiatrists lived in the heart of the asylum, among the patients. Most of the time they encountered only patients and a few caregivers with whom they would discuss the patients; even when they went to seminars or professional meetings, they spoke about the patients. They encountered them in the clinic, in the courtyard, in the gardens, in the evening over dinner, in the film-club sessions. For years on end, they rubbed shoulders with mental illness. The spectacular aspect of the illness hardly affected them. Facing delirium, feelings of persecution, crises of rage or anxiety, they reacted like surgeons facing an appendicitis—with a calm, professional manner. For Ostaptzeff, it was neither a scandal nor a distortion of the world's order. I could summarize his view of psychiatry in one sentence: 'The reasons of an illness are stronger than Reason itself.' Moreover, he never dissuaded me, never assumed any condescending airs towards my illusions and dreams of innovation. I owe him an infinite debt. When I got to know him better, when we worked together on many projects, we became bound by friendship. It must have been three or four years later that he confided to me that he was an emigrant like myself, that he had gone through the same early experiences in France. The only difference was geographic. He'd come from Russia, I from Egypt; he'd grown up near the slums in Asnières; I 13 kilometres away, in Gennevilliers. I took all his suggestions; he accepted all my audacity. At a time when all the practitioners of psychiatry brandished psychoanalysis like a fetish, he did not believe in its virtues. He had a more social conception of care. He believed that a workman, a daily companion of the patient in the menial or trivial tasks like cooking or cleaning, was far more useful than psychoanalytic sessions. Looking back today, I think he was not wrong. Some serious psychiatric problems are not accessible to any known treatment, neither pharmacological nor psychological. The task of the psychiatrist in such cases is to re-educate the patient, to adapt him to the singularity of their being. When we spoke together about psychiatry, he mocked the theories. Still, he let me be. I often asked him whether he himself had undergone an analysis He'd draw on his pipe and grumble something like, 'What for?' One day, he disappeared. He did not show up for work, nor did he come in the next day, for a whole week, nor the following week. The rest of us, his collaborators, anxiously telephoned his secretary at the hospital. No one had seen him. He had not set foot there, nor in the clinic. He was gone for two full weeks. Then he reappeared at the clinic's Monday meeting, without offering any explanation. In the evening, after the the last patient had departed, we sat on the benches in the waiting room where we would relax for a few minutes before returning home, I asked, 'So where were you?'

'On a lion hunt,' he replied absently.

'Come on, be serious . . . Where were you?'

'On a lion hunt,' Ostaptzeff repeated, 'in Kenya.'

He explained that, tired of hearing me proclaim the benefits of psychoanalysis, he'd put some money aside to undergo his own. When he found himself in possession of a large enough sum to pay for an analysis of three or four months, he thought it was absurd to give all that money to a shrink. Instead, he decided to go on a safari, a real one, with the opportunity to hunt wild animals. He concluded his explanation with a broad smile: 'It's amazing how much good it does. For me, it's far superior to an analysis.'

I will never know if he actually paid for this lion hunt, but it's certain that, for him, a lion's head was worth far more than an analysis.

When I was hired, the place had just changed its name, after the reform establishing district psychiatric clinics. Previously, it had been called a 'Social Hygiene Clinic', a holdover from the immediate post-war period, when the policy had been to care for three major aspects of public health: tuberculosis; sexually transmitted diseases, especially syphilis; and mental illness. These three posed a danger to the community, whether it be from contagion or from the disorder they spawned, and so it was deemed necessary to encourage those who were ill to seek treatment. That is why treatment was obligatory and entirely free, with no registration fees, no administrative forms to fill out. Patients met their doctors immediately. It must be said that such availability proved effective: by the end of the sixties, tuberculosis and syphilis had been largely eradicated. That was why, as a sign of the times, the clinics substituted 'mental' for 'social' hygiene. But although the administrative designation had been changed, and psychiatric teams took over, no one had assumed the responsibility of changing the plaque above the door. For as long as I worked there—close to ten years—I fought without success for them to instal a plaque conforming to what actually went on there. Everyone balked at the thought of explicitly engraving 'mental hygiene' over the entrance. It smacked too much of insanity. It wasn't until the eighties, a decade that so loved euphemisms, that they began to call these places 'CMP', still not daring to say 'Medico-Psychological Centers'. I'd already left for the university. While at the clinic, I'd taken seriously the implementation of the new politics of the district. For it to be known and accepted, it was imperative that the psychiatric clinic insert itself into its community, so that it would be called upon during a crisis, before the emergency services or the police. Being one of the first 'psychologists of the district', I set up spaces where we could meet the population. I led discussion groups with patients and their families to prepare for their discharge from the hospital. I went to the buildings where a hospitalized patient lived, I met with the family and the neighbours to explain our treatment strategies. I even organized a film club at the youth centre, to discuss the problems posed by mental illness in a film. I believed in this work. Bonds were beginning to be formed, the team to be known. The institutions were beginning to trust us. A year after my arrival. I had a chance to evaluate the effect of all this in a real clinical situation. The concierge of a building just across from the clinic had begun to present psychiatric problems. First it was her family that showed up, asking us to hospitalize her. I explained that this was exactly what we were hoping to avoid. They were dubious. It was not her first crisis. On each occasion, she'd been interned in the psychiatric hospital. Why lose time? No! We proposed taking care of her in her home. The caregivers would visit her daily, and if the psychiatrist determined she would benefit from medication, the nurses would administer the drugs right there. With everyone's help, we would avoid the violence of a hospitalization, the loss of familiar objects and the resulting disorientation. But anxiety was beginning to engulf the building. I met with this woman's daughter, then her son. Then I received the building's owner, and, one by one, all the tenants. I explained to each that the crisis was transitory, that we would do our best to abate it as soon as possible. Every day, I spent close to an hour with the patient, discussing her life, her concerns, her delirium—her delirium above all. It seemed that Mitterrand, who was her lover, came to see her every night. Of course, they were a little noisy, but what could one expect from a couple in love? She was being reproached for making noise? Yes, of course, she was making noise!—but they were pleasant noises, cries of pleasure. It wasn't like the couple on the third floor, two fools who roughed each other up whenever they'd had too much to drink. One night, when her lover was leaving, the neighbours surprised him. Mitterand had tried to hide in a trash can. In his haste to conceal himself, he'd misstepped and all the trash cans had clattered down the stairs. The other tenants reproached her, but it was nothing but jealousy. The tenants' version was different. They claimed that in the middle of the night she urinated on the trash to avenge herself. They'd seen her, perched astride a can, like a witch. She was touching, this grandmother in her fleece robe and slippers that had worn grooves into the stairs, thousands of times, for decades. She'd guessed, through her madness, the behaviour for which the man who would be elected president would later be reproached. People were already talking about the possibility of François Mitterrand's candidacy. Many believed he would win against Giscard. In that commune that had voted for the right since the Liberation, the building's inhabitants had likely not appreciated the concierge's socialist and nocturnal passions. Come on! She knew very well what they were saying. Yes, the psychiatrist had been to see her, but he was not like me. He'd only stayed a few minutes and had prescribed those dreadful drops that smelt like death. Halopéridol was the name of the psychotropic the nurses gave her to drink, three drops a day, in a glass of water. She would not be fooled: '*a l'eau, peris et dors*'—'take with water, die and sleep.' We were expecting the amelioration that would calm her and ease the neighbourhood's tension. But as is so often the case in such situations, our efforts were unsuccessful. It was a Sunday morning. The clinic was closed. I'd stopped by to see her the night before, on Saturday, finding her especially anxious, as typically happens before the weekend. She warned me. 'They'll get me, little psychologist' (her name for me) ... They'll lock me up, I know it.' And winking, she added, 'I know too much about it.' On Sunday, she went to buy her bread at the corner shop. Impatient, she shoved another customer. The baker said something. Our patient threatened to call her lover, the leader of the socialists. The shopkeeper called the police for help. And so the concierge, caught in her illusions of grandeur, found herself hospitalized.

I liked those home psychotherapy sessions.

I conducted many, always willing to go and see people, 'real' people, to speak with them about their worlds, to examine with them the objects they loved, the photographs they'd chosen, which they'd hung on their walls, to discuss their neighbours, their neighbourhoods. Simple people have difficulty talking about their lives and their problems in a clinical office. At home, they are unstoppable. Now that I think about it, I realize that this was the method of my great-grandfather, Rabbi Yom-Tov, who would take himself on Shabbat to visit his faithful who were having difficulties. It is only tonight, as I write these words, that I see the connection.

That's how I was earning my living. Not even 1,500 francs a month, at that time the salary of a schoolteacher or a novice agent of the peace. I had a profession I was passionate about, that filled my time and my thoughts, but I knew that I was at the very beginning of my apprenticeship, that I would have to engage in the psychoanalytic training, towards which all the fibres of my being had been yearning since adolescence. Naturally, I went to see Devereux, who had a place on the list of the Psychoanalytic Society of Paris, who knew everyone. Surely, he would be able to point me in the right direction. He suggested two individuals who were not sticks in the mud, who didn't rigidly follow all the rules: Sacha Nacht and Nata Minor. I met Sacha Nacht only once. At the time, he was head of the Psychoanalytic Institute, president of the Psycho-analytic Society of Paris. He looked at me with amusement when I confessed my desire to engage in psychoanalytic training, I who was no one, he who was the summit. 'But you will never be able to pay me!' he warned right off. The minimum fee for a session with Nacht was 250 francs. At three sessions per week, a month of psy-choanalysis would easily add up to more than twice my salary. I'd liked him, this grinning little man, with a somewhat old-fashioned elegance, with his bushy eyebrows and sparkling eyes. I also liked his name, *nacht*, 'night'. I saw in it a sign; it corresponded to me. When he asked me why I wanted to undertake an analysis, if I was suffering any psychological troubles, I was at a loss. I wasn't doing badly; I wasn't doing well either. I was wandering in a sort of netherworld, not really myself, not really another, not fully in my body. I couldn't manage to figure out why I was in the world. A strange feeling, as if my surroundings were a stage set, as if real life lay elsewhere. I had no symptom to present, nothing other than some peculiarities of my existence. I preferred night to day—I still do. I only feel peaceful when the world retires, as if I were watching over it. That's when I can write, practically the only time, in the uninterrupted hum of silence. However, I wasn't an insomniac. I slept soundly during the day, and for a long time. I liked to wake up around noon. But I was beginning to have problems ever since

I'd taken the position at the clinic. I had to get up, to arrive at the office by 9 a.m. And then, there was my constant quest for women. Was it a symptom? Women—I wanted to know them, and then I wanted to know more. For me, it wasn't so much the behaviour of a Don Juan, rather a fundamental curiosity, as if sexuality and intellectual knowledge had somehow merged. I can't claim that frustration led me always to seek elsewhere. I've never been disappointed in a woman. I lived each relationship fully. Some lasted for several months, some for no more than a single night. It was as if I were reading a new novel each time. I was fascinated by the immediate intimacy only love can produce. And in the morning, I liked to witness the deployment of the complexity of their being. At that time, the prevailing mood in France encouraged casual encounters whose only motive was to know each other more deeply. We were all communists back then, a communism of feeling and flesh. Fundamentally, I was not collecting women, I was collecting stories and dreams. I'd discovered that these stories could only be gathered during the course of a night of love. Is that a symptom, doctor? Some remarks I'd heard here and there, from certain women at times of rupture led me to fear it. So, if it was the symptom of an illness, it must be hereditary. I suspect my father was also like this. I'm not certain, but snatches of conversation with this aunt or that cousin have led me to suppose so. The sole business of humans is the continual effort to perceive one's own peculiarities and come to terms with them. I would spend a long time trying to understand this one aspect of myself, and still I have not, not fully. Jews have a special relationship with the marked divinity of sexuality. In this respect, they are like the other Semites and the peoples south of the Mediterranean. The divinities of the ancient Near East—Babylonia, Mesopotamia, Assyria and Egypt—were accustomed to having sexual relations with mortals. The Near East gave birth to Adonis, Cybèle, Aphrodite, Astarte . . . all the divinities of love, not to mention Agdistis and Osiris. Although the populations of these civilizations have disappeared, they have left an inheritance. The populations mingled, changed the names of places and gods. What relationship do the Greeks of today have with the divinities of Antiquity? They are satisfied with taking care of their stone patrimony. Additionally, the Greeks have preserved the language, which is clearly not the case with the multitude of peoples who occupied this region in Antiquity and who have fallen into the trashcans of history—the Akkadians, the Ammonites, the Aramaeans, the Babylonians, the Canaanites, the Chaldeans, Hittites, the Medes, the Nabateans, the Phoenicians, to name only the most well known. These, who for the most part, spoke Semitic languages, have surely been victims of the global success of Arabic which integrated into its corpus the vocabularies of their tongues. Today, I see no more than three of these languages still: Amharic, Hebrew and Aramaic. Only the peoples with a project survive. It's absurd to oppose the identity Devereux termed 'ethnic' to the multitude of attachments that bind an individual. The identity that ties a person to their people has no existence unless the people have a political project. A person's other attachments stem from their own decision. I am not Jewish because of my own will, but because of the fact that the Jews have chosen to exist as a people. And this impalpable will, collective, unfolds in the public sphere. It is never a given, but a triumph against adversity, against the accidents of history. *Identity is not a nature but a choice.*

It is a characteristic of these peoples of the Ancient Near East that the sexual relation bound humans to their gods. Greek mythology is full of the amorous passions of gods for mortal women, sometimes even of goddesses for mortal men, such as Aphrodite for Adonis, or Anchises, Aeneas's father. As for the Semites of the Near East, not satisfied to recount the myths, they put into action a ritual coupling of gods with mortals. We know that in ancient Babylon, as in a great number of Semitic civilizations in Antiquity, there was a strange obligation of sacred prostitution. According to Herodotus, virgins were brought to the divinity's temple and offered to a passing stranger for their sexual initiation. This stranger incarnated the god. The Hebrew language has preserved the memory of this custom, designating the husband by the word *baal*, which also signifies 'master' and 'owner', as, for example of a building. Baal is also the name, we recall, of the god of the ancient inhabitants of Babylon. Thus, these peoples from Antiquity were profoundly marked by the sexual sampling, the lord's right, permitted to their gods, their *baal*s. One can imagine the excesses to which such a custom might lead, the abuse by priests and others in power. And, as so often, such excesses gave way over time to a moral reversal. Judaism is likely in part born from this rebellion. Nevertheless, it has preserved the notion of a sexual relation between God and mortals, but has transformed it. It is no longer with an individual but with a couple that the Jewish God manifests His 'radiance'. God comes to visit the couple. Hence Sarah, at the age of ninety, becomes pregnant from her ninety-nine-year-old husband, because God honours the couple with His presence. Ever since, for a Jewish man, his wife is necessarily his path towards his God. I imagine that this is what was unconsciously stirring deep within me, during my adolescence and early adulthood. I thought I was seeking a woman; in fact, I was erring on the path towards my God. I do not know how Sacha Nacht, a Romanian Jew, received the recital of my amorous pranks; all he did was advise me to find other symptoms if I wanted to engage in psychoanalytic training. Not long before, no doubt influenced by the Lacanians, more and more influential each day, the Psychoanalytic Institute had renounced the infamous 'training analysis'. Since then, if one wished to become a psychoanalyst, one simply had to engage in an analysis, plain and simple, a therapeutic cure. I was in fine shape with my preoccupations that must have seemed the mannerisms of an intellectual. In other words, although my sexual restlessnes might prove to be a path towards God, it was not a path towards institutional psychoanalysis. Whatever the case, the grapes, unripe, were also out of reach. I did not have the means to pay for a cure with Nacht. Hence I decided to try my luck with Nata Minor. At that time, I was living again in Gennevilliers, and I traversed the city in my ancient Citroën 2CV. Minor saw patients in her apartment on boulevard Saint-Germain. It took me a good hour to get there. I'd taken that route, I recall, with François, a fellow student who went to his psychoanalytic session with Lacan on the rue de Lille, a few doors down from her place. I dropped him off at the intersection with the rue de Bac. After finding a parking space, I saw Francçois walking back to me.

'Didn't you tell me you were going to see your shrink?' I asked.

'I'm leaving,' he replied.

'But you hardly had time to arrive.' He'd not stayed more than five minutes in his session with Lacan. He explained that the 'scansion', the untimely ending of a session after a few minutes, had a ruthlessly revelatory effect. Caustically, I asked him if during the time gained through the 'scansion', the analyst saw another patient or if he sat calmly in his armchair thinking of him. François saw me as ignorant, confusing psychoanalysis with other professions, like running a grocery or plumbing. I didn't know then that this practice of short sessions was one of the reasons for the expulsion of Lacan and his disciples from the International Society of Psychoanalysis. I left François on the pavement and went off to my appointment. As I entered the building, I ran into Didier, like me one of Devereux's students.

'What are you doing here?' he asked.

'The same thing as you, I imagine.'

I found myself in a tiny waiting room. A small room in a bourgeois apartment, tastefully furnished, expressing ease. It must have been November or December. Outside, the damp cold penetrated your clothes. In that waiting room, it wasn't warm either. Bundled in my coat, I was leafing through journals of contemporary art, letting my distracted eyes rest from time to time on dark paintings that resembled Rembrandts. I found all this old fashioned, not terribly cheerful, but classy. From the other side of the wall, I could hear the door opening, steps in the corridor, an exchange in low voices, the entrance door slamming, then nothing more. For a few minutes, I thought of escaping. I had the sense that my destiny would play out here, in this office, and I was enjoying the thought of altering its course—to disappear, without even speaking to her . . . What did I have to do, after all, with psychoanalysis? After my first interview with Nacht, I knew she would be expecting symptoms, real symptoms, psychopathology—obsessions, compulsions, hallucinations ... No, not hallucinations! They wanted people who were ill, of course, *ma non troppo*, not too much—first of all, people who could be cured. And me, I wanted training. A curious paradox. I had to be ill in order to become a psychoanalyst, but in good enough health to earn a living and to pay them—or else be an 'heir'! No doubt it was these patients they would prefer, the 'heirs'! People were speaking of arrangements. Rumour had it that Laplanche, one of the two authors of the prestigious *Vocabulary of Psychoanalysis*, and in possession of a veritable fortune, had left a good part of it to Lacan. Me, I was earning a modest living, and all I had inherited from my family were memories. At that time, psychoanalysts could permit themselves anything. Theory had the wind at its back and had become the principal reference point, not only in psychiatry and psychology but also in literature, in anthropology, in the media, even in politics. Requests for a cure were numerous and practitioners were few. Their conditions were draconian: the fee for sessions reached astronomical heights, and they had to be paid in cash, from hand to hand, without cheques or receipts. If one wanted to protest, all one had to do was to go elsewhere while thanking heaven that the psychoanalyst did not call the police. The publication in 1969 of 'Man on the Tape Recorder' by Jean-Paul Sartre in *Les Temps modernes* had created a scandal. Reading it left a bitter taste. The patient had come to ask for an accounting from his psychoanalyst. Armed with a tape recorder, he'd insisted on recording the session. The psychoanalyst had refused. They'd vigorously debated. The psychoanalyst's arguments were so weak, the patient's so persuasive. The psychoanalyst had

175

ended up calling the police. Some were saying that the patient had a psychotic break. Too easy to clear the clinician while incriminating the patient. It was also said that Pontalis, the other author of *The Vocabulary of Psychoanalysis*, had resigned from the editorial board of *Les temps modernes* after this publication. The territory was mined, and I did not have the map.

Nata Minor was—I imagine she still is—a woman of refined elegance, wrapped in large oriental scarves. A small face, gracious and sympathetic, she smiled—a rarity among psychoanalysts, her head leaning to one side as if she were nursing. She punctuated her listening with a multitude of encouraging little 'yes'-es.

'Yes?'

'Oh well, what can I say? I want to engage in a psychoanalysis.'

'Yes, yes.'

And then what, 'yes'? It's easy to practise this profession. To the one who has just said everything and also invented the way of saying it. My mother used to characterize such people, stingy with their words: 'This one, she only buys—she never sells.' Nata Minor only bought. Before this good little woman, curled up in her easy chair like a chilly cat, I remember having experienced a sense of revolt. The radical asymmetry of the relationship seemed absurd to me. A professor is named, designated . . . a priest as well, a prophet is chosen by the people . . . but a psychoanalyst? By whom are they anointed? Come on! They would not hold their position unless you granted it to them. Of course, I understood the implicit theory. Facing nothing, with no counterpoint, no respondent, I was forced to seek my motives within myself. But did I have any? After the requisite exercise of presenting myself, the narrative of my emigration, my nostalgia for the lost world of my childhood in Egypt and the sense of unreality I felt in this world, I interrupted myself and looked around. A strange painting hung on the wall. I'm not sure it was as I'm about to describe it. And yet I saw it three times a week for five years. A sort of inhabited carapace, a man, or perhaps a child, in wooden armour, walking down a road. 'I'm like that, like that little man in his carapace, the man who can be seen in your painting . . . ' She looked surprised. 'What little man?' she asked. 'I don't see a little man in this painting.' Perhaps he wasn't there, after all. Perhaps it was simply a wooden individual wandering through the countryside. At the time, I had much more imagination than I do today. But it was definitely how I felt, forced to hide my true nature, like the man in the wooden carapace, out of fear of being attacked, pursued, destroyed. I know today that this is a very common feeling among migrants, who must hide their ways of being and doing if they want to appear like the others. I also spoke to her of my love for literature, of the novels and poetry I was writing. Years later, perhaps twenty years after the conclusion of my analysis with her, I would learn that she had emigrated from the Russian Empire at the age of four, that she was haunted by an infinite nostalgia for her native city, Odessa. She also had a true passion for literature, and much later she published four or five novels, written in a limpid style, in which she described the small problems of existence. This remains my general impression of psychoanalysis, both its theory and its lived experience: the niggling interest in trivial questions. That is what renders it both fascinating and contemptible. Nata Minor, my psychoanalyst . . . I never really knew her; I guessed at her. I smelt her perfume, watched her movements, heard her sighs, her clearing of her throat—for years. It allows one to construct, month after month, year after year, a detailed, deep image of the person. I did not know her, and yet I know so much about her, leading me to believe that in psychoanalysis it is the patient who discovers his psychoanalyst and not the reverse. And still I remain incapable of describing her, as she if she remains enveloped in the mists of myth.

She addressed herself not to me but to a sort of superior authority hovering above us, which she called *the Unconscious*. I never had any interaction with her, beyond my cure . . . but I would have liked to have known her. From silent, subtle contacts, I've preserved the memory of a deep woman, with a propensity for the imaginary that she curbed only with difficulty. In the practice of her profession, it was as if she were possessed by her 'psychoanalytic-being-in-the-world'. For the rest, she spent her time at an impossible work, stubbornly repetitive, a sort of absurd task, as if she were trying to reconstitute a sugar cube dissolved in a glass of hot water, or enclose an aroma, a scent, in a flask. The remarks she chanced to let fall during these years all had the same function: to return one of my perceptions back to myself, to transform it into a singular fantasy, an interior thought. Her office was the grotto of the ghost train; everything one claimed to see was purely imaginary.

I concluded my first meeting with her by revealing my desire to become a psychoanalyst. She opened wide, astonished eyes.

'But . . .' she replied, 'you know very well that the rule for having your psychoanalysis considered a training analysis, is that it must be with an incumbent. I am not a full member of the Institute, as of course you must know!'

'Yes,' I retorted, 'but it is stipulated in the brochure of the Psychoanalytic Institute that, *as a general rule,* the student must undergo an analysis with an incumbent. As a general rule—that means there are exceptions, doesn't it?'

'Why do you want at all costs to be considered an exception?'

That was her commentary. It presaged everything that would follow, bringing each of my words back to my inner world. According to her, I took myself to be exceptional. The truth was much simpler. I'd chosen her because she was more conciliatory than the incumbents; because she'd agreed to lower her fee. She'd agreed to take four times less than what Nacht was asking. I did not want to be considered an exception; on the contrary, I was searching for a way, with the means at my disposal to do as the others did. I acted as if I accepted her commentary as a kind of truth about myself. In reality, the two of us were caught in a false pretense. So goes psychoanalysis, just like life! Each one speaks to the other, each believing they are taking part in a dialogue, while each one like the other sings his own song to himself.

I showed up for my psychoanalytic sessions three times a week for five years. They were my peaceful years. I was advanceing in my profession and making progress in my research. My universe was expanding and becoming populated. I was discovering professional life, its constraints and its rewards. I saw patients at the Mental Hygiene Clinic, which was teaching me my profession far more effectively than the university courses. For my thesis, I conducted complex research; I published my first articles in specialized journals. Life was taking care to complete my training. But three times a week I devoted three hours to this strange return to myself. I drove to Saint-Germain-des-Pres from my suburb, a trip that took an hour each way, and the sessions lasted, like my Lacanian friend François's joke, forty-five minutes, not one minute more, not one less. On the way there, I would ruminate about what I would say, or tried to remember as precisely as possible my dreams of the night before. During the return, I would endlessly go over the words my psychoanalyst had used, weighing them, dissecting them, imagining others. The sessions lasted a good three hours! And continued in my mind for hours more . . . Nata Minor remained immoveable, year after year, like a sphinx, forcing me to accept her stony bearing through the genuine warmth of her welcome. No doubt she thought of herself as perseverant, with the undisciplined patient that I was, with whom it was so difficult to stay on track. And as for me, I thought I'd submitted without reservation, that I'd accepted all the constraints demanded by the cure: the payment for missed sessions, the departure on holiday for the same month as the analyst, the a priori acceptance of her words. It's one of the characteristics of psychoanalysis, a sort of blank cheque accorded the practitioner, an offering to the passing of time. In exchange, psychoanalysis offers you hope. You understand nothing about your symptoms, about the problems that paralyse you, but one day you will . . . Nevertheless, once, during the course of a session, she tried to persuade me that the woman who'd appeared in my dream, one of my co-disciples, a pretty blonde with long hair that descended to the curve of her buttocks, represented her. I didn't see the reason for this substitution, since that pretty blonde was quite real, as was the attraction I felt for her. Irritated by her insistence, I threw back at her: 'How do you expect me to feel the least attraction to you, when I don't even know what you're like?'

I have to say that I barely saw her, except for a few moments I entered or left her office when I greeted her, a little longer at the end of the week when it was time to pay her. Even today, I have the greatest difficulty picturing her to myself.

'That's exactly it,' she replied, 'exactly because you don't know what I'm like, that you represent me like this in your dreams.'

I considered it to be gratuitous sophistication, like all the wordplay she indulged in. Another time I dreamt about a car, as I often do. It seemed natural to me, I love cars! I was driving an Autobianchi, a little red A12, and speeding down a winding road. She repeated, 'Autobianchi.' I realized that she meant me. 'Yes, an Autobianchi, it's a kind of car, a small Italian car, powerful and agile.'

'Autobianchi,' Nata Minor said again. She must have repeated it three times before I understood her pun: Ô *Tobie en qui?*—'Oh Tobie in whom?' This time I didn't protest; I realized that her witticism expressed her view of me, the impression I must have given of chasing every skirt. But so what? I would spend many years, first on the couch, then in the armchair as a psychoanalyst, before I understood that psychoanalysis practised in this manner, orthodox and rigorous, does not convey any content. It reveals nothing but the inner thoughts of the person on the couch, it does not lead to any truth. It's an inner experience, a sort of asceticism, a 'phenomenological reduction', as if one wagered to think, 'If the world were nothing but an illusion, if all my perceptions arose from my own impulses ...'

And yet, I clung to my project: to become a psychoanalyst ... With hindsight, I might tell myself today that all this was in vain.

No doubt! But psychoanalysis had entered my head, had settled in all the recesses of my life and thought.

The Heights of Saint-Pierre, 1990

In 1990, on the island of Réunion, I attended the healings of Louisa, a good little woman with an iron grip. Early in the morning, we'd threaded our way through cane fields until we reached the little village announced by the flowering bougainvillaea. It was a Sunday. The narrow street was jammed with cars; and in front of the house, an unusual turmoil reigned. It was the day for consultations. Some fifteen patients were awaiting their turn, accompanied by spouses, parents, children. In large cardboard boxes, chickens—mostly white, with a few red—were cackling. In a shack in her garden, Mamie Louisa was beginning her interviews. Those who were ill outlined their problem in just a few words She rarely had the patience to listen for long. To understand the source of their illness, she relied on a miscellaneous array of tools. She examined the palms of their hands with a kitchen knife, drew Tarot cards, and with the look of an inquisitor, studied the depths of their irises. Then she ordered them to wait in the courtyard with the others, and, allowing them to leave, rubbed them with foul-smelling lamb fat, most likely to protect them. Bad smells have always repelled evil spirits. The odour was dreadful and enveloped the person for weeks.

On this particular day, I'd remained in the courtyard, chatting with the sick people who were patiently waiting. There was a robust matron who'd come to ask for the return of her husband; there was a Tamil woman with an amputated leg, suffering unbearable pain in her phantom limb; and an epileptic young man, brought by his parents, an elderly couple. Taking me aside, the old woman explained that ever since their daughter had killed herself by jumping off a cliff, her husband would not eat a thing. I glanced at the man who was indeed very thin. His head was bowed. A tear slowly trickled down his cheek. I ventured a timid, 'Are things hard for you, sir?' 'Useless,' his wife warned. 'He doesn't unclench his teeth. It's been two years since he opened his mouth, not even to say good morning or good night.'

She could no longer sleep. All night long, she watched over him as he wandered through the house, anxiously wringing his hands.

11 a.m. Louisa clapped her hands to assemble the crowd, which settled in front of her on wooden benches. I found a place among them. She began with a rapid 'Marseillaise', then went on to sing religious songs everyone seemed to know. She had a lovely high voice, reminiscent of Edith Piaf, and she sang on key, leading her congregation in a pagan mass whose forms she'd invented. And we sang, pressed against one another, guided by the voice of this magical mistress. Like the others, no doubt, I felt a strange sense of communion. While we sang, Louisa's assistant, a former patient who'd been healed, was busy using a hose attached to the garden faucet to fill an enormous metal barrel. After a brief half hour, Louisa was warmed up, and we were ready. We could move on to the healing sessions.

'Whose turn is it?' Louisa asked loudly. No one wanted to be first. The old woman thrust her husband forward. 'Him?' she asked timidly. Louisa conducted the old man, lost in his suffering, into the centre of the courtyard, in the middle of the group. Aided by her assistant, she undressed him and asked him to sit on the earth, wearing only his undergarments. First she addressed us, her public. 'Have you seen him? And you see how he's suffering? This is what evil spirits can do.'

She spun him around while uttering imprecations in Creole, in which one could recognize fragments of Catholic prayers. Then, as I had seen Visnelda do, she addressed the spirit beyond the patient, or, rather, the spirits. The formula was the same, leading you to think they'd both learnt it from the same source

'Who are you? Comorian spirits? Malabar spirits? Malagasy spirits? Troubled ghosts of the dead?'

Anguished, and frightened by Louisa's gestures, the man rolled his eyes, sweating profusely. Louisa approached him, carrying an old enamel pot filled with cool water drawn from the barrel. Again she questioned the spirit: 'Comorian? Hmm? I was sure of it! Sitarane?' she asked again.

At the beginning of the twentieth century, Sitarane, not a slave but an indentured labourer from Mozambique, had embarked on a series of sorcery murders that had terrorized the population. It was said that, after killing and robbing his victims, he drank their blood. When he was finally captured, he was condemned to death and executed. Until his last moments, he remained unrepentant, insulting his judges and spitting on his executioner. Ever since then, Sitarane continues his evil deeds, but in the invisible world, the embodiment of absolute resistance, that of the dead, who fears neither judges nor the police. His grave, in the Saint-Pierre cemetery, is a pilgrimage site even today. People come, pray, leave offerings, asking for the gift of invisibility or the courage overcome trials. I placed a glass of rum there, come what may.

'Oh, Sitarane, I know you!' Louisa groaned.

Suddenly, she rushed to throw the contents of the pot in the old man's face. He snorted, slowly brought his hands up and stared at her angrily. Mamie again launched into her defiance of Sitarane. She condemned him, turning him into an object of derision, warning that her power was infinitely greater than his. The old man was slowly calming down. Then she went towards the box where the chickens were stirring. She grabbed one by its wings, shook it in the man's face. 'This is what you want, isn't it? That's it! I know you, Sitarane!' Then, turning towards us, she explained: 'Blood. It's always what he demands.'

With the help of an assistant, another healed patient, she held the chicken spread out above the man's head. She brandished her knife, a huge butcher's knife, and then pierced the chicken through its heart. It's absurd, but hearing the sound of the bones cracking filled us all with the same dread. The bird's wings beat desperately over the stricken man's head. Louisa covered the unfortunate man's cranium with the eviscerated animal. Proudly shaking her knife, defying Sitatane's spirit, she circled the man, now covered in blood, 'I know you. You cannot resist the call of blood. I know you.'

Then she brought out a dish of meat cooked as a ragout with rice and beans that she'd prepared especially for her cures.

She undertook to coat the man with the food, first his legs and feet. Then she lifted the waistband of his underwear and placed the curry on his genitals.

'You're hungry, aren't you? Eat, then, eat!'

The procedure lasted maybe half an hour, from the initial shower with cool water to the sacrifice of the chicken, to the smearing with curry, and concluded with a final sprinkling of water.

'Go now. Go take a shower at the back of the garden,' she commanded, pointing to the hose.

Later, I asked Louisa to explain. I was not harbouring any exaggerated illusions. I'd noticed quite often that healers were concerned primarily with action, certainly not with theories. She'd not seen the same man as I. For me, it was clearly a case of a depressive reaction following his daughter's death. For her, it was a completely different story. The girl, Louisa explained, had been invaded by a cannibalistic spirit, surely Sitarane's, which had devoured her from within. Of course no one could see it. Once she'd been emptied of her substance, the girl had nothing left to do but kill herself. The true death was not at the moment of her suicide, but much earlier, when she'd been eaten. When the spirit was done with her, he'd cast himself, eternally starving, onto the afflicted father. Again a request for explanation. And what had Louisa done to be rid of Sitarane's spirit?

She'd appeased it with the blood of the sacrificed chicken. Having enticed and captured it in the ragout, she'd driven it, in the trunk of a car, in pursuit of the rest of the dish, all the way to the foot of the cliff, where it had gone to join the soul of the drowned girl in the sea. What was most striking is that by the end of this strange therapy session, the sick old man had begun to speak, to smile, to live.

Louisa had a great deal in common with my psychoanalyst—a love for her profession, a poetic view of life, a weakness for beautiful texts— but she absolutely distinguished herself through her genuine rage to heal.

8

George Sand

I possess two or three photographs of Rabbi Yom-Tov Israël Sherezli. The most impressive shows him flanked by his three sons: First, Michael, the eldest, the grandfather of psychoanalyst Jacques Hassoun—a man of conviction and culture, who died too young in 1999; the second, Mayer, father of my maternal grandfather; and the third, Moussa, about whom I know nothing. In the photo, the rabbi's beard is long and white. His kindly eyes are open wide, but the overall impression he gives, outfitted in a long ceremonial caftan with an image of Mount Sinai as a backdrop, is that of a patriarch posing for posterity. He holds his hands out like fetishes from Bénin, his fists closed, his right palm facing the earth, his left facing the heavens. I've heard that, in Africa, that's how men in touch with the things of this world and the world beyond present themselves, one hand for the visible and the other for the invisible—one hand for the Torah, the one holding the book, and another for the unseen, the one with the closed fist. The elderly aunts who'd interpreted my mother's dream were older than my parents, and had retained a vivid impression of the rabbi. In their day, a memory of him still lingered in the minds of the living, and he remained haloed in mystery and fear. They respected him so much that   they were incapable of pronouncing my first name. They called me *geddi*, 'my grandfather', in Arabic. That was how I grew up, a child-grandfather so to speak, at least in the eyes of my amused great-aunts. Did they really believe in reincarnation? Surely no more than that; but it was better not to take any chances, especially with such a personage. A good while later—some fifty years—I engaged in a theoretical debate with Professor Serge Lebovici, in relation to his 'precocious interactions' with newborns. That day, he'd just met a couple from Cameroon. The woman called her young son 'papa', and Lebovici wanted to interpret that as a sign of her incestuous attachment to her own father. The poverty of psychology! It was useless for me to insist that if the son bore the name of her father, his mother had no choice but to call him 'papa'. Surely she knew he was not the reincarnation of her father, that was not the problem! Calling her son 'papa' was both a mark of the respect she owed her father, and a way to imprint him in her son's destiny. I was in a good position to know, I who'd been called 'grandfather' throughout my childhood.

You don't name a child capriciously, randomly; you come to know their identity as you create it. If they'd given me the name of my grandfather, it's because they'd recognized that he wished to return to the family. By engraving him deeply into my soul, they were offering him to me as my destiny. It was no use. Lebovici would not hear of it. If things were as I claimed, how then could he continue pursue his particular fantasy? Typical of a debate that today might seem outdated, but which at the time often earned me the ostracism of the self-righteous.

In 1891, Mayer, Yom-Tov's second son, had a twelfth child. The old rabbi, seventy-one at the time , was the *sandak*, that is, he held the newborn at the time of his circumcision. A few weeks later, he departed to join his ancestors. The child, his last grandchild, who should have been named Isaac, like my grandfather's grandfather, was instead named Zaki, thanks to an ambiguity between the two languages. For a Jew, 'Zaki' could pass as a diminutive of 'Isaac'; but they were living in Egypt, where Zaki is also an Arab name that means 'lively', 'intelligent', the equivalent of 'clever' in English. Zaki was my maternal grandfather, my mother's father. He had a skull like a billiard ball; he smelt good, of precious perfumes and rubbing alcohol. He worked as a pharmacist in Cairo for thirty years, until 1956, then spent his remaining days in Geneva. Transmission of identity, at the same time fragile and self-evident: the rabbi had carried the infant Zaki on the day of his circumcision, a child who should have been called Isaac, the name of the rabbi's grandfather. I myself should have borne the name of this grandfather in turn; I should have been called Isaac or Zaki. However, my mother for-tuitously had a dream. And in this way, from grandfather to grand-father, the rabbi Yom-Tov returned to dwell in our family. As my father liked to say, history does not really exist; the same events repeat themselves endlessly; and so it will be until the end of time.

Rena, Zaki's eldest, my mother, was a genius. It has already been more than twelve years since she departed this world. She had an aptitude for everything, with an absolute intelligence, the way one speaks of a musician's 'absolute' or 'perfect' ear. Only matters of the mind motivated her. She was interested in children only for what she could teach them. She regarded them the way she regarded the cats she adored and which she educated, or like the parrots she raised on her balcony. She was drawn neither to their beauty nor to their ability, but she was in raptures over their intellectual feats. As an intellectual herself, she related to others largely by way of their intellect. There was a kind of passion for the differences in others in the way she considered creatures, even those closest to her. Children or adults, animals or objects, were all entities to know, particles of thought in motion over which to exert her own thinking. Even the most familiar things that interested her had to continually stimulate her mind. If they stopped doing so, they would immediately disappear from her universe. When she hadn't seen me for over a week, she would say to me, 'You did well to come today, I'd forgotten your face.' The relationship she established with her children—with all children—was the opposite of that tendency towards complete identification that psychoanalysts attribute to mothers. For her, the child was another whose contours must first be explored, and then, if they were capable of it, made into an apprentice, a companion in her mental adventures. That's how she raised me. At the age of four, I could recite all of Victor Hugo's 'The Retreat from Russia', down to the last verse. I knew the names of all the animals and discussed with her the existence of God. She claimed she loved me; I knew that I interested her, the way she was interested in the origin of the species, or the structure of gypsum, or the history of the pharaohs. Meanwhile, I reciprocated in kind. I cannot say that I loved my mother, but it's certainly true that she interested me. More than anything, I loved spending long hours beside her, talking about the world, about beings and things and theories—theories above all. During all those years, I was never bored in her presence—not once. Of course, she spoke words of love to me, but from her lips they were hardly believable; I had the feeling that she only wanted to act like the others, to pretend to be a mother. It made me smile. Expelled from Egypt, refugees in Italy, not knowing whether we would go to Israel or remain in Europe—or even if we would return to Cairo—at a standstill—the family frozen in confused perplexity, living in that dump on Via Sorrate in Rome, her pleasure was still that of having me practise my maths problems. I was attending the neighbourhood school, in Italian, but every afternoon I had to study French with her—because one never knows! I must admit that I enjoyed our mutual defiance of school. I've retained the conviction that school can't teach you anything—it can only present the material. Learning is easy with a teacher who loves to teach! With her, I learnt, for that was where her pleasure lay, her sole pleasure. She saw to all the housewifely tasks—cleaning, cooking, etc.—but she did so reluctantly. In the early afternoon, when she could finally settle into her armchair with a maths book or a classic novel, she looked like a cat curled up in front of a fire. She could have become an Einstein, a Karl Marx or a Marie Curie, but she was no more than a lost emigrant. After crossing the threshold of that small apartment in a Garges-les-Gonesses housing project in 1964, she emerged only on Saturdays to run her errands. She died there, thirty-five years later, having travelled the world through books and the tales of her two sons. How many brilliant women are hidden away behind the grey windows of the banlieues' public-housing projects?

My mother, she was George Sand. Born in 1917, gracing her family like a shard of pure intelligence, all she wanted was to learn and to teach. She was a lifelong student, and a lifelong teacher. She learnt everything, everything she'd ever come across: French literature, which was her passion; and calligraphy, which gave her the sort of perfect handwriting that is now a thing of the past; mathematics, which she taught until her last breath; geography, which she knew in the old way; plus all the traditional occupations: sewing, cooking, the art of making preserves and the art of household management. In addition to her deep learning, my mother had an aristocratic side, whose source was for a long time a mystery to me. 'In our home, we don't do this,' she would say. But why? Because we were not like the others. The 'others' were *baladi*, 'the common people'—the 'others' were the rest of her family, her innumerable cousins, the Cohens for example, with whom she shared cousinship with my father, and above all, it goes without saying, the Nathans, my father's family, those primitive Yemenites, the least emancipated and the most backward. She was not condescending towards them; rather, she conducted herself like a militant paternalist, seeking to educate them. We had an implicit reference point, the *hara*, the Jewish quarter. Those who still lived there or who had only recently moved away were the very quintessence of *baladi*, except that she herself was from the *hara*. She'd been born there and had spent her childhood there—as had my father. They'd both grown up in that same house, although they probably never played together. He was older by five years, and she had left the big Cohen house at the age of five or six. For her, the *hara* was the primordial clay from which her humanity was moulded, though her mind was dedicated to extricating herself from it. She thought she'd made the choice of modernity. She believed herself to be an avatar of the Enlightenment. I would learn much later that she was in fact the custodian of our family's legacy. Once a year, we would go to see the old Esther, my paternal grandmother's sister, whom we called *nonna-autre*, 'the other grandmother'. Esther still lived in the *hara*, and it was all my mother could do not to hold her nose during the course of the visit. As for me, I liked the odour of that tiny dilapidated room, smelling of mildew and old age. At Esther's, we spoke only Arabic, exchanging the latest news about the family and lamenting that we'd lost sight of one another. We would piece our memories together, and we would leave feeling somewhat uneasy. The *hara* had once been us, but it was so no longer! This was where we were from, certainly, but it would take me decades to understand that it was also our source, the place where we would find the strength to renew ourselves. After Esther's, with relief, we would make our way to Groppi's, downtown Cairo's elegant Swiss patisserie, where we would order overpriced vanilla and pistachio ice creams. Surely my mother had acquired her aristocratic pretensions from the family, passed down from generation to generation. She'd decided to incarnate their antique splendour, from the days when our family was at the head of the community, was prosperous and respected.

My mother, she was Sarah Bernhardt! She too, like the man who'd been unhappily married and then unhappily divorced, had tangled with the Nile. During the 1920s, the rabbi Entebi, whom we called the *'akham* in our Arab-Hebrew sabir, presided over Cairo's Rav Moshe synagogue, the one that had housed the remains of Moses Maimonides before they were transferred to Tiberias. At that time, my mother was still living in *beit el Cohen*. Most of the *hara*'s children knew the '*akham*, to whom they turned for moral guidance and everyday psychological help. Aside from his strictly religious functions, the rabbi was a specialist in healing. On the portico, abutting the synagogue, was a tiny wooden cabin where he would often sit cross-legged on a wooden bench, his eyes half shut. With his long white beard, he could have been mistaken for an Indian fakir. He wore a turban and a *galabaya*, the traditional Egyptian robe, beneath his black caftan. Before the entrance to the cabin, dozens of children would await their turn, growing impatient on the benches, sitting beside their mothers, aunts, friends of the family, servants. On this particular day, my mother was even more afraid than she'd been when she'd come to see him before. Over the past few nights, she'd been having nightmares that would jolt her awake. She'd call for her mother and her aunts to help her. One morning, her mother said to her younger sister, Aunt Engela, 'Take five piasters and accompany the child to Entebi. *Ou y er ilha*, go, so he can calm her.' My maternal grandmother did not believe in the therapeutic abilities of rabbis. Wasn't she married to a pharmacist who'd completed long years of study in the region's most prestigious university?

But her daughter's suffering was beyond her, and there seemed to be no other way. Five piasters was not nothing! With that sum, you could purchase a whole family's daily bread. As for my mother's young aunt, she made out pretty well—she would leave one or two piasters for the rabbi and keep the rest for herself. The two women were anxious about the consultation. The evening before, my grandmother had wrapped some salt and a shard of alum in her *mandil*, the scarf Jewish women used to cover their heads. She'd knotted it *zay el sorra*, 'like a wallet', then circled my mother's head with it seven times in one direction, seven times in the other, then slipped it under my mother's pillow before she fell asleep. Thus my mother spent the night letting her soul freely communicate with the mineral amalgam. No doubt the material of her dream, cleansed of its slag by the salt, had steeped into the alum. In the morning, my grandmother enclosed the little packet, alum, salt and dream in a sheet of newspaper, and gave it to my mother. 'You know what to do, don't you? You give it to the rabbi and you do whatever he says!'

Which brings us back to the little lady, five or six years old, perched on the wooden bench, swinging her feet while awaiting her turn. Engela, her aunt, was trying to distract her by telling stories.

The old rabbi examined the wallet filled with alum and salt, still warm from the child's sleep. Then he asked Aunt Engela, 'What is her name?'

'Rena Israël.'

'And her mother? Tell me her mother's name also.'

'Bertha el Cohen.'

'What happened? Why have you brought me this child, and from what is she suffering?'

'She screams a great deal,' the aunt lamented, 'and at night, she wakes with a start.' (Literally, 'she arises', in Arabic.)

'Well,' said the *'akham* Entebi calmly, 'we'll see.'

His words were to be taken literally. As he prayed, he would 'see' the evil that was causing my mother to suffer. He took hold of his old book with the threadbare binding, then placed it for a moment on my mother's head, then on her chest, all the while murmuring blessings in a Hebrew she did not understand. Entebi kept his eyes closed throughout. And that day, he did not yawn! For when the 'akham yawned, you could be sure that the child was suffering from a *nefs*, a 'wind', that is, an evil spirit that had come to disturb her. Or it could mean that someone, most likely a family member, had envied her, and had 'cast the evil eye', *el eïn*. And so they had to deeply purify the victim, to wash her, or donate a rooster or a hen to the poor, as a *sadaka*, an offering. But that day, as he recited the blessings, or perhaps during the prayers he'd read over the child's head, a vision came to him. In Arabic, he told my great-aunt, '*Lazem te rou'hou te namou fel maam,*' 'Both of you must go to sleep in the crypt.' And if she dreams there, you will come to tell me the dreams.

It was 10.30 in the morning. My mother and her aunt descended into the crypt. The tomb was still there, although the remains of the old philosopher had 'gone up to Palestine' ages ago. The place was renowned. People came from afar, on pilgrimage, to be healed. And by no means was it only Jews who revered the place. Muslims and Copts also eagerly sought the healing powers of the philosopher-doctor. Sometimes all four rooms were occupied, and you had to wait for hours until the pilgrims had finished sleeping and dreaming, communicating with the saint. Everyone knew that Saint Maimonides was so powerful that the stones that had been in contact with his remains would remain charged for centuries, for millennia, like a magically radioactive substance. To benefit from this *baraka*, the seekers would fall asleep, their heads touching the stone worn by centuries of devotion. My mother, for whom sleep was often so difficult, dozed off shortly after entering the sacred cave. It often happened that Maimonides himself appeared in the sleeper's dreams. It was certain that this doctor to kings would offer them some way to cure their illness. Perhaps the communications were coded formulas the *'akham* Entebi would have to interpret? And yet, despite her aunt's pressing requests, my mother could not remember her dream. Perhaps Rav Moshe had been content merely to brush her cheek or whisper in her ear, as the rabbi Entebi sometimes did. There is no longer a single Jew in Cairo, but I know that Rav Moshe synagogue is still as it ever was, that in this respect at least, nothing has changed. The true therapies are techniques, methods that ignore culture and race. There is a kind of immanent justice in these popular practices. If Maimonides, who was Salah al Din's personal doctor, had spent his life caring for the rich and powerful, it is only right that he dedicate his death to the care of common folk.

My mother was a nervous child. She went quite often to visit the *'akham* because her mother was pragmatic. She would say, 'It's not about believing in devils or magic. If the rabbi calms her, it's good. That's all there is to it!' Although married to a pharmacist, she was open to traditional ways of healing. Her most spectacular treatment had set the family abuzz. She'd been suffering for over a year from a nasty case of sciatica. My mother was probably twelve at the time. Her mother, nearly paralysed, spent her days bedridden. Her husband had given her all sorts of injections—certainly all the painkillers he knew. But one day, tired of seeing her suffer so, her young sister, the same Aunt Engela, announced: 'I'm going to take your scent and bring it to Aïsha, the healer!' Once night had fallen, she wrapped grandmother's hair in a *mandil*, and recommended that she keep it on all night. The next morning, at first light, trembling a little and of course feeling guilty, she brought the fabric to the seer. What of it? Someone had to do something. As soon as Engela crossed the threshold of the healer's door, Aïsha immediately had a vision and called out: 'She is paralysed in her bed, the poor woman. What can you do?'

Astonished by Aïsha's divination, Engela took a few moments before answering, 'You're the one who must tell me what to do!'

'Will you do exactly as I ask?'

'I will! For the good of my sister, the poor thing, yes, I will!'

'Bring me a black hen,' the matron requested. 'I will prepare it, and then I'll give you something to to throw into the Nile.' With the chicken meat and some other ingredients—herbs, plants and powders, the healer concocted three small meatballs. When my great aunt returned two days later, Aïsha handed her the meatballs, wrapped in an old newspaper: 'You will go to the centre of the Kasr el Nil Bridge. Once there, you will turn your back to the river and you will throw these behind you. Like this,' she demonstrated, swinging her hand over her shoulder.

'And then?' asked my great-aunt.

'You will leave quickly . . . without looking back, without turning around, O unfortunate one.'

But my great-aunt Engela, who more than anyone else possessed women's intuitive subtlety, told my mother, barely adolescent,

'Since you're the closest to the invalid, you're the one who'll toss the little balls into the Nile.'

The next morning, the two of them went to the bridge. I can only imagine their apprehension, looking to the right, looking to the left. Surely they would be taken for sorceresses! My mother took out the blackish little balls, one by one, as Aïsha had recommended. Obediently, she turned her back to the river, and, trembling, her gaze fixed on her aunt, she threw them backwards over her shoulder, murmuring, 'May God forgive me!'

Her mother recovered immediately. The family avidly debated various hypotheses. Aunt Engela was certain that it was indeed Aïsha who'd cured her older sister, and moreover merely for the price of a simple hen. But my grandmother had also begun a course of electrical stimulation. And perhaps all those injections by the pharmacist had finally taken effect. And then, Uncle Youssef had a Russian friend, Makine, recently returned from America, who'd tried out his newly acquired, ultra-modern physiotherapy techniques on her. Was it really Aïsha's chicken that had accomplished the miracle, or was it the injections, the electrical stimulation or American-style physiotherapy? Back then, Egypt was a land of multitudes; today it has become a land of calculations.

My mother, she was Shirley Temple in the films of the 1930s. Her father must have been in his fourth year of medical school when he was conscripted into the Italian army. Until then, no one had taken seriously the nationality that our family had purchased two generations earlier. They were Italian, yes, but only to escape contraventions. And now Italy wanted them to go to war! The Jews of Egypt were profoundly resistant to nationalisms, never so content as under Ottoman rule which had granted them a degree of autonomy in direct proportion to the taxes and tariffs they were subject to. They knew that a nation-state was too ephemeral to constitute a person's identity. Some select individuals managed to colour a nation's identity now and then, but never the reverse. Nationality was nothing more than the papers, a way of playing cat and mouse with the administration. The truth lay elsewhere, in the depths of history, in presence of the Pyramids, in the imperturbable placidity of the Sphinx. But after the war of 1914–18, the nations came to claim them. The Jews of the Nile, Egyptians from the time of the pharaohs, ancestors, in part, of the Copts, did not take seriously this Muslim Egypt that modernity was giving birth to. On the contrary, many were out fighting for a modern Egypt, democratic and secular: for example, the celebrated James Sanua, a Jew and a sheikh who founded the first liberal newspaper, *Abou Nadara*, 'the man with the spectacles', a name by which he would ever after be known. Exiled by the British for 'subversive activities', he took refuge in France, where he ended his days. Later, many Jewish intellectuals were engaged in the struggle for a socialist, communist Egypt. But what is left of them? Those who were politically engaged as well as those who were content to take life as it came were equally chased out. One cannot resist the impetus of the times. In France, my parents never applied for French citizenship. They both died as Italians. What difference did it make in this end-of-the-century, united Europe? My grandfather must have been twenty-four or twenty-five when he left for Italy to fight with the Allies. He was a medical student and a senior officer during the war, where he began his practice of medicine. He learnt emergency medicine in the field, the common, minor surgeries that would stand him in good stead throughout his career. He was already married, and it was during a leave that he made his contribution to my mother's existence. He was away when she was born on 18 April 1917. When he returned to Cairo after the war, he chose to discontinue his medical studies because the time commitment was too much for a man already responsible for a family. He transferred to an accelerated programme and obtained his doctorate in pharmacy in Beirut in 1921. My mother, four years old at the time, climbed onto the stage with him, and it is to her that the dean handed the diploma. She considered herself deserving of this doctorate, since she'd studied the material alongside her father. She was a child genius, a doctor at the age of four, and the science of the body continued to serve her as she dealt with the entire family's hypochondria. Her father was a pharmacist; she was a doctor.

I don't know what impelled my grandfather to pull my mother out of school, She was made for that, so curious, so passionate, a virtuoso to a romantic degree.

'*Le saule*' ('The Willow'), Musset's poem that she taught me before I learnt to read, best approximates her desire:

> *Il se fit tout à coup le plus profond silence*
> *Quand Georgina Smolen se leva pour chanter*
> There was all of a sudden the deepest silence
> When Georgina Smolen stood up to sing . . .

These lines are inscribed in my memory. She wanted to be Georgina Smolen; she was searching for her Musset. Her song was not musical, but the one of theoretical maths. My mother, she was

George Sand. But her father wanted to confine her to conventional femininity, to turn her, despite herself, into a marriageable young woman. Too serious to understand that he'd guessed she might have a demanding sexuality, she resented him—a feeling exacerbated by the accidental death of her mother, killed by a potato. My grandmother had gashed her finger while carelessly peeling a potato; she'd shown it to her husband Zaki, the pharmacist, who'd reassured her and promptly disinfected and bandaged the wound A week later, she was dead from tetanus. Although my mother never admitted it, I know that deep down she held her father responsible, and this she would never tell him. 'How could it be that you, a doctor, a pharmacist never thought of tetanus? How can anyone be so little attentive to their beloved spouse, to their other half? My mother was twenty-three, her father fifty. Six months later, he'd decided to remarry. What did they expect?—he was a man; and furthermore he ate meat. Distressed by her father's attitude, my mother let her studies go and sought a husband. How did they end up together, Ranou the intellectual and Sousou Hantoussou? Close through family ties, but almost opposite by any other standard, they'd known each other since childhood. They must have felt an unspoken complicity, each having lost one parent, he his father, she her mother—a loss that shaped their destiny. But their demeanours, their tastes, their interests differed widely. He was handsome, a womanizer, a gambler, a man of the night and of empty words. She was sullen, serious, loving her books more than anything else, finding pleasure only in her one passion: learning and teaching. He was thirty years old, and hadn't managed to decide among all his conquests. And besides, to whom could he confess the infirmity of having remained whole, uncircumcised, if not to his cousin, his sister Adèle's close friend? My mother, for her part, wanted to spite her father, to prove that she was able to succeed at everything, including marriage. They came to terms. You couldn't call it an arranged marriage, but it was a good arrangement for them! My father had had many adventures during his nighttime escapades. He'd even had an intense relationship with the celebrated Leïla Mourad, also his cousin. When my father knew her, at the beginning of the 1940s, Mourad had already recorded dozens of songs and starred in several musical comedies that drew crowds of Egyptians. The beautiful singer was even more difficult to pin down than my father. She sang of the power of desire and love: 'Love Is Beautiful', 'My Heart Turns Me Upside Down', 'Why Did You Let Me Love You?'

Egypt during those years was Hollywood on the Nile. Concerts drew audiences of thousands. The songs of Umm Kulthum, Samia Gamal and Farid el Atrache gave rise to veritable cults, immense trance rituals. They all sang of desire. Women fainted, photos of stars filled the magazines. The cinemas screened Western and Egyptian films in rotation. Western style became the fashion. Bouffant skirts à la Marilyn Monroe, dark sunglasses and sophisticated hairdos, a passion for American convertibles that seemed odd to me: 'When a girl says she hates you, it's because she's in love with you.' Strange words, surely based on her experience as a woman, but which also expressed the preoccupations of the time, an obsession with love. She and my father played at being a loving couple, interlaced in public, striking the poses of actors in front of the camera. But it was cinema. Quite a while later, in France, my father confided in me, 'With your mother, you see, it was never like that. If she hadn't been Jewish, she would have become a nun.' In truth, her interest in love was of the same nature as her interest in maths. She wanted to know, but she cared very little to feel. She therefore displayed a genuine enthusiasm for my adolescent loves, which offered her a window of sorts onto this new world that surrounded her. At eighteen, I was bringing my one-night stands home, and they would spend the night with me in my childhood room. In the morning, she would enter without knocking and pretend to be surprised: 'Last night there was only one head, and this morning I see two.' She would lift up the end of the bedspread. 'Four feet, too. I see four feet.' During breakfast, she would question the girl: 'And what does your mother do? Does she work or does she only take care of the house? Perhaps she was worried not to have seen you come home?' The world outside, the world of which she knew practically nothing, was making its sudden entrance into our home. She was quivering with excitement. Once the young beauty had left, she would barrage me with her reactions: 'So, in France, mothers allow their daughters to spend the night away from home? They're not worried . . . imagine that! I myself never spent the night elsewhere myself. I slept only at home. I was grateful for that.' I shared with her my first readings of Freud, talked to her about infantile sexuality and repressed desires. She offered her critique, read the books herself, annotated them and resumed our discussion at the first opportunity. 'Sexuality seems to be very important to people,' she observed. 'But this Freud you so revere .. . he's certainly very intelligent but his mind is *ma'woug*, inside out. The things of which he speaks exist, but he assigns too much importance to them. For example, yes, I was in love with my father. He was intelligent and no one could tell stories the way he did. I could well have married him. I thought about it often. But I didn't give it any more importance than that.' I bemoaned her lack of respect for my new idols. I expounded, argued, produced examples, recited psychoanalytic theory. She listened willingly, joined the game and countered me when it was her turn.

9

Anthony Perkins

We were a tad British in Egypt. We called my mother *Mummy*, and used several expressions inherited from the British soldiers which always cracked us up. When, for example, *Mummy* wanted the maid to open the curtains, she would say to her, while carefully rolling her *r*'s, 'Ouahiba, some *morre* light, please.' My brother, he was Anthony Perkins—he *is* Anthony Perkins! the same lean, taut beauty. His name was Edwin, the first name of an English lord, although his namesake is actually David Nathan, my father's father. How did David become Edwin? In Arabic, David is pronounced 'Daoud'. 'Daou' led towards the 'dw' of Edwin, my mother's coinage, to sound modern. The whole family was happy to accept this innovation. From then on, David would be Edwin. But my brother considered it to be his first name, belonging to him alone, 'Lord Edwin'. And he really was a British lord, his posture erect, his chin thrust forward, his hair parted on the left. He took up fencing, adopted a curt manner with everyone. Our family preserved the vague memory of a presence on the island of Rhodes, among the English. Much later I would learn that indeed Rabbi Yom-Tov's grandfather, Moshe Israël, and his son Isaac, had both been Grand Rabbis of Rhodes during the eighteenth century. More problematically, however, one of their descendants committed some embezzlement and took refuge on Rhodes, where he eventually died. Our Britishness was thus not entirely commendable.

As the first child of the unusual couple my young parents were, my brother was welcomed like a prince. But he was born prematurely, after only seven months in the womb. It was in January 1944, still wartime. Of course the German threat had been averted in 1942 by Montgomery's victory at the Battle of el-Alamein. Still, the world was not at ease. My brother is the child of el-Alamein. Conscious of having escaped mortal danger, my parents had resolved to marry and start a family. But raising a first child, premature and sickly, during a time of war and anxiety, drove my mother wild with worry. She was obsessed by the little one's weight. What did she need to do to make him grow, to plump him up? When would she know for certain that he'd chosen to live? And the little lord had his whims. He only accepted certain foods, vomited the rest and caught every passing illness, which made him immediately lose the several hundred grams he'd gained. Yellowed photographs of the infant Edwin show him swathed in layers of woollen clothing during Cairo's winter months, when the temperature rarely went below 18 degrees. In the photos, he already has the frowning, severe face that would continue to characterize him as an adult. But his greatest distress occurred when I arrived, five years later, in November 1948. By then he'd recovered from his prematurity, and was developing well; yet he took a turn for the worse after my birth. He lost weight again, and acquired a yellow hepatic complexion that never left him and earned him the nickname of 'the Japanese'. Joking as little boys do, I swore he'd been exchanged at the hospital, that the nurses had replaced my true brother with the son of a Japanese woman and now this one was ours. My brother remained thin like Anthony Perkins until he was close to forty years old. You could say it took a long time before his reaction to me was finally played out.

Although everyone claims that children are not interested in adults, only in children, I had strong feelings about my parents: I found my mother captivating and enjoyed discussions with her; although he was an enigma to me, I respected and admired my father. As for my brother, I loved him, quite simply, I loved him. I still love my brother. As children, all we did was play complex games of our own invention and engage in discussions about people and the state of the world. Each time we had to ascertain the facts. We had the same thoughts, the same passions—cars, for example. From the balcony of our fifth-floor apartment on Farouk Street (which in 1953 became el-Guesh Street, 'Army Street'), we'd spend hours identifying the makes of cars. Odd how some mistakes follow you, like something for which you must atone. One day, I was unable to identify a Volkswagen Kombi; he could! We both also kept a certain distance from events—a nihilistic, disillusioned philosophy. We might have remained Egyptian . . . perhaps we would now resemble the son Leila Mourad had with her Muslim husband, surely a perfectly integrated Egyptian. We could have become Israeli, like many of our cousins, whose parents had chosen to make their *aliyah*. Today, then, we would resemble Yossi, or Dror, or Jacky. We might have remained as Italians in Italy, or, more precisely, as Romans. We could have emigrated to Switzerland, like our maternal grandfather, Zaki the pharmacist, or to South America, or Canada, or Australia, like other cousins. We know that in each case we would not be who we are today. We would have spoken another language—Arabic or Hebrew, Italian, or Spanish or English. We would surely have chosen different professions as well. We would have been someone else. Of course, anyone can tell themselves the same thing, but for us it was not an idle fantasy, a theoretical speculation. We knew from experience that it was entirely possible. I believe that this plethora of possibilities that marks our history causes us still to have some uncertainty about our identity, as well as an acute awareness of its contingency. Knowing that our 'self' is purely the product of chance, how can we possibly be proud of who we are? What we're left with is a fundamental anxiety, a kind of fear of being and a certain mockery that renders the most unrealistic theories thinkable.

I am my brother's twin. It's possible—twins born five years apart! We have that 'geminal' mental closeness, each anticipating the other's next move before it's been initiated. It's an understatement to say that we know each other—we know everything about each other, without needing to say a single word. The way we regard each other is inherently shameless. What one says about the other is always a revelation. What one thinks of the other is his own thought. We are twins in the antique manner, with the vague feeling that if fate were to become aware of our existence, it would make one of us disappear. Nature abhors doubles. That is why, to deceive providence, we avoid each other.

We're not identical. Edwin succeeded brilliantly in business. From his position as the elder, he has preserved a predilection for being in charge. Doubtless more anxious than I, he blended in with his surroundings more adeptly; he does not stand out as I do. But, fundamentally, we are the same person.

Raised on biblical myths, we identified with the two sons of Isaac the patriarch—he with Esau, I with Jacob. At the time, we hadn't realized that they were twins, although in fact they are. Esau, the elder, just came out a little earlier. Re-enacting the tale, my brother one day sold me his birthright, not for a plate of lentils but for an artichoke. Ever since, I no longer eat artichokes and he still loves them. Did we take the ceding of the elder's right seriously, though? Within this traditional yet utterly dislocated family, it was not simply a childish game. The right of elderhood is a lynchpin in certain systems of relationship that have the distinctive characteristic of always being doomed to failure. In principle, its function is to resolve a problem stemming from patrilineal filiation. In these systems, the ancestor is a male. He transmits his name to his son, along with the capacity to regenerate the line. The problem arises as soon as there is more than one son, the rule reserving the privilege of transmission solely to the eldest. What, then, do the other sons do, the latter-born? They would have to remain for their entire lives in the position of children, which is obviously impossible. The problem is complicated when there is an inheritance, especially when it is landed property. The older son inherits everything, both the name of the father and the father's possessions, and nothing remains for the others except one solution: exile. In cultures where the eldest does not rule, the younger sons can establish themselves in turn and pass on their property. This is one of the reasons for the emigration of African men who are governed by such rules of filiation. Where the right of the eldest is the law of the land, it is either circumvented, or it generates exiles and ruptures.

In the case of our family, which no longer possesses any goods other than memories, the right of the eldest might seem to be a mockery. It is not. Each of us has been Aeneas fleeing Troy in flames, carrying his father Anchises on his back. Which of us two would manage to be the founder of Rome with the remnants of the core he'd managed to save and transport throughout his wanderings? Such were the stakes for which we were playing, my brother and I, at the dawn of our exile from Egypt.

I remember my brother wearing his magnificent white chest protector, at the centre of the fencing team of Cairo's lycée français. He was good-looking! I remember him in his scout's uniform with the beret slipped under the epaulette. Martial! I was too young to join, but I did not feel jealous—no. What I felt was that I was living out his adventures by proxy. He was my hero; he is my hero still. Although he was not very forthcoming, whatever he experienced, I experienced. He was thirteen when we emigrated. He'd had the time to learn a few things about life, to get to know people, to have opinions ... perhaps even to have had some tentative sexual experiences with the young maids. I was just a bit older than eight, barely hatched, so to speak. As a result, he developed the habit of acting, I of thinking. He always had a grandiose side, Lord Edwin, though it was tempered by our mother's constant anxiety. To her, he'd remained that fragile infant, hesitating to take hold of life. The anxiety one feels for loved ones has its foolish side, not because it is unfounded (it isn't always) but because it provokes a reciprocal anxiety—the response of the shepherd to the shepherdess. My brother has always been very anxious for my mother, for my parents. As a result, he lavished anguished attention on them, which would then worry them, and so on and so forth, an infernal circle of anxiety provoking anxiety that intensifies at every turn. The only way out is to break the circle, to choose egoism, which is what I did. I kept everything for myself.

The upending of the familial order is at once the great benefit and the great drawback of emigration. There's an Arabic proverb that states, 'Whoever knows my father, let them go and tell him, and whoever signed my marriage contract, let them go and annul it.' In other words, 'I'm a foreigner. I have nothing to do with your laws.' It perfectly describes the émigré's fascination with that vertiginous freedom that opens up before him—the freedom to think, to act, to defy, to trespass. The price one pays is that the world becomes disordered. The father becomes the child in the eyes of his son, for this father cannot master the new elementary rules which the child follows effortlessly. The child is a father to the father who asks the way, for the translation of a word, for how to fill in the social-security forms. The family fractures into so many feverishly individualistic members, engaged in the same adventure, sometimes misadventure. It's not unusual that eventually they will not be able to bear each other. I cannot bear the sight of this father who exposes who I am, who cannot speak without an accent, who acts as if we were still back 'home', in the wheat fields, in the village, in the *hara*. Emigration has a god, and he is Christian. The child abandons his father and mother in order to follow the prophets of the new god. I was fortunate in that I was never ashamed of my father. He was the guarantor of my originality, and whenever he chanced to speak, he inevitably uttered unexpected truths. In December, when the trees were covered with garlands of lights, when the town halls were lit up with glad tidings, he would mock the artificiality of it all. He would say, 'All this, you see? It's nothing but smoke in your eyes, nothing but smoke in your eyes.' What he was really saying was that we emigrants were not moved by these conventional displays. Though we were in a position to be exploited, we were fortunate not to be manipulated at will, we were not sheep. My brother, who was older, had a harder time accepting my father's way of seeing things. He desperately wanted to appear normal; I knew that we were not, that I was not.

Many years later, in the nineties, I published an article in a major weekly, *l'Express* I believe, in which I described our arrival at the housing project for migrants in Gennevilliers, sandwiched between a huge junkyard and an immense slum. My classmates lived in the slum. We would thread our way through the junkyard, pretending to be nabobs behind the steering wheel of a Cadillac without tires. In the article, I described how 80 per cent of the children in my new CM2 class were emigrants—Portuguese, Italians, Kabyles, and even a few Polish Jews who'd emigrated before the war. At the time the article appeared, Edwin was the CEO of a large pharmaceutical firm. He did not appreciate his colleagues' questions. When I think about my former classmates, I realize that some twenty of them, a good half, died well before reaching fifty. Some succumbed to an overdose, others to AIDS. It's odd that three of them died in the same way, during an attempted escape after their incarceration for armed robbery. Emigration puts you in direct contact with the underbelly of society. My brother, the worrier, felt he was too good for it. I must admit, to do him justice, that it was not his responsible position that made him want to forget the poor neighbourhoods where he'd spent a part of his youth. Even back then, he would walk around Gennevilliers like an aristocrat. Here's an interesting incident: he must have been barely seventeen and dating the prettiest girl in the project (who would become his wife and remain so). The two would stroll hand in hand, sometimes intertwined. I'm sure they took advantage of dark corners to fool around. There weren't very many private spaces for young lovers at the time. Displays of affection flourished out in the open, on pavements, in the recesses of entranceways, in movie theatres, on public benches. Their budding love incited the jealousy of a gang of toughs in black leather jackets, my classmates' older brothers, revving up their Vespas, the tips of their cowboy boots in the wind. The gang cornered the couple in an alley and were preparing to teach my brother a lesson, to beat him up. Instead, he started speaking to them, telling them that they were a social force, that the future belonged to them. He compared them to the members of the workers' uprising in Paris at the time of the Paris Commune. They listened to him, dumbfounded, asking questions, seeking to learn what became of the rebels. I doubt whether he specified that most of them had been killed. The gang ended up letting the young couple go, without harming either of them. My brother did everything he could to leave this world behind. I, on the other hand, embraced it wholeheartedly.

When we arrived in Paris from Rome—it must have been August 1958—disembarking after twenty hours on the train, we needed to find a place to stay. The hotels refused to take children. My brother and I crawled in on all fours to sneak past the reception desk at the Hotel Brébant de Beauséjour on boulevard Montmartre. For months, all four of us lived there clandestinely in a room no more than 10 square metres, my mother cooking on an alcohol burner, my father leaving every morning to type in a secretarial pool for 45,000 old francs per month. Fearing eviction, we would hide under the table or the bed whenever a hotel employee entered the room. My parents were haggard, my brother clenched his teeth, but I was happy with this reversal of the world's order. Children's reactions cannot be foreseen, which is why one should never believe psychologists' predictions. I was happy with a sort of mental freedom that I felt each day. Nothing was as it had been, and I liked the changes. The rules had radiantly flown off, routine had disappeared, urgency compelled us, necessity was loosening all the bonds. I don't know what might have happened had this situation persisted. Perhaps the family would have broken up. As it happened, I was the one who resolved matters—by falling ill with tuberculosis: physical exams, endless waits in the neighbourhood clinic, sessions with aerosols whose scent remains in my nostrils to this day. Tuberculosis? The word alone was enough to terrify my mother. She forced my father to find us an apartment. That's how we finally arrived in Gennevilliers.

In December 1958, cité Claude-Debussy, the housing project, was barely out of the ground. The street was still a construction site. We had to traverse hills of mud to access the building's entrance. The tiny, three-room apartment seemed like a palace to us. News of the project spread quickly to other recently exiled Egyptians. Many found their way to the cité Claude-Debussy. Most were from

Cairo; a few from Alexandria. Some had already known each other in Egypt, others were from entirely different social circles. There were the Pardos, several Cohen families, two Israël families, the Saadias, the Gallimidis, the Harraris, a good many Levys, the Avayous, the Kodsis, the Hadidas, the Khodaras, the Hassids, the Politis, the Sassouns, the Alboukers, the Menaschés. Listing their names is like reading the Bible. There were also a few Ashkenazy families from Alexandria, the Bercoviches or the Geigers. These Egyptian Jews, tossed here by the winds of history, reconstructed a ghetto, a sort of *hara*. One of them, the most religious, perhaps, or else the most nostalgic, named Ouahba, set up a synagogue in his apartment. The men assembled there on Friday evenings for the Sabbath service and on religious holidays. At first, the street had no name, it was solely 'la cité'. Eventually, the municipality put up a plaque that read 'avenue Claude-Debussy'. On the eve of Yom Kippur, this avenue, which ran between the cemetery (Christian), the junkyard (Roma) and the slum (Kabyle), would become 'the street of the Jews'. The boys strolled along in their new clothes, while the fathers rushed to be on time for the service, each clutching plastic bags with their prayer shawl and prayer books. There were also a few 'Frenchmen', Frenchmen from France, 'regular' folk, workers who'd found homes here during those difficult post-war years. They too were dislocated, already beginning to express their incomprehension of public politics: 'We're in France here! Go back home.' If only we could have.

Even if someone had asked for our opinion, we would never have left Egypt. I believe it was Bondy Albouker, the first to be naturalized (or was he born French?), who had the best comeback.

In his tenor voice that rose above the rest at the end of Yom Kippur, rolling his *r*'s with the sound of a machine gun, he spat out, 'Sirrr, I'm morrre Frrench than you! I *chose* to come here—all you did was go to the trouble of being born!' Blessed Bondy Albouker! He looked so much like Fernandel that one day, when he drove down the Champs-Elysées in his brand-new Peugeot 404 convertible, waving to the passers-by, he was applauded as in the synagogue.

The Romans had understood, as did the Greeks well before them, and the Babylonians too: let the Jews have a temple, and they will soon be assembled as a community. That's why, for close to a thousand years, these peoples never stopped destroying the temple in Jerusalem. Our synagogue in the *hara* Claude-Debussy allowed us to keep our heads above water for a good while, several years—enough time to learn about this new country where we'd landed. In its first year, a Talmud Torah was organized there, a school where on Thursdays and Sundays children were taught the rudiments of their religion. I bless this place, our first synagogue in France. It was there that I felt my first sexual stirrings. Her name was D. I won't say her real name—I don't think she'd like others to know about our adolescent romance. She had dark hair, frizzy like a lamb, and sapphire-blue eyes—Isabelle Adjani's eyes. There was not enough room for two separate classes, one for boys and another for girls. All of us sat together to learn our prayers, the rituals and Jewish history. One day I found a little note on my small schoolboy's desk. 'Do you love D. the way she loves you?' I must admit, I had not thought about it, but now that I was being asked, I was sure that I loved her. She was fourteen, I little more than eleven. It's well known that the God of the Jews brings couples together. We petitioned him with our childish prayers and He responded. I'm convinced that God always responds. He's proven it to me again and again. D. and I arranged to meet in a cellar. Children's secrets have always inhabited the depths.

The cité's rascals knew the cellars like the backs of their hands. We organized games and snack times there. In later years, they served as places of discussion. The cellars sheltered all our loves. D. was my initiator. She taught me the power of desire, which overturns the rules and braves the forbidden. Desire, the incomprehensible alchemy that lets me think for a moment that I am myself. We spoke very little. We would meet sporadically for years, to ascertain each time if our desire was still present. Afterwards, D. entered even more deeply into me: she haunted my dreams; she still appears in them from time to time. Above all, she left an indelible imprint on me. Humans are creatures very susceptible to imprinting. My affair with D. gave shape to my desires going forward. I like nothing better than the surprise of a woman revealing her desire.

For all these Egyptian families who'd been brutally uprooted from their home by political events, the *hara* Claude-Debussy constituted a refuge, an acceptable environment, where the familiar, the traditional, enabled them to withstand the new, the incomprehensible, sometimes the unacceptable. In this provisional shelter, they could take the time to process the trauma of expulsion, to marshal their strength before confronting the new world. These families made use of this moment of communitarianism, the better to savour the Republic later. At that time, the word 'communitarianism' did not exist, and the antagonist of the Republic was still fresh in people's memories. He even had a name: Philippe Pétain.

I must admit that this notion, of the benefit of a moment of communitarianism for the ultimate adaptation of families, is something I think of only today, after many years have passed. At the time, on the contrary, most of these Jews of the Nile were seeking to escape from the cité Claude-Debussy, all except for a few children. I was one of those. Some of the older ones, the almost-adults, left in the morning, hugging the walls on their way to the lycée, or the office, or the factory, to convince themselves that they were just like everyone else. The girls were the first to take the path of normalization, the prettiest ones especially, the ones wrapped in the arms of the boys in black leather jackets. We younger ones would sometimes surprise them in the cellars we knew so well. The adults, of course, were also trying to appear 'normal' but had a harder time than the young people, betrayed as they were by their accents, their choice of words, their ways of perceiving the world.

Some adults—those who were the most mature I think, the most accomplished—arranged their lives to deny the exile. There was one woman whom I recognize as my double in nostalgia. We called her 'Aunt G', because she was in fact the aunt of one of us. She'd decided to live in France just as she'd lived in Egypt—a life made up of endless conversations over a glass of whiskey while playing cards. During the day she more or less took care of her home and her three children. But at nightfall her real life began. A taxi would pick her up to take her to the Enghien casino. There she would find other Egyptian women like herself, along with Algerians and Tunisians. She would spend the night there, returning at dawn, her face and clothing in disarray, sometimes accompanied by a casual beau. In order to withstand the situation, her

husband drove a night taxi. He changed his name, choosing a surname that evoked an older France. He wore elegant clothes and
adopted the mannerisms of the well-to-do. But everyone knew that
his wife's nostalgia was making his life impossible. He ended up
leaving her. For a good while, she won at cards, enough to not have
to work. Eventually her luck ran out. She'd squandered her meagre
savings. She was barred from the casino. She grew old in one day,
as if the twenty-year reprieve she'd been granted had crashed down
on her without warning. She contracted every illness and ended up
dying alone in her small apartment in the cité. There was also Mr
J, a man who terrified all of us. He claimed that we could not run
from him indefinitely, that the dead would finally catch up with us.
He would call to the children and invite them to make the glasses
turn with him on a cloth he'd inscribed with the letters of the
alphabet in a circle. And the glasses turned, and the dead arrived.
They were unmistakably the old dead, the ones who'd passed away
in Egypt and who were now asking for the services owed to the
departed. Mr J was obsessed with all those we'd left behind—alone,
lacking prayers, lacking visits. My ancestors, the Cohen family, the
forbears of my parents' two maternal grandmothers, had been
buried in the Bassatine Cemetery in Cairo since the dawn of time.
There were perhaps twenty successive generations beneath the
earth of that cemetery, perhaps twice that number, who knows. The
story went that an old rabbi had used a subterfuge to obtain the
concession for the cemetery from the sultan. The rabbi had healed
the sultan's daughter. To thank him, the sultan asked him to express
a wish. The rabbi asked for a plot of land on which to construct a
cemetery for the Jewish community.

'And how large should this plot be?' the sultan asked warily.

'The size of this camel's skin,' the rabbi replied.

'Your wish is granted,' the sultan decreed.

And so, the rabbi cut the camel's skin into narrow strips that, laid end to end, would delineate the perimeter of the immense Bassatine Cemetery.

We had learnt that after their military defeat against the Israelis, the Egyptians had desecrated the graves. It was even said that they'd stolen the stones to build little shelters on the roofs of already tottering structures. One cannot claim that the dead left behind in Egypt were thriving. But they had found an advocate in Mr J, a bizarre and worrisome advocate whose influence was confined to this single alley in Gennevilliers. Later, our dead would find a more effective advocate in Mrs Carmen Weinstein, who tirelessly petitioned the Egyptian authorities until they finally agreed to restore the Bassatine Cemetery, at the expense of the Egyptian Jewish diaspora of course!

All the children knew one another in the cité Claude-Debussy—in fact everyone knew everyone else. Of course, there were a few flirtations; even some that lasted, but most of the children married and founded a family with outsiders, generally French from France. Almost all the young people decided to leave, to find love outside their community of origin. The boys married girls from families newly arrived from the provinces, and were thus able to put down roots somewhere in France through their in-laws, be it in Picardie, in Morvan, in the Eure, in the Creuse or in the Var. As for the girls, if they left the cité, they did not go very far, marrying the sons of grocers or plumbers. If you wanted to measure the degree of a community's adaptation by the mingling of its children with the new population, you would have to say that the Jews of Egypt, at least those who wound up in the cité Claude-Debussy, adapted in an exemplary fashion—with a few exceptions, including my brother Edwin and I, who both married girls in the cité from Egyptian Jewish families, themselves also born in Egypt. When a Jew from Egypt like me has a child with a Jewish woman from Egypt, what is the nature of this child? There was a moment of hilarity when the teacher at my firstborn Michaël's school told us that in response to the question of nationality she'd posed to the class, the little imp, at the age of four or five, replied 'Egyptian.' Yet Michaël was born in Paris, at the Saint-Antoine Hospital, to two parents, both French. There are logics that belie appearances.

This period of beneficial communitarianism in our lives came to an end with my brother's marriage, at least for me. Real life, everyday problems, suddenly imposed themselves, overwhelming, impossible to ignore. Everyone knew one another on the avenue Claude-Debussy, you cannot say that everyone loved one another, far from it! In Egypt, my mother would never have spoken to the women of the cité, not to any of them. They were all *baladi*, peasants. She would not even have crossed paths with them in Egypt. They did not live in the same world. So goes emigration, completely overturning the order of things. What she could never tolerate was being associated with these women; she could not bear the thought that someone might think she was one of them. And so, she never left her home. From the moment she arrived at the cité, to protect the image she had of herself, my mother took refuge in her apartment, the Republic is imposing for common folk. 'For whom does she take herself, this one? Queen Nazli? Oh, my dear, she gives us such looks! She walks before us with her nose a mile high. She barely manages to acknowledge us . . .' Over time, my mother eventually reclaimed some status for herself. She began to offer private lessons to the cité's children. To teach them was acceptable, to help them rise above their vulgarity was even salutary, but as for spending time with them, that was out of the question! I truly believe that none of the boys my age—not even the oldest— escaped her maths courses—the dunces who were trying to get into the superior class as well as the good students hoping to place in a competition or enter an exclusive school. I have to admit, she was gifted! Not only in maths, but also in her ability to teach these somewhat lost youngsters, caught between overwhelmed parents and a school system that ignored their specificity—because its first principle is to ignore all specificity. She was for them a sort of intermediary, could present the subject to them in an accessible manner. There are so many children who never take to learning, for it comes to them like a poison. She knew them, these rascals! She knew them well. Every so often I run into some of her former students, who always remind me that my mother saved the day, that they might otherwise have amounted to nothing, still stuck on the same dead-end road. Benny, Doudou, Roby, Gougou, Peewee, Zaco, Zizi, Zouzi . . . we all had nicknames. But there was one problem: the problem of marriage. The marriage of their children always poses something of a problem to migrants! They have the dim sense of being the last link in a chain. Before them, from generation to generation, like joined with like. But now, in their lifetime, they were going to see their children marry strangers, thus breaking the hundred-, perhaps thousand-year-old chain. They felt themselves responsible for this inevitable betrayal, even while knowing that a marriage to a son or daughter of the host society is the strongest guarantor of being firmly settled in the new land. The problem is exacerbated when religion comes into play. Back then, to marry a French person was almost certainly to marry a Catholic. The feeling of betrayal acquires more weight, echoing like a familiar refrain, violating traditional prohibitions, recalling the old sayings. Doesn't the law state that when a Jewish man marries a non-Jewish woman, their children will not be Jewish? How could a parent assume the responsibility of denying the community to their own grand-children? Most of the time, the parents did not express their anxiety, for fear of planting the thought in their children's minds— to avoid misfortune also, in a sort of apotropaic denial. This was clearly the case in our family. For my mother, the question of her children's marriage was further complicated because, for her, if either of us were to choose a girl from the cité, albeit a Jew from Egypt, we could be forming an alliance with a family not to be fre-quented, one of those families she kept at a distance with fierce determination. However, that was what my brother did, and at a very young age, little more than nineteen. The one consolation: the wedding was held in the grand synagogue on the rue de la Victoire in Paris. They were young, they were in love, they were good-looking: Tony Perkins and Audrey Hepburn. Stunning! They must have been the first in the cité to so resolutely step into this new life. I don't know what my brother was thinking. He must have been roiled by the same storm of emotions that had deluged me then, and which I spent years trying to identify. Since our departure

from Egypt that February morning in 1957, we had been the characters in a history written long ago. The rabbi Yom-Tov Israël
Sherezli had been Joseph in Egypt, he too an advisor to the sultan,
on equal footing with those in power, even while protecting and
leading his community. The generations had succeeded one another
'until a leader of Egypt appeared who had not known Joseph'. That
leader's name was Gamal Abdel Nasser. Every year, at Passover,
we'd been told the same story. In every prayer, the pious Jew tirelessly thanks God for having brought him 'out of Egypt'. One day,
the Exodus from Egypt, *yetsiat misraïm*, actually occurred and we
were its protagonists. Without a doubt, we were the contemporaries
of the myth, and we were the last generation to live it. There will
not be another exodus from Egypt after us, for there is no longer a
single Jew in Egypt. As the subjects in a narrative already written,
we watched the events unfold like an ineluctable mechanism to
which we had no choice but to submit—until the day when my
brother made a choice, against his parents' wishes, a difficult choice,
a free choice. Another life was about to begin. I'd had the presenti-
ment on the day of our departure from Egypt—not in my mind,
but in my hands. The gesture they accomplished without my knowing it had been my first leap into individual liberation.

When, in February 1957, we embarked from the port of
Alexandria, on an auspiciously named Italian ship, *L'esperia*, our
bags had been ransacked, every object of value confiscated. We'd
also been strip-searched for hours—a violent, humiliating body
search—the whole family, including the children. Money, jewellery,
watches, silverware—everything—had to stay behind in Egypt.
Nothing of value could leave the country. Despite it all, the customs

officers, God knows why, spared a signet ring I had on my finger, a gold signet ring with my initials stamped in bas relief. The ship very slowly pulled away from the dock. To my left, I could see my father's trousers, to my right, those of a stranger. My mother and brother were in the cabin, nursing their first seasickness. A pleasant breeze came to caress our faces, bringing with it an incomprehensible sense of well-being—a consolation? I was on the bridge, contemplating Egypt receding into the distance. I knew that everything was over, without grasping the significance. I then very slowly removed that ring tossed it into the sea. Later, I would claim to have lost it.

After my brother's wedding, my friend Jean-Loup and I slipped away through the narrow streets of the ninth arrondissement. We walked for a long time, until we reached rue Saint-Denis. There, we sauntered, hardly able to believe what we were seeing, our astonished eyes devouring the prostitutes strolling by. We drew close, but backed away when they offered to initiate us. We had no intention of going upstairs with them and, besides, we didn't have a penny in our pockets. We only wanted to approach, to imagine. Apparently, my brother's marriage had given us notions.

10

Ouedraogo

Ouagadougou, 2000

It was in 2000. I'd been invited to teach a course in clinical psychology at the University of Ouagadougou, Burkina Faso. Accompanying me were several members of the team: Lucien Hounkapatin, now a doctor—and what a doctor!—the voice of the depths; Emmanuelle, a keen-eyed filmmaker; and Peter, a medical biologist with an always-open heart, as wide as the Boulevard de la Révolution. After nightfall, we would spend hours at the Independence Hotel, rehashing the clinic, dreaming up new research topics, seeking to understand what the Burkine students were telling us. That night, our conversation was especially animated. We were returning from a visit to the village of Ouedraogo, a Mossi healer. There are times when the brain refuses to accept what the eyes have seen. That's why Emmanuelle accompanied us in the tiny hut that measured no more than 3 by 3 metres. Everything we'd witnessed had been recorded by her camera, but we could barely make out the details on her tiny screen.

We'd wandered for a good hour through that desert dotted with a handful of shrubs before reaching the hut at the centre of a tiny hamlet. On large mats in front of the door, grains of red sorghum were drying from which dolo, *the millet beer, would be brewed. Ouedraogo was a short, lean man, dry like the hot wind that made the palms quiver. We found him standing on the threshold, as if awaiting us. A healer must never be surprised. He began by introducing himself, speaking an incomprehensible French that had atrophied through lack of use.*

Assuring him that our interpreter would translate without a problem, we urged him in vain to express himself in the language of the Mossis. He did not know his exact age, but claimed to be close to a hundred. He spoke to us of a war he'd fought for France. Initially, I thought it might be the first, from 1914 to 1918. On further consideration, this seemed impossible, even if he'd been born in 1900. As proof of his time in the army, he showed us the rusty old revolver hanging on the wall, the only decoration in his monk's cell. He sat down cross-legged on the mat placed on the floor of beaten earth and invited us to join him. Outside, it must have been at least 35 degrees Celsius, but inside it was much worse, as hot as a steam room, causing us to sweat bullets. In front of him, a hen was standing motionless on one leg, looking towards the door with one eye. It was not reacting, not moving its head, not seeking to peck. Until then, all the hens I'd seen had been anxious, moving every which way, ceaselessly searching for a worm or a grain, raising their heads up to spy a rooster. This one was decidedly atypical. No movement, no cry, she seemed stuffed with straw. Ouedraogo asked us what we wanted, what we were expecting from him. We replied that his reputation extended as far as the outskirts of the capital. We were wishing to meet him, in order to know him, to learn about his work. He wiped the lenses of his eyeglasses, which must have been transparent in some distant past, and I noticed his eyes. They were strangely clear, an opalescent green. Until the age of forty, he'd never dreamt of becoming a healer, and, to tell the truth, he was no longer one today. It was his cousin who was the keeper of 'the thing'. With his eyes he indicated a large mass at the back of his hut. 'The "thing"?' I asked, opening my eyes wide, but all I could make out was a tuft of feathers. The 'thing' must have been about 1 metre high, of indefinite shape, of a consistency impossible to discern. Perhaps a large earthen mound covered with sand and bird feathers? While he was speaking, he was shaking in his hands a fistful of cowries, little bits of porcelain, pierced on the back and on the belly. Centuries ago, during the time of the Portuguese, these shells had served as money; today, they permit one above all to penetrate the invisible world and to predict the future—still a kind of money, the price of a passage into the world's hidden realms. Before the war, his cousin had been a healer, here in this village, in this very hut. When Ouedraogo returned from Europe, he found his cousin dead. It seemed that the other had waited to die until the very day of his return. The elders interpreted this death as a sign, and so they designated him, Ouedraogo, as the successor. That was when they gave him the fetish, the 'thing' we could see behind him. At first, he'd refused the charge. He was returning from the battlefield; he was returning from France. All he cared about was drinking and having fun. He left the village to try his luck in Ouaga. But over there, he ran around in vain. Nothing worked. Both women and luck fled from him. He ended up on the street, like a stray dog, without friends, without work, without a roof over his head. And when he fell seriously ill, with an incomprehensible disease no doctor could diagnose, he finally resolved to return. Could he give us the date of his return to the village, the year at least? He no longer knew—a few years after the war, that much was certain—five years, maybe ten. The strangest thing was that no one had taken care of the 'thing' in the interim. Apparently, the elders had waited. Yet one cannot evade one's obligations indefinitely. As soon as he agreed to accept them, his illness disappeared as mysteriously as it had come. What did he have to do but to serve the fetish? He had never ceased doing so ever since. You could not call it a vocation, a gift or anything like that. No! A servitude, rather. The elders had appointed him. After some hesitation, he'd ended up obeying. Which is why he'd clarified to us that he was not really a healer. No one had taught him anything, neither how to question fate, nor how to make medicines. To answer our questions: to heal illnesses, to identify the causes of misfortunes, he did nothing. The fetish took care of everything. As for Ouedraogo, his task was simple. It consisted solely of feeding the fetish.

He interrupted his narrative to interrogate the cowries. As I was sitting beside him, I was the first on whom he focused. He tossed them several times, observing the figures they drew, picking them up tossing them again, tracing with his finger a few strange signs in the sand. Then he removed his eyeglasses and looked at me with his large, clear eyes.

'I know that you come from afar,' he began. 'I can tell you today that you will travel for a long time yet.'

He closed his eyes, considering if he'd said enough, then gathered up the shells and resumed the narrative of his imposed vocation. To feed the fetish was not so complicated after all. It was sufficient merely to place a live hen on top of the 'thing', and it would absorb the creature's substance. He looked at us and solemnly declared, this time in Moré: 'I've never used a knife to cut the hen. I never choked it, nor did I poison it, nor anything at all.'

Intrigued, we questioned the interpreter. Could he provide details? Why did the old man insist so vehemently that he'd never killed the hen offered as a sacrifice?

'He's explaining that the fetish kills the hen, takes hold of it, deprives it of its strength, and that's why it dies. It dies from one moment to the next, abruptly. Ouedraogo sets it down and it dies. That's all! Do you understand? That's what he's explaining.'

'Oh?' I was astonished. 'The fetish can kill a hen?'

The old man was carefully listening to our interpreter's words, examining the translation and nodding his head. Satisfied, he simply added, 'It can kill more than a hen . . . It even knows how to take a sheep! You just place the sheep on top of it. You don't have to attach it. You place it, that's all. The fetish kills without a knife, without violence. That's how it is . . . You place the sheep and it dies . . . I'm telling you the truth. Me, I do nothing other than to serve the fetish.'

It was very dark in the corner of the 'thing'. It was useless to scrunch our eyes. All we could see was a shape, an indefinable mass. Ouedraogo asked Peter if he also wanted to have the cowries tossed. Peter approached and looked dubiously at his hands, dry as sticks of wood, as they played with the cowries. Ouedraogo tossed and re-tossed the shells. What he saw seemed to intrigue him. He looked at Peter, then at the shells, then at Peter again. Then he picked up his game and began again. He must have started over five or six times before concluding with a sibylline sentence, something like, 'A man never lives alone because we who are on the earth are all born twins.' While Ouedraogo persisted in making the cowries or the earth speak—do we know who speaks when we toss the shells?— the hen remained immobile, like a soldier keeping watch. I had to satisfy my mind. I made a movement of my leg, thinking the hen might take fright and flee. But no! She did not flinch, did not react to sounds or ges- tures. The healer questioned the cowries for Lucien, who was laughing at each question. These tales of fetishes did not surprise him. He'd spent

231

time with them as a child, and the old man's divinations seemed doomed to failure from the start. As a result, Ouedraogo hesitated, retraced his movements, so dissatisfied with the responses he received, that he left to search for other shells before beginning again. He concluded by giving up, announcing that this time, for this man before him, he saw nothing. We remained a good two hours in this tiny hut, six or seven of us squeezed together, in the stifling, damp heat. When the healer rose, giving the signal for departure, the hen suddenly came to life. She escaped outside, moving, running, pecking, cackling. One might have said that until then some force had constrained her with invisible bonds, gagged, fixed. She suddenly began to live as a hen.

That night, at the Independence Hotel, I anxiously asked Emmanuelle: 'Tell me, did you film the hen?'

'I filmed nonstop for two hours,' Emmanuelle replied, 'until my hand went numb, from gripping the camera. But it was as black as in an oven in there. I doubt whether you'll find the hen . . .'

It was in 2000. Ouedraogo shall remain in my memory as the perfect healer, the one you trust without reserve. He did not boast, did not display a gift or a familiarity with the invisible ones. He did not claim to know the plant that would cure AIDS or quell the desire for drugs, the secret prayer that renders one invisible in combat, the amulet that lets you win at lotto. He did not even describe the initiation he must have undergone before leaving for the war, nor his purification when he returned. No! He presented himself as a modest technician, the servant of a mechanism, complex and singular, which he called 'the thing'. Today, if I had to define the art of healing, I would use the same words as he. A world in order, a happy world in which one knows that healing is a matter of forces, and caring is a manipulation of 'things'. My training in psychoanalysis was revealed to be at once less limpid and far more problematic.

* * *

Paris, 1977

I'd passed the third cycle of my doctoral thesis the preceding year.

I was established in my position as a district psychologist, and my appointment book was full. And yet, I could not claim to be happy in psychotherapy—the way one is said to be 'happy in love'. I rigorously applied the principles of psychoanalysis as I had read them in books, and as I experienced them myself three times a week in my own cure. Yet I did not feel the effects. No eurekas, no great upheavals. The truth was slow in arising from the words, and when a little light came to illumine the scene, there were fleeting moments of happiness without tomorrows. Still, the patients liked the sessions—it is indeed the paradox of psychoanalysis; they never missed their appointments, took pleasure in the staggered process, endlessly voiced their trivial, everyday concerns and their existential questions. But they never got any better. I repeated to myself the same consoling words I heard everywhere, soon even from the mouth of the President of the Republic: 'One must give time some time.'

It was idiotic! Time went by ... I also told myself that indeed, if the healings were slow in coming, it was because I didn't know how to proceed. Too impetuous, too full of references, too anxious to succeed, too . . . too . . . much—yes, definitely too much! As a general rule, the patients felt better—or, to be more exact, they were carried along by the momentum of the cure that infused them, in a regular rhythm, like a transfusion, drop by drop, with a dose of hope. But I did not see the dawning of the radical transformations I was expecting. The psychoanalytic texts, published by the hundreds, overflowing with examples of miraculously successful analyses in which the decisive turns had occurred after a dazzling interpretation. Why did this never happen for me? Like so many of my psychoanalyst apprentice friends, I was in awe of the amazing formulations of our elders—Pontalis, André Green, Masud Khan. Masud Khan above all, the English psychoanalyst of Pakistani origin. Come! I needed to learn more! Still, I was a little put off by my most admired heroes: I needed go to London for a conference. I wanted to take advantage of the trip to approach this man whose texts I revered. I dared to write a letter to Masud Khan, requesting an interview to discuss some questions I was wondering about. I received a reply that left me speechless. 'Sir, I am a prince of royal blood. One does not address me in a letter typed on a machine.' Indeed! The man might be a prince, but I was not aspiring to be his subject. I didn't bother to answer. Much later I would learn that Masud Khan was a bizarre character, who acted strangely with his colleagues, his patients, strangers on the street. One of his patients had filed a lawsuit claiming Khan had beaten him.

Later, I would often hear stories of physical violence perpetrated by psychoanalysts against their patients. At the time, I did not believe them. 'No one is as deaf as he who will not hear.' People said it was customary for Lacan, and some of his followers imitated him. One of my patients, years later, definitively unsealed my eyes when he told me he'd been slapped by his previous psychoanalyst, a follower of Lacan. I fell from the clouds. Why had he not lodged a judicial complaint? Why had he accepted such humiliation? As for Khan, who regularly had sex with his patients, who'd broken so many rules of an elementary deontology, including those of ordinary ethics, he ended up being expelled from the Psychoanalytic Society of Great Britain. He'd been stricken by a cancer of the throat and the larynx for some ten years, and up until the last moment his colleagues thought his death might avert a scandal. He died during the year after his expulsion. In this way, psychoanalysis, through a sort of internal necessity, produced submission, dependence and delinquency. But in those days, the casserole cover was screwed on tight; it released only a distant wisp of steam. Lulled by the psychoanalytic routine, my revolutionary fervour had slumbered, evidence that, even without medication, psychology possesses soporific qualities. I became strangely concerned with respectability. To justify this, I would tell myself that anyone in charge of souls cannot help but act like a savage. If psychoanalysts so often act entitled, it's because, feeling themselves considered as models by their patients and students, they end up embracing the role. I felt that this role clung to me. And then, the work of the psychoanalyst is a kind of slavery that leaves little time for imagination. Still, I obtained some therapeutic successes, but labouriously, without ease. For those, as the saying goes, I 'paid my dues'. I didn't yet know how to put it, but I sensed that my patients improved in proportion to the sacrifices made by their therapist. I remember a woman just entering into delirium, whom I saw at the clinic four times a week for hour-long sessions. In addition, I'd authorized her to come whenever she felt the need, if she was suddenly overcome by anxiety. She would burst into my office while I was in a session with another patient or in a discussion with a colleague. I would take her aside into the hall for five minutes or a quarter of an hour, and she would leave, calmed. She would call me too, at all hours of the day or night—at the office or at home. I would sometimes fall asleep, my ear glued to the phone, after an hour of conversation in the middle of the night. So much effort, over so many years, was eventually recompensed. The young woman ended up okay. She was able to earn her baccalaureate, to find work, to return to a life of normalcy. I hope she did not have a relapse. But I would ask myself: was it psychoanalysis that cured her or the massive and stubborn investment of her psychoanalyst? At that time, I did not know that the only force that heals patients in psychotherapy is the *furor sanandi* of their therapist, 'the passion for healing'.

But if that first condition is necessary, there is yet another one, also active: therapists prove to be effective when the cures they bring about enable them to know the world. As soon as they stop learning, as soon as they think they know, their therapeutic abilities decline, as if by magic. That is why the young ones, the apprentices, the ignorant, often obtain therapeutic successes that surprise their elders. I also regularly taught psychology to cohorts of young women at the School of Social Work on the Boulevard du Montparnasse. I was committed, of course, to preparing them for their future profession as social workers, but often my own concerns took over and I focused instead on what was driving me: my interest in psychoanalysis and in distant worlds. At that time, each new consultation, each new patient, was a source of discoveries. I cared for people in order to learn; I learnt in order to teach; I taught in order to retain what I'd learnt. As for my own symptoms, my 'sufferings' as we put it then, they were not improving, far from it! I was not like myself—with each passing day, I grew further and further away from myself. I always had the feeling that I was playing a part in a bad theatre piece. A muffled revolt always accompanied me, a sort of fundamental frustration. And then what? The combination of the most modern ideas about a liberated sexuality and of the street, that cauldron in which our dreams of a revolution in morals had simmered, had produced nothing but this insipid dish. I wasn't even thirty years old and I was in the process of becoming a functionary of conventional thought.

I was saved by my son. As I'd heard it shouted in Brazil during condomblé rituals, when the faithful greeted the arrival of a divinity or a spirit: '*Sarava!*' My wife was pregnant. I was sure it would be a boy. I rifled through old texts in search of his name; she went through the first names of friends and family, asking whom she should honour. I knew that he would be my firstborn son and I wondered what name would be fitting for the first to be born so far from the land of Egypt where our ancestors had succeeded one another, generation after generation, for centuries. As the due date approached, we were still unable to agree. She found my proposals too ponderous, unsure of a child's ability to bear a name so charged with meaning. I found her proposals commonplace, too distanced from the substance of which we were made. One morning, it was like a revelation. I don't know whose idea it was. What about Michaël? It would be Michaël! We had many friends who were so named, Michel Sapir, for example, who, when he saw my son, barely one year old, exclaimed: 'Your name is Michaël? Like me! I'm sure your parents gave you that name to honour me.' And Michaël had burst out laughing. 'You're a man,' Sapir added, 'you must eat camembert. Men, you see, must become accustomed very early to strong substances.' My son spit out the cheese. Like many young children, Michaël liked only buttered pasta. But his name suited him so well, in Hebrew, *Michaël*, 'like God', he who was surely as handsome as a god. During the initial days, Michaël was my sole joy. Like me, he seemed to be of the night. Until he reached the age of six months, he woke up at two every morning. Lying in my bed, I would place him on my legs, and there, face to face, we would converse for a long while, without his mother's knowledge, in an incomprehensible language invented for the occasion. Perhaps it was a case of that 'primal tongue' humans share with spirits? We had a lovely Siamese cat named Electra. Her brother, Orestes, a sturdy tomcat, had left us to chase tail; he never returned. Michaël was more interested in the cat than in his father. When she walked in front of him, he grew frenzied, trying to catch her attention with overtures that I imagined were sensual. One night, when he could not have been more than five months old, he looked at her for a long moment and, grimacing, making an effort that to me seemed unnaturally strong, he distinctly uttered: 'Electra!' I jumped. I asked him to repeat it. Again he said, laughing, 'Electra!' and again, repeating it some dozen times—and then, no doubt drained by the effort, he fell asleep. The next morning, it was impossible to elicit anything other than his usual babble. It would take another year for him to speak. His mother was convinced that I'd dreamt, or imagined, or simply invented the tale. But no! Michaël, as a five-month-old infant, had spoken the cat's name.

Children know how to speak before they speak. Who knows what lies hidden in the mental universe of very young children? Before becoming humans, bound in a network of constraints and words, children convey a message that arises from the depths of time. If Michaël had captured my attention, if he'd planted a question in my mind, I did not know its significance. It was not until ten or twelve years later, when I discovered an Internet site put together by a cousin in Australia, detailing Rabbi Yom-Tov's genealogy, that I was finally able to put all the pieces together. The eldest son of Rabbi Yom-Tov, who'd informed my mother in dream that he was coming to settle in her house, was named Michaël. According to the elderly aunts, I was the reincarnation of Yom-Tov. My wife and I had searched for a name for weeks. We'd clashed, but something had driven us to keep on searching. And this was the one that had arisen. We thought we'd created it, had imagined it for him; in fact, we'd simply rediscovered it. His name was Michaël before we named him. Yom-Tov's son was named Michaël; it was also my son's name. Furthermore, my son, before knowing how to speak, had come to remind me that I could study all I wanted to, learn from books and from the world, but I would never obtain the essential knowledge. My son had filled the same function as Ouedraogo's elders, who'd imposed on him the service of the fetish. Michaël had come to announce an absolute truth: that humans are born attached. They grow and they learn, they circulate and forge new bonds, but their primal attachments remain. They are of course akin to animals, who can move their bodies at will, but they are also like trees, whose roots hold and connect them through an infinity of fibres and nerves to the past, as well as to other trees with which they share the earth. Today I believe that Michaël had come to deliver me from a mad thought that necessarily flowed from the practice of psychoanalysis, that of believing in the existence of a naked man, an individual desiring, impelled solely by his own will, belonging only to himself. I suddenly became aware of an immense solitude, I who was living in my new country, France, without my ancestors, without my ritual places, without the objects, my ancestors' 'things', without the rituals that beat out the rhythm of the world's order . . .

Rio, 1998

In Rio de Janeiro, in 1998, I'd been invited to present a series of lectures at the university, in the department of the late lamented Flavio Pessoa de Barros, a professor of anthropology who knew both how to touch 'things' and how to theorize them. Again: 'Saravá!' Hail to the elders who dared to defy conventional thinking in order to further advance the religion that the enslaved people had brought with them from Africa. He studied their history, offered analyses and established his own congregation, a terreiro. *Thus Flavio was both a university professor and a* païdos santos, *in Portuguese, a 'father of the saints' or if one prefers African terminology, a* bababalao *in Yoruba, a 'master of the secret'. We traded stories, talked all night, drank, sang, danced. He invited me to participate in the ritual whose proceedings he'd meticulously reconstructed and which he opened to his group of students and professors, as well as people who were ill, whom he welcomed in the ritual manner, with immense feasts in homage to the African gods. It was of a hybrid undertaking, traditional in their careful respect for knowledge gathered during field research and perfectly contemporary, adapted to the concerns of present-day Brazilians. Every day, Brazil demonstrates that the most forward-thinking modernity is enriched by these teeming resources that unbridle the imagination and bring joy to the people. Flavio was deeply respectful of the traditions he'd gathered from across the country in other terreiros of condomblé, which he then taught to his—how to put it?— 'faithful'? patients? subjects? There were songs in Yoruba. Although they did not understand the meaning, they sang fervently, a little like the peasants of another era reciting the Latin Mass. Lucien, who was again accompanying me, recognized the words, translated the songs, explained, commented. The adepts of ondomblé suddenly saw their mythology emerge from the intellectual haze, finding a voice and acquiring a body at the heart of the music. I saw them overcome, somewhat frightened, perplexed, happy. They didn't want Lucien to leave, following him everywhere, asking him thousands of questions. The members of the terreiro, some of whom perhaps had Yoruba, Ibo, Fon or Goun in their ancestry, acted as if one of their forebears had miraculously arisen from the past to explain the passage of time to them. I owe these moments of intense discovery, infinite interrogations, to Flavio, unfortunately dead too young, and to Inês, forest spirit, agile and fecund, a waker of sleeping worlds. One day, we were shopping in a supermarket with Flavio and Inês. In front of us, in the line that led to the cash register, a man, quite dark-skinned, engaged us in conversation. We introduced ourselves. He was a taxi driver, Flavio and I, both professors, Inês, a psychologist She explained that her profession consisted of healing. 'Is that so?' the man asked, 'Did you notice the spots scattered on my arms and legs?' We hadn't noticed anything, but now that he called our attention to it, we did. 'Two years ago, I was covered from head to toe with large, festering boils,' he explained. 'Look!' He held out his arms, rolled up his pants to show us his legs. Indeed, innumerable dark spots, the size of coins, gave him skin like a leopard, covered with eyespots. 'Doctors were giving me up for dead. They were expecting septicemia, which would have killed me.'*

'Boils?' Flavio asked, surprised.

'Yes, sir,' the man replied. 'Huge boils, filled with pus, and terribly painful. I could no longer move. I could no longer go to work. People turned away from me, disgusted. My children no longer wanted to come near me ...'

'And now?'

'Now, as you can see. I'm fine. The boils have dried up. My skin is as smooth as satin.' One thing leading to another, he described how his illness had been cured. At the time, he'd been a practising Catholic, a believer who attended mass as often as possible. It was actually at church that one of his friends suggested that he visit a terreiro *of condomblé. For him as a Christian, all these practices had seemed like the work of the devil. But he was suffering so much that he eventually let himself be convinced. When he arrived at the* terreiro, *the mother of the saints cried out 'Obalouayé!' the moment she saw him.*

'Obalouayé is the god of smallpox,' Flavio remarked.

'Yes! it's my orisha,' the man said. At the terreiro, *they used the occasion to profit from the feast of the divinity, known as Sakpata in Togo and Benin, to organize a healing ceremony for him. He danced, he danced like a madman. He spun, infinitely. He could no longer stop.*

When the mother of the saints saw that he was falling into a trance, she clothed him in a large straw mask, from his head to his toes. There were only two eyeholes. And he danced even more beautifully in his heavy costume. Then he fell, went into convulsions and lost consciousness. He was surrounded, caressed, given something to drink, taken to a cell within the 'convent'. He slept for two days. And when he awoke, the boils had dried a little. His treatment lasted for a full year. He danced frequently, for Obalouayé, his orisha, for the others as well. He learnt the songs and the tales. He ate the consecrated food and drank the substances, the waters, the oils, the powders. He washed the statuettes, learnt the scents and the colours. For close to a year, he was treated like a nursing infant who knew nothing of the real world. It was a treatment, but also a teaching. In a word, he learnt his orisha, this god, this 'thing' of which he was made.

'They must have taught him Sakpata's story,' Flavio told me.

It is said that, as a young man, Sakpata had been covered with smallpox pustules. In love with a young woman, he didn't dare approach her, for fear that she would be revolted. That's when he thought of creating that great straw mask, beneath which he went everywhere—in the village, at the market, on the road. And it was in this costume that he courted the young woman. He spoke to her every day, he spoke to her every night. His words became the most beautiful love poems a man can compose. He sang for her every day; he sang for her every night. And these songs are precisely the ones the faithful intone on Obalouayé's nights, during the feast of the earth, the feast of the harvest. For Sakpata is the divinity of the earth; Sakpata is the earth. Whoever does not recognize its power, whoever hinders its production, whoever corrupts it will one day be overcome by corruption, covered in turn with pustulent

243

boils. The suffering earth, too dry, will come and inscribe its mark on his skin.

Thus the man was healed, both by discovering his roots and the group that enabled him to honour them. He was Black, most likely of African origin. There was no evidence that his ancestors came from Benin, Togo or Nigeria, where one finds Sakpata's adepts. Perhaps they came from Senegal or Mauritania, perhaps even from Mozambique or Tanzania. Or were his ancestors primarily Portuguese or Spanish or even French? But at the conclusion of the ritual, he was certain he'd descended in a direct line from the Yorubas of Dahomey. His healing had shown him that he had been sick because he thought he was a naked man, belonging only to himself, governed solely by his own will.

* * *

Healing is a very powerful process of affiliation.

The retort one always hears, the claim that 'he was healed because he believed', is wrong. The opposite is true. First one is healed, then one believes. He believed because he was healed. Healing creates the faithful, groups, religions. Jesus Christ, a specialist, healed to make people believers. He was not the first, far from it, but his example was followed. Today hundreds—perhaps thousands—of Christian believers have proliferated all over the globe—in Africa, to be sure, but also in Polynesia, in America, in the old Soviet empire. To each of them, healing is offered in exchange for membership. One must recognize that in the healing market, symbols are the only currency. That is where the webs of influence that move the political levers of the most powerful are woven. In 1977, I was unaware of that. Innocent, I was trying to slip into one of them, the Paris Psychoanalytic Society. By then, I'd completed five years of psychoanalysis and was presenting my candidacy to become a student at the Psychoanalytic Institute. Nata Minor, my psychoanalyst, didn't exactly jump for joy when I announced my decision. Of course she didn't say a word, but I sensed that I'd irritated her. I knew what she was thinking and could have said it for her. 'Why did I need institutional recognition? Wasn't it infantile to chase after such baubles?' I was interviewed by the dean of studies. And so began the reproachful attitudes, the knowing looks—as if I didn't know that in order to present my candidacy, I had to be arising from the couch of a senior practitioner, a 'didactitian', as they were called back then. Of course I knew it, but . . . 'There is no "but" with the Unconscious.' And this too, as I must know, the 'Unconscious does not recognize 'negation'. Indeed, yes, it was a question of means, you see. Nonsensical, of course . . . most rationalizations are attached to financial arguments. Surrealistic exchanges between an iron pot, the omniscient Big Brother, and a clay pot, me, shaking in my little shoes. And so, if in order to be admitted to the institute, the candidate who'd respected the procedure passed in front of three 'commissioners'— so named most likely because they were part of the teaching commission, and also perhaps in memory of the statue of the 'commissioner of the people'—then the one who came from an ordinary couch was entitled to a double ration: six commissioners. I've lost my memory of these Kafkaesque interrogations in which the candidate I was did not know what the investigator was expecting, and tried by all means to answer questions that had not been posed. All I remember is one moment that left me speechless: 'Were you married at the beginning of your analysis?'

'Yes, sir!'

'Are you still?'

'Yes!'

'To the same woman?'

'Well, yes . . . '

'You should surely ask yourself if your psychoanalysis has truly taken place.'

I must say that I couldn't manage to take my commissioners' questions seriously. Of course I understood their theoretical underpinnings. For example, in this case, it was assumed that my infantile neurosis had taken refuge in my matrimonial relation. If I had dissolved the neurosis during my analysis, then I should have dissolved the marriage and been divorced. All this irresistibly reminded me of a Woody Allen movie. That year, my candidacy was rejected. Nevertheless, I was authorized to present a new candidacy after a twelve-month hiatus. Echoing the commentary my psychoanalyst had not articulated, what began to infiltrate my consciousness was a feeling of inanity, as if a page had been turned without my knowing it. In that autumn of 1977, my situation had imperceptibly changed. Devereux had secured a teaching post for me at the École des hautes études, and I was beginning to lead a seminar on clinical general ethnopsychiatry, the continuation of the main seminar on general ethnopsychiatry which Devereux was still conducting. I prepared for each session with maniacal care. I made it a point of honour that each meeting contain some original reflections. That same year, I'd also begun to teach in the medical faculty at Bobigny. It was an introduction to medical psychology, a reflection on the complexities of the relationship between doctor and patient. The least one can say is that the usefulness of such teaching is obvious, but putting it into practice is terribly difficult. Each time, it was a challenge to interest the medical students in these questions that combined philosophy and day-to-day practice. Ignoring me, they remained obsessed with their exams in biology and anatomy. It was also the year that we launched our first journal, *Ethnopsychiatrica*. A very young editor had suggested to Devereux that he create a new periodical in which would be free to develop his own line of thought. Devereux had had his fill of editorial committees, reading committees, censorship committees, at the initiative of American journals that had blocked research in the social sciences, by then completely sterilized. This new editor was offering him freedom, true freedom, Devereux agreed to direct this journal on the condition that he not be constrained by any committee of any kind. As it turned out, the editing of the journal was confined to two people: editor-in-chief Georges Devereux, and deputy editor Tobie Nathan. And that was it! He read all the proposals for articles. When one interested him, he personally corrected it word by word, then gave it to me to review. The result was that all the articles in all the issues seem to have been penned by the same hand. In this way, things seemed to be in good order. Ethno-psychiatry was enjoying a small audience, and Devereux's prediction was in the process of being fulfilled. I would end up as his successor. In any case, I was on the road to becoming.

But the world is so constructed that order arises from disorder, and life from decay. Noticing worms milling about in rotting meat, Aristotle concluded that life was born from filth and corruption, what has improperly been called 'spontaneous generation'. A misinterpretation. To him, life was born from nothing but its own degradation. It is also in the degradation of an orderly world that I began to perceive beings and movements that eventually transformed my thinking. The first time was in a seminar session, during the analysis of a clinical case brought by an intern in medicine. The intern's patient, a Senegalese man about thirty years old, had emigrated to France some time ago. In vain he he'd searched for work; unable to resolve to return to his country empty-handed, he'd finally set himself up as a marabout, a holy man. He sublet a room, outfitted himself in a long wool djelaba and cap, and distributed ads in mailboxes, promising success in love and business, the return of one's loved one, the reversal of fate. The amazing fact is that, within a few weeks, his consultation was full. His reputation had spread beyond the confines of the few alleys in his neighbourhood. People from all over Paris crowded into his maid's room in the Goutte-d'Or. Immigrants from West Africa of course, from Senegal, Mali and the Ivory Coast, but also people from elsewhere, even sometimes well-heeled people from wealthy neighbourhoods. He began to wonder what was drawing them there. He realized that the prayer he was uttering had a special power. But, associated with this prayer, an unpleasant memory arose in his mind. He'd stolen this prayer from a true holy man. Yes, stolen! It was a matter of a secret sura, unknown to even the most learned believers. He'd encountered the old man seeking to embark for Europe. In exchange for the passage he'd arranged with a fisherman, the old man had shown him the paper hidden under his clothes. Having absorbed so much dust and sweat, it looked like parchment. Holding it in his hands, the old man had prayed over his head while uttering the secret names of God. The next day, when our patient found the marabout asleep on a boat, he'd stolen the precious prayer, skillfully calligraphed in Arabic, framed by a multitude of names of angels, spirits and demons. He never again saw the old marabout. Had he completed the voyage to Europe he'd envisaged? Had he taken his turn in the shelters for migrants in Paris, Brussels or Rome? He didn't really want to know, had not asked a single question, concerned only to preserve this prayer he thought of as his protection. For a long time, he kept it against his chest, without trying to decipher it, without even looking at it. When he'd decided to play at being a marabout, on what could he depend? He'd used it. He copied the words onto a wooden board. Later, he'd dissolved the writing in the water he gave to his clients. It was also the sura he chanted before sleep, hundreds of times, seeking to shed God's light on the questions he was trying to resolve. That was how he worked. He asked a client to tell him his mother's name and his true name, the real one, the one he'd received at baptism, not one he'd invented since, a nickname or circumstantial pseudo-name. He mingled the two names with the names of the spirits he'd discovered on this sheet of paper folded a thousand times. He recited the prayer and recited it again. And evidently, the patients were healed: the unemployed found work, the fickle lovers returned. He'd even succeeded in reviving the tired sex of an old diabetic who had not had an erection for years. Little by little, in the solitude of his prayers, our makeshift marabout, this usurper of talent, began to be haunted by the spirits he'd invoked. At first it was only in dreams. But the dreams multiplied, taking on troubling aspects, turning into nightmares. The spirits changed shape. They had fiery red eyes, burning hands, with flames shooting from their mouths like a welder's blowtorch. They approached him in troubling ways, as if they intended to transport him into a volcanic universe of explosions from smoking embers. He stayed up later and later to satisfy his clients, slept less and less, became isolated from the Barbès Senegalese community. One morning, after a sleepless night, he saw the spirits appear in his room. They were exploding before him like fireworks. They advanced, threatening, brandishing fiery swords, until they brushed against him and collapsed to leave room for others, then resumed their diabolic dance. He rubbed his eyes, and when he opened them again, they were still there. He wanted to flee, but he felt that the true marabouts of the neighbourhood, those from Myrha Street and even those from Stalingrad, had set him spinning. He understood that he was done for. And he had a sort of eureka moment: he'd been found out, he was sure of it. They knew he'd stolen the secret prayer, the unknown sura the elders had handed down from generation to generation. To take revenge, they were sending cohorts of devils, armies to fight him. Now he was terrified. It was not so much the fear of dying as of being bound to this hell of which he'd had a foretaste. He threw himself onto a police officer, wringing his neck while begging him to protect him from the *djinn*s and *sheytan*s pursuing him. At the psychiatric hospital, he was lucky enough to be taken in charge by that young intern, serious, devoted and full of curiosity about distant worlds.

We discussed him at length during the seminar. Of course, the intern recognized the symptoms of the onset of schizophrenia, as he'd been taught. But also, the unravelling of the crisis, the patient's awareness—all of it—conformed to what we'd read about the anthropology of Senegalese marabouts—and especially the description my friend András Zempleni had set forth in his doctoral thesis. The man had been overtaken by a well-known esoteric experience reported and described in the literature, the *listikhar* which, in its forms, resembled the practices of Jewish kabbalah. In Senegal, as in Jewish tradition, there was a warning that the faithful who ventured into esoteric domains without having been prepared through long study, without having been purified, especially those who approached God without having been authorized by a master, would be dragged into a world of madness, the *ngueleum*. One couldn't entirely blame the poor marabout patient. This sura indeed existed. Who knows the effect of secret prayers on a believer?

I was profoundly moved by this man. I knew him. He had tried to live alone, detached, cynical, modern, and the beings and forces of his world had caught up with him, knocked him down. He resembled me. I'd been beset by the same temptation, which had made me miserable, from myself. And then the experiences to which he'd delivered himself, the problems of all those people he'd taken under his care, had enriched him. I refused to disenchant his world. I sensed, without having an elaborated idea, that a treatment ignoring the forces against which he'd rubbed, would be doomed to failure. To consider him as a detached, solitary individual, trapped in an inner world similar to that of a Viennese neurotic, would only aggravate his distress, because the treatment—separating him from his god and the constraints of his world—would resemble the causes of his illness. By all logic, it was necessary at first to interpose between him and the spirits that were pursuing him; and, second, to encourage him to set himself right with his obligations. Perhaps he would end up being initiated into the healing techniques whose threshold he'd trespassed. The young intern in psychiatry devoted a great deal of time to this patient. He dedicated both his doctoral thesis and numerous presentations at professional meetings to him. Afterwards, the patient went to Senegal to meet the healers, the *boro-xam-xam*—a word in Wolof that signifies 'master of knowledge'—to deepen the knowledge he'd brushed up against. As could have been predicted, the patient overcame his crisis and reoriented his life.

Spirits, *djinna*s and *sheytané*s, were strangely familiar to me. I'd known them since childhood, like everyday beings. My mother, unlike my father, truly believed in neither God nor the devil; yet she always uttered a conjuration before pouring boiling oil in which she had browned fries into the sink: '*destour ya s'hab el ard.*' Literally, 'May it be according to your law, o owners of the earth.' In answer to my questions, she'd reply, 'It's better.' It's better? Better than what? She claimed that, this way, she avoided anyone getting burnt. I wasn't satisfied by this response. Then she would tell me that beings were said to exist beneath our feet, invisible beings we needed to respect, *afrit*s, a sort of local devil, it was said... 'By the old women,' my mother would confess, 'like your grandmother, for example. They claim that the inhabitants of the earth who live beneath our feet also have families, and if the oil we spilt ended up burning one of their children, their anger could be terrible.' She didn't know if it was true, but she'd found that whenever she uttered this formula, there was never an accident. According to the saying, 'it's best not to tempt the devil,' right? 'How does it hurt, after all, to utter a little sentence without any consequences if it could allow us to avoid difficulties? But there was much more to her formula, and she was not unaware of it. If humans use the word *destour*, 'according to your law', it's because they consider their own law—human law—to be subordinate to that of the owners of the earth, the *guen*s or *djinn*s in Egyptian Arabic, or *afarit*. Among all the invisibles that populated her everyday stories, I experienced some difficulty grasping her true feeling. She both laughed about the *afarit*s of believers even as she took them seriously. Because commerce with spirits is based not on a contract, not on honesty but on deceit or cunning, not on a word freely given but on constraint and a way of escaping. She told me about a legal case that had taken place in Cairo during the 1850s. A woman had pleaded before a religious tribunal that a spirit, an *afrit*, had made use of her body—in a word, had possessed her. The judges invoked the spirit. The woman presented herself. They had interrogated the spirit and it had responded through the woman's mouth. They had severely scolded the spirit for having shamelessly obstructed the unfortunate woman's mind. And the spirit had excused itself. In conclusion, they'd ordered it to leave the woman's body. And the spirit promised to go. My mother hooted with laughter—as if the spirit would obey a tribunal! It was evident that one could not trust an *afrit*'s word. And here I was finding these beings in the midst of my work, among people who not only knew them but were weakened by contact with them, coming up against their rules and their laws. My mother, who had known them as a child, was for a long time protected from them by the prayers of the good 'akham Entebi. No doubt they'd returned to pester her during her moments of panic or grief. At the end of her life, she would find them again in the suburban hospital where illness had thrown her. When I came to visit her, still befogged by the vapours of painkillers, she would tell me. 'They're at the end of the corridor, a whole family with bizarre heads. Seem to be Chinese.'

'Chinese? But what Chinese?'

She had seen them lining up in front of her door grimacing. One night, two of these beings had even come to make love right in front of her. She'd called for the nurse, but she was in cahoots with the devils and all three of them had lain together. ('On the Sabbath, can you believe it?') Her doctor had immediately sent in the psychiatrist on call. He questioned her, concluded that it was nothing more than a memory from the night. The psychiatrist confided in her, spoke to her of his studies, his divorce, his children . . . She gave him advice, suggested new ways of practising his profession. He emerged saying that a specialist in psychopathology had been hospitalized. But when night fell, anxiety invaded her again. 'I saw them last night,' she insisted. I would go to make sure that there was no one at the end of the hall and return to reassure her. She would say, 'Of course you didn't find them—they hid in your watch.' At that moment I had to act like the old rabbi, reciting a prayer over her and crafting a protective amulet I slipped it under her pillow so they would not return to disturb her during the night.

In 1978, I once again presented myself before my six commissioners at the Psychoanalytic Institute on the rue Saint-Jacques.

After all, although the dean of studies was the same, the others were all different. Yet they were also similar, with the same indifferent looks, the same way of making you feel you were seeking entrance into a private club or a secret masonic ritual, and that such a privilege had to be earned. One exception, however, was the beautiful and gentle Joyce McDougall who, during the interview, whispered that at the Psychoanalytic Institute they did not appreciate originals like me, but that was not how she thought. She concluded by distinctly letting me know that she would defend my candidacy. I thus had a reason to persist, like the flame of a Sabbath candle that refuses to be extinguished. I would continue on this quest that had possessed me since adolescence, but it no longer held the same importance. After all, it wanted nothing to do with me ... In my theoretical reflections, my interest in 'the Unconscious' was slowly beginning to dissipate, replaced more and more by my investigations, increasingly more complex and documented, into the spirits. The spirits were everywhere, in all the worlds, in all cultures, in all latitudes. I perceived them from afar, through the prisms of rationalistic condemnations, and from up close, enshrined in my family history, in the traditions of the world into which I'd been born. The spirits were beginning to seem more intelligent than the Uncon-scious, their pursuit less demoralizing, their knowledge richer and more complex. After all, before a 'manifestation of the Uncon-scious', one has only one option: to submit to its law. While withspirits, one can scheme, skirt around them, flatter them, bind them, lose them in labyrinths of amulets, toss them onto other victims or, for the most seasoned, enlist them in service to the therapist ... And this crafty commerce, now that I think about it in this moment of accounting, was more in keeping with my Levantine character. The concept of the Unconscious demands a quasi-Protestant transparency, its cult promoting that Platonic, terrorist idea—that the truth heals—to dominate, solely through its pronouncement. If it were unfortunately revealed to be true, Big Brother would in short shrift have set up his kingdom a long time ago. Already Foucault, in his courses at the College de France, was beginning to denounce the society under surveillance that a generalized psychoanalysis would foster, right up to the last little soldiers of social charity. In the end, I was admitted into the Psychoanalytic Institute as a student. I was delighted! At our next session, I greeted my psychoanalyst with a magnificent smile. Settled on the couch, I announced: 'I've just learnt that I've been admitted to the Psychoanalytic Institute.' She replied, tit for tat: 'And I most likely will be resigning.'

A grim story of exclusion lay at the origin of an uprising, and my psychoanalyst was part of it. Nicolas Abraham, who was only a provisional member of the society despite his experience and reputation, had again sought to be admitted to 'full' membership. He was one of the most creative clinicians of his generation. The reception of his truly strong and original published works by the wider psychoanalytic community was enthusiastic. His concepts were adopted, widely cited in the publications of other practitioners and discussed in seminars. Despite all this, the commission had again rejected his candidacy without explanation, as usual. But this time the 'youngsters', the practitioners between fifty and sixty years old, had protested, asking to learn the content of the deliberations. They discovered that Bela Grunberger, Abraham's analyst, had opposed his election by using against him some confidences he'd made on the couch. In itself, the fact was unsurprising. The psychoanalytic world lives in a generalized state of shamelessness. Each psychoanalyst has been on the couch of a full member to whom he has for years revealed the details of his life and the peculiarity of his character—and it is these same full members who judge the candidate and determine his progress within the institute. It is the most sophisticated system of surveillance, being the most economical, since the persons surveyed voluntarily discloses the information about themselves. But this time it was too much. The death of Nicolas Abraham, barely fifty-six, had not calmed things down, quite the opposite. The psychoanalysts of his generation, who'd worked with him and appreciated him, felt it was their duty to bring an end to the reign of self-denunciation. Nata Minor offered me no explanation, just a brief indication, something like, 'It's because of Nicolas Abraham.' I laughed in response: 'You're leaving the Institute! Be real. Leopards don't change their spots.'

She did in fact resign from the Institute on the rue Saint-Jacques, but I was comforted to learn that she was as rebellious as I. I could stop attributing my doubts and critiques to my invisible neurosis. The following year, I passed the test and began to teach psychology in the universities of the northern suburbs.

11

Prudence

1979. In those days, university admittance was a transparent process. My doctoral thesis on sexual communities had not gone unnoticed. Jean Guillaumin, professor of psychology and president of the Lyon Psychoanalytic Society, was on my thesis committee. He was a man of integrity, a true psychologist with a wide range of professional experience, including both experimental psychology and psychoanalysis, and a man who appreciated innovative ideas and case studies. He was impressed by my combination of field studies of sexual communities accompanied by meticulously documented clinical cases. He'd telephoned to alert me that his written evaluation would be favourable. Thus I found myself on the lists of candidates qualified for an assistant professorship. All that remained was for me to present myself to the universities. But there were hardly any positions. Alice Saunier-Deïté, the minister then, had decided to take revenge on students and universities. In order to neutralize the Great Fear, the legacy of the Red Plague that had threatened the powers-that-be, she was drastically cutting the funding for universities, imposing a hiring freeze, especially in the more vulnerable disciplines of the social sciences. Wasn't it there that the rebellion had fomented? from there that the hellions had arisen? The minister's grudge was deep-seated. Some institutions were seemingly completely abandoned, left to their own devices, it being only a matter of time before the faculty fell to the ground, crushed like rotten fruit. The minister had ordered the dismantling of the most turbulent and most active institution in the years following the events of 68—the University of Vincennes. She'd exiled it to the outskirts of Saint-Denis, on the site of a lycée still under construction, intended to accommodate less than a quarter of the enrolled students. 'I don't understand why they're protesting,' she complained, 'I've set them up on rue de la Révolution between avenues Lenin and Stalingrad. They should be happy there, among the Communists.' Even today, one can read, in gigantic letters at the entrance of the establishment, the strange inscription: 'University of Vincennes at Saint-Denis'. A short circuit, it was nothing but a short circuit. The faculty never accepted this expulsion to the edge of the highway in the middle of a concrete desert.

The minister's second gift to the Communist municipalities could be found 2 kilometres away in Villetaneuse, at the University of Paris 13, mired among wastelands, muddy roads and public housing projects. On early summer mornings, before the students and teachers had arrived, when only a few researchers were taking advantage of the calm to watch over their ants, spiders and mutant rats, you could see long lines of plastic chairs making their way to the cité Salvador-Allende—the spontaneous redistribution of the state's wealth to the neediest. I taught psychology there, as a lecturer. A position of assistant professor opened up, but only one. Many had been cooling their heels in front of the door, and for a long time. Serge Lebovici, who'd just been named professor of child and adolescent psychiatry at Bobigny, was part of the commission of so-called specialists judging the candidates. I'd met him two or three times before, at faculty meetings. He'd heard me present my views, had questioned me on my interest in ethnopsychiatry. He'd had my thesis in his hands, had perhaps even leafed through it. I made an appointment to see him.

He was a short man, quite corpulent, but with a supple and lively walk. My eyes were immediately drawn to his hands: surprisingly large, a mechanic's hands, hairy and muscular, as if they'd continued to grow after the rest of his body had abandoned the effort. But when you looked up at his eyes, you stayed fixed there, unable to turn away. They were of a transparent blue, limpid, a combination of curiosity and innocence, a child's eyes. He came towards me, greeted me warmly keeping my hand in his for a long time. 'I know why you're here,' he said straightaway, with a look of amusement.

I had assumed he'd be able to guess my intention. I could not have been the first to present himself like this; one could tell from the cohort of candidates lining up to see him. I remained silent, waiting for him to continue.

'I'm convinced it's an excellent idea,' he declared.

Was he telling me right off of his support? It didn't seem like him. He was rather of the give-and-take variety. He began to smile, then observed me for a moment before continuing: 'With the clientele in Bobigny, and your competencies, I think it would make sense to open an ethnopsychiatry clinic here.'

I must confess that until that moment, up until Lebovici uttered the words, I'd never thought of it.

Indeed, for several months we'd been discussing how to put ethnopsychiatry into service for migrant patients. I'd enlisted three friends from the seminar: Albert, an émigré from Morocco who spoke perfect Arabic; Inês, the Brazilian psychologist who evoked the ambiance of a song by Vinicius de Moraes; and Philippe, comrade-in-arms since childhood. But our ideas were still entangled in the web of theory. I gave a look of acquiescence, but continued to act as if I'd come for a consultation. It sometimes happens that events progress more quickly than our thoughts, as if a curtain were rising, allowing the world's intention to appear, within the space of an instant. Why then do we say that we are born from our past? Quite the contrary, we are children of our future.

Several days later, I ran into Antoine Guedeney, who has since become a renowned professor of child psychiatry. At the time, he was an intern in the agency. He hailed me: 'So, you came to propose a consultation in ethnopsychiatry to Lébo? Wonderful! When do you begin? I already have two or three cases to present to you.'

This was not the first time that events turned out this way, my body resisting, as if an exterior will was scheming. Chance? Unless it be something else, an unseen hand pushing me towards some unknown place. But to where?

Within half an hour, I undertook to present to Lebovici the project of this consultation that had been born right there and then, through the will of the unseen. The ideas flowed, emerging from nowhere. There would have to be several of us, because we would need to bring together the greatest possible number of languages spoken by the patients. And then, to tell the truth, we did not know, we'd never done it before . . . We would have to discuss, to formulate solutions step by step, as the problems presented themselves. Oh well, I envisioned holding our discussions in front of the patients. We would need at our disposal several competencies, several opinions, several languages. This consultation would also be pedagogical, open to interns and externs of the agency. In this way, we would be contributing to their training. Lebo was a little surprised, but saw the relationship between the modalities I was proposing and the psychodrama he was already leading with children. He too received patients amid a group of clinicians. The matter was quickly settled. He gave me his approval, set the day for the consultation, Friday morning, and requested a delay to alert his colleagues. He assured me that he would be present at the first session, to signify his full commitment to the project. I left his office with my head in the clouds, my entire being in a tumult.

The following Saturday, at lunchtime, not without pride, I presented the project to Devereux and the entire seminar. We would finally emerge from our little chapel, the ghetto in which we'd been confined, to publicly experiment with the revolutionary ideas of ethnopsychiatry, to demonstrate their power, as much to explain disorders as to contribute to their cure. I was fully aware that this was a radical innovation: there had never before been a consultation of this sort. But I did not think of myself as a creator, much less as a dissident. I saw myself as an agent, a kind of ambassador of Devereux's thought. He'd listened and rejoiced with me, then gone off to lead the seminar as he did every Saturday. The rest of us stayed behind with my acolytes to refine the project. That very evening, it must have been around 11 p.m., he called me on the telephone. His voice was graver than ever. After a few words of introduction, there was a long silence. He was waiting, as if expecting me to reveal something to him.

'Tobie, you have betrayed!' he finally ended up saying, 'Tobie, you've betrayed.'

'What do you mean, Georges? Why are you saying "I've betrayed"? And whom have I betrayed?'

'You know very well what you've done!'

I knew nothing at all and did not understand. I rapidly reviewed the events of that day and the preceding days. At first, I did not see what he could be alluding to. I had for a long time discussed with him the possibility of a future ethnopsychiatry consultation; I'd hidden nothing from him. He'd given me his blessing and even suggested that he might participate in it. Perhaps it was something else, perhaps that article for the journal I'd defended against his judgement? But we'd ended up in agreement. We would ask the author to review our edits of the second part of his text. During the preceding days, I had not advocated for any of his adversaries, one of the many who'd slipped from one day to the next into the category of 'enemies' or 'psychotics'. I truly did not understand. There was nothing with which to reproach myself. And Georges was refusing to provide the least explanation, solely repeating that 'I'd betrayed'. When I finally understood, my response was immediate. I had a true reaction of anger, one of those cold, deliberate angers that determine the course of a life. My voice flat, I replied slowly, weighing each word: 'Oh, I see!' I said, 'I understand what you are saying. In truth, your view of me has just been reversed. From an object of love, I've become an object of hate. I'm not the first and I certainly won't be the last. I've often seen individuals you admire suddenly lose your esteem, earning instead your spite and contempt. You played out this same scenario with Dick, with Arnaud, with Nicole . . .' I rattled off a long list of those who before me had fallen into disgrace with the master, perhaps a dozen of my fellow students. Surely, I even forgot some of them.

'We know each other too well,' I added in conclusion. 'You would like to spare me what comes next. Let's leave it at that.' And I abruptly hung up. We never again said a word to each other. I held strictly to the stance I'd adopted, ignoring the messages he sent me later through the intercession of one person or another. I'd worked with him for close to a decade, since the time of my apprenticeship, during my immersion in the infinite meanders of his thought and writing, dating as far as my early experience as his 'spiritual heir'. Well then, it would all end here, right now, on this Saturday evening in autumn. It was over. I refused the excommunication—mine, firstly, which I considered to be without cause, and also his. I refused to condemn him in my heart or mind. I had to preserve what I'd learnt, to not direct my anger against the theory he'd passed on to me. Devereux's judgement of people and events was very sensitive to the terrors that would suddenly overcome him. I knew this; I'd had occasion to witness it many times over. That's how he was, moulded by suffering, but proud, too, unconquered, distinctly antisocial. What came back to mind was a small ceremony organized at the École des hautes études in honour of Lévi-Strauss's seventy-fifth birthday. Levi-Strauss's colleagues were offering him for this occasion a book of homages. Each speaker had to state what part the old master had played in his development. As they succeeded one another at the microphone, each more pompous than the last, Lévi-Strauss remained as stiff as a commander's statue, accepting without reaction these conventional accolades that must have weighed on him. When his turn came, Devereux, who'd obviously not prepared anything, was content to describe an episode of a joint trip in 1946 after the war, during which they'd flirted with two girls on the boulevard, like tipsy young men. He used expressions such as 'you remember, don't you? you chose the blonde ... I was much bolder than you.' The audience burst out laughing, but the professors were not amused. 'Frankly, you can't take this one anywhere.' Surely, he'd done it deliberately. Devereux never submitted to social rules, or respected the conventions. That's what explained his isolation within the university community; but it was also his greatness, the measure of his freedom of thought.

As for me, I understood that in this difficult moment of rupture, he remained where he'd always been—in the position of master, to guide me for one last time. I decided that was his final lesson, teaching me how to take my leave.

Even today, I continue to think that in abruptly changing his attitude, he'd propelled me into the world, the way a father pushes his hesitant child into a deep pool. With one motion, one flick of his wrist, he'd transmitted to me the rage to keep on going. I saw him again one last time, five years later, in the meditation room of the columbarium, a few moments before his cremation. He'd requested that his ashes be scattered on the lands of the Mojave Indians, in accordance with their customs—a final thumbing of his nose at the collective. He who considered himself a child of nowhere, rejected by all, had decided to spend his death on an American Indian reservation. We were not very many, perhaps about twenty, all former students. With Andras Zempleni and Mariella Pandolfi, we isolated ourselves in a corner of the room. Mariella described his last years, choked by emphysema, rarely leaving his apartment. Andras and I could not accept what was happening. Strangely in accord that day, we both thought that the dead belonged to their community, no matter what wishes they'd expressed before their departure. Devereux's death deeply grieved me, not that I'd intended to see him again.

I felt that his death was as sad as his life, without family, without children. I was devastated. I kept mechanically repeating, like an automaton, 'One must not burn a Jew, even if he has requested it. It isn't done, especially not after the Shoah.'

Bobigny 1985

Like many senior psychoanalysts, Lebovici drew his clients from among the upper classes—very upper, in his case. He often gave me appointments for supervisory sessions in his luxurious apartment near the Pont de l'Alma, at 11 p.m., after the departure or his last patient, whose languorous fur coat I would brush against at the lift door. As I spoke with him, his eyes would droop with fatigue. He was falling asleep, suddenly waking up to toss out an unexpected remark. He ended his workday after midnight. He confided in me several times that that's when he could dedicate himself to his true interests. He too was 'of the night'. Fired from the public health service in 1941 by the Vichy laws against Jews, he'd for a long time remained outside the staff and hadn't obtained his position as a professor until the end of his career, in 1978. His admirers had followed him from the Alfred-Binet Centre all the way to his agency in Bobigny. Known as 'the women of the 13th', these student psychoanalysts under supervision cultivated the art of dressing well as much as that of speaking. It was odd to see them arriving there, in the heart of a working-class suburb, a few steps from Drancy, in their fancy cars that endlessly circled the hospital as they searched for parking. Every day, they took over the agency, skipping from one office to another seeking 'Lébo'. But on Friday mornings, when the patients from the ethnopsychiatry clinic arrived, Kabyle or Malian families with their many children, their sounds and their colours, along with the cohorts of social workers and teachers who accompanied them, the lovely adventuresses promptly disappeared. I should specify that Lebovici had given his office to me, and that there was always a crowd.

That particular morning, there were a good fifteen of us to welcome Prudence: psychiatrists from the clinic, the two interns, my students. Prudence was accompanied by a young psychologist, she too an apprentice psychoanalyst, surprised to see so many gathered for a single consultation. Prudence had been taken in by the shelter with her child, a little girl of two. For several weeks now, she'd been inactive, prostrate, as if dazed. She was seen several times by a psychiatrist who diagnosed her with depression and prescribed some strong medications, which had had no effect. Her condition was the same as on the first day.

'We've been able to establish that this sadness, this apathy, the inability to work and to take care of her child, in brief, her depression, dates back to her father's death,' the psychologist observed.

She turned towards Prudence to ask for her assent. Prudence answered in a barely audible voice. Yes, she felt that it was indeed since that moment, since her father's death.

She was from Cameroon, with Douala as her mother tongue; she spoke perfect French. A large woman, very large, of an imposing corpulence. After the psychologist completed her presentation, Prudence sank deeply into the armchair. She was impressive, a good head taller than me. I must have seemed very slight, sitting opposite her, at the heart of this assembly. She had a round, harmonious face, carefully made up. She was also beautiful. It was clear that she did not want to speak, that she felt any relationship with others was beyond her strength. Rather than questioning her, I drew closer and placed my hands on hers, for a long time, until I could feel their warmth.

'Close your eyes!' I asked, but she continued to keep them open, still a bit dazed. 'Relax, let yourself go,' I pressed on. 'Close your eyes now.'

She accepted. She closed her eyes. After a moment, I sensed that she'd grown calmer; she'd stopped blinking. The silence in the office thickened, as if it acquiring a kind of density. You might have thought she'd fallen asleep. That's when we heard her breathing grow more rapid, louder and louder. Her eyelids began to flutter, then her lips opened, as if she wanted to articulate some words that weren't coming out. She was shaking her head as if fighting against something, or someone. We heard gurgling sounds, saw furious inner movements. Then all her limbs began to quiver. Her chair was agitated, scraping the floor. I sensed my colleagues trembling. Prudence was grimacing. She seemed to be suffering. Anxious, the psychologist rose, hoping to wrap her arm around Prudence's shoulders. With a slight gesture, I signalled that she should return to her seat. Suddenly, Prudence opened her eyes wide—too wide, much too wide—fixed. And then there was something was like an explosion. A strong voice, a man's deep voice, emerged from her—not from her mouth, but from much deeper within, from her chest, her belly.

'Who are you, who are you?' the voice violently asked me. I jumped; I suspect my co-therapists, who'd been sitting still, were even more surprised. It was incomprehensible—and frightening—to suddenly hear such a powerful male voice emerging from this woman who, a few minutes earlier, could not utter a single word. Our minds were racing, imagining that the being that had possessed this powerful body might project itself against the objects in the room, would throw itself on us. Fear is congealed imagination. We were afraid. To top it all off, the voice was speaking to me familiarly,

'Who am I? But what difference can it make to you?' I replied, forcing myself to remain calm. 'I'm the one who should be asking you this question. Who are you?'

Again silence. I insisted: 'I asked you who you are, you who came here uninvited.'

'What is this? Who am I? But I'm her father!' the voice thundered.

Was that it? The deceased man briefly mentioned at the start of the session had arisen without warning. I was overcome. It was the first time such a thing had happened to me. Of course, I know I could have ended the session right then and drawn Prudence from her state, interrupted this improvised shadow drama. But I pursued the dialogue, I crossed the line, overstepping the bounds.

'Her father?' I continued 'I don't believe it, not one bit! A dead father who comes like this to persecute his daughter until she becomes ill, melancholic . . . is most certainly not a father.'

Again, a long silence. Prudence still had her eyes closed. I confess I was afraid at the thought that the being I'd just defied, which for the moment was manifesting itself solely through words, would decide to move, or even to push against me. I must say that if it had decided to take me by the collar, I would have been unable to resist it.

'Yes, I am her father,' the voice concluded, sounding less violent, more conciliatory. 'I'm taking care of her, here where I am. I've even found a husband for her.'

'A husband from among the dead?' I jeered, 'That's a good one, that's really something! And you claim to want good for your daughter? Here's proof that you're not her father.'

Another prolonged silence. Then the voice finally declared, 'I want to see my children.'

At this statement, Prudence rubbed her eyes. She groaned as if waking up.

'Gently,' I cautioned, 'return gently.'

She was holding her head in her hands. I felt the assembly relax, reassured by the restoration of the world's rational order.

'She must have a very bad headache,' said Loubaba, then a very young intern and later an accomplished translator of both Moroccan languages and the language of the spirits.

Loubaba hastened to Prudence's side, bringing her a glass of water, stroking her cheeks. Prudence drank greedily. She had some trouble returning to us.

'Why does he insist on seeing his children?' I asked.

'It's strange, what you said a little while ago,' replied the psychologist accompanying Prudence. 'It's strange because you didn't know that he's not actually her true father, not her progenitor. Prudence is the child from her mother's first marriage. It was not her biological father, after all, who died.'

The patient rose, adjusted her clothes and stood up quite straight in front of me. She now looked as if she'd somewhat returned to earth. We arranged to meet again in two weeks. I asked her if it was possible for her brothers and sisters to attend the consultation. It would be difficult—the whole family was living in Cameroon. But she would ask them ... Considering the gravity of what had been broached here, perhaps they would agree. Everyone in the family knew that the father had left 'with his eyes open'.

'With his eyes open?'

'I'm not sure,' Loubaba ventured, 'but among us, when we say that someone has left with "his eyes open", it means they died while carrying a secret to the grave.'

'Yes,' Prudence confirmed, 'that's also what we say back home.'

Chatting at the end of the session: retrospective terror, doubts, questions, debates. The responses were all over the place. 'And so? Do you believe in revenants now?'

'It wasn't a question of believing in this or that. Had I even asked for anything? Not the least induction: I never once suggested that the father could return. He imposed himself upon us, with all the strength of his voice. Do you remember how surprised you were?'

'Yes, but why did you open with that moment of relaxation? Why did you ask her to close her eyes? Aren't you the one who provoked this hysteric scene? What got into you? What were you thinking?'

'I don't know. She seemed to be suffering so much, as if she were straining to hide a secret. Once the voice appeared . . . her father's voice, you will note, not Prudence's voice, but a deep male voice.'

'Okay, yes, of course, but once we heard the father's voice, why did you engage in a dialogue with it? Didn't you sense you were in the presence of a charlatan?'

'But why do you say "charlatan"? . . . If the Doualas of Cameroon have the custom of controlling their succession in this way . . .'

'Okay, okay, we didn't use the right word. Usurper, then?'

'You say "usurper" . . . Now you've correctly understood the course of this session. The voice, which did not seem to recognize my legitimacy, was accusing me of usurpation. Here you are then on the side of those who want to make this woman ill.'

Two months and several sessions later, the other children arrived from Cameroon for Prudence's consultation. They were gathered one Friday morning in the office of the chief of psychiatry at the Avicenne Hospital in Bobigny. Present were Pasteur, the eldest, a strapping fellow close to 2 metres tall, with a refined look, a distinguished man who'd managed to leave his real estate business for a few days. And Justin, an elegant steward for an airline company. And Amandine, a sort of 'Mama-Benz' who sold luxury lingerie in the villages in the north of the country. Two of Prudence's siblings were missing. Still, she seemed satisfied to have convinced the eldest, the most influential. She'd also invited Justine, a Cameroonian friend living in France, to help with the translation. During the preceding session, the father had expressed his desire to speak in Douala. There had never been so many people in the consultation. We had to leave in order to bring chairs from the internal medicine clinic.

Prudence, who was beginning to get used to it, sat in the same chair, awaiting that little moment of relaxation that had become our ritual of entry into the matter. Her two brothers and her sister, along with her guest, Justine, were clearly terrified. They seemed to be anticipating what might arise. This time, I'd barely brushed Prudence's hands before the voice roared.

And the father began to enumerate his demands. Pasteur, the eldest, should take charge of the family, and above all organize the funeral. 'The funeral?' I was confused. Hadn't their father been buried? Pasteur briefly explained: 'A burial is not a funeral.' Ah! He must mean a 'second funeral', during which the entire clan gathers in order to establish the deceased among his relatives in the world of the dead. Pasteur, who managed the family's real estate, should also watch over the family plot in the village, located today in

Douala's large suburb. He knew what he would have to do there: meetings with the elders, offerings, sacrifices.

I cast a look in his direction.

He'd paled. His lips were trembling, as if he were about to burst into tears; or as if he too would offer his body and his voice to the wandering soul. But no, he was frightened, that's all. And then, as is often the case with those who come from worlds that have not renounced the multiplicity of beings, he dreaded the traditional charges. He knew what they would cost in time, money and responsibilities. But after what had just happened here, he would do it, that's for sure!

Then the voice addressed Amandine: 'Money is like cowries. It is made to circulate, to pay for the passages between the worlds, not to be hidden under beds deep inside calabashes.' Why didn't she give some to the family? Didn't she know that in truth she was the head of the family? I looked at the three visitors who'd come from so far. They were shocked, perplexed. They did not understand. But they did not for a moment doubt that their father was present, that he was speaking, that he was stirring them up, calling them back to order.

Again, as in every consultation we'd had with Prudence, a long silence ensued. We'd learnt that as long as she did not stretch, as long as she did not rise from her chair, he was still present. No one reacted, each firmly in place, those who believed in the return of the dead and those who did not, all struck by the same stupor.

Then, the voice addressed me: 'And you, what are you doing here?'

Prudence was not moving, not one gesture, ensconced in her armchair. The others lowered their eyes. I assumed they were hoping that reason would triumph in the end, that they would obtain an explanation.

'Why are you listening to our family stories?' the voice resumed. 'You're not even Black.'

I took my time before replying: 'There are some people, you see, who are white on the outside and black on the inside.'

That's what I finally said ... A formula that was like a riddle or a charade, and which, I knew, bound him in knots of perplexity. He might well be her father, but he lived under the law of beings. Beings are not reason. They are lies; they are cunning; they are brute force. In Hebrew, we say *ched*, 'spirit', but the root of the word means 'force', neither positive nor negative, a wild, untamed force. I thought of Odysseus grappling with Proteus. He needed to resist the lies, the metamorphoses of the old man of the sea. One cannot convince beings—one can only deceive them.

It was then, after this formula I'd invented on the spot, that Prudence emerged from her—what to call it? hypnotic? sublunary?— state as painfully as during the preceding sessions, only this time she was crying. Loubaba and the psychologist rushed to her side, surrounding her, trying to console her. Her sister, Amandine, offered her a tissue from a distance, not daring to draw too close. She knew that beings had the propensity to leap from one human to another. Prudence was still crying. I turned towards Pasteur. In answer to my unspoken question, he declared, distraught, 'This time he's really gone. It's now that everything begins.'

I was thinking about the distance that separates an ethnologist from the other worlds he manages to study. Devereux had died a few months earlier, alone, with no one to say the least word on the day of his funeral. Years later I learnt, from one of my students who'd gone to visit the Mojave reservation in Parker, Arizona, amid the cactus and the rattlesnakes, that the Mojave had accepted Devereux's remains without much enthusiasm. Very few of the elders who'd known him were left, and it was only after a long council that they finally agreed to welcome his memory. There was hardly anything in their minuscule museum—nothing, only his first book, *The Sexuality of the Mojave Indians*. What a difference from that man who'd died in Cameroon, who could summon all these people from thousands of miles away to signify his will to his survivors. I left the session a little destabilized. I had the sense of having accomplished something, that I'd done my duty as a therapist, relieving Prudence of a burden that was oppressing her. But as I reread the notes on the series of consultations, I felt that I was more like a notary. Surely the father had left to his children, his family, indications about his legacy. Although adopted, Prudence was his favourite. Perhaps that was why he'd designated her as his messenger. Or had it been her position as the eldest? Or what?

Four or five years later, it must also have been a Friday morning, I climbed onto a bus at the Saint-Lazare Station in Paris. I was on my way to the Sorbonne, to take part in a thesis jury. I noticed a seat in the back. I wanted to take advantage of the trip to reread my notes. I sat down, absorbed, automatically apologizing as I took my seat.

'Excuse me, ma'am . . .'

The woman turned to me: 'But we know each other,' she exclaimed, astonished.

I looked up: that same round face, the same deep look. She was beside me again!

'Yes,' Prudence insisted. 'Don't you remember? You took care of my father, a few years ago, in Bobigny.'

Of her father? Yes, certainly, but also of her, I hope. I didn't know what to say. In some ways, she'd been so close, yet so enigmatic at heart. After the last session, during which she received the dead man's recommendations, I'd never had any news—only a telephone conversation with the psychologist who informed me that Prudence had left the shelter and resumed her work.

'How's it going?' I asked Prudence now.

She gave me an odd look. I repeated: 'Is everything okay?'

'Do you mean me? How am I? Yes, I'm okay, but . . .'

'What's wrong?' I asked.

'It would be best if I went to the other end of the bus,' Prudence replied. 'You'll understand why.'

* * *

In 1996, in Cotonou, still with Lucien, we were returning from a dinner at the home of Therese Agassou, a psychiatrist from Benin, an exceptional woman, who knew how to make modern science compatible with the respect owed to the dead and to the divinities. In Africa, intelligence is always multiple.

It must have been around midnight. The day had been intense, among the Gibigowiwés, 'the white souls' of the evangelical church where we spent our days observing strange ways of caring for psychological suffering. As always, I was playing the game. It was much harder to convince Lucien to prostrate himself, to sing the psalms, to go into ecstasy, in the true meaning of the word, before the trances unleashed by the priest as he sought the diabolical beings he was exorcizing by the score in the name of Jesus. We'd decided to return on foot to take advantage of the relative coolness of the night. At the intersection, the residents of the neighbourhood were gathered for an intense festival. They'd brought out their drums of all sizes, and all the young people were taking turns in amazing displays of virtuosity. All around us, the dance contest was giving way to acrobatic feats such as I had never before seen. I asked Lucien if he knew what was motivating this nighttime exuberance. Without hesitation, he replied that they were honouring a dead person. And to see the intensity of the festival, the number of participants, it must have been someone important. Sadness is not a necessary reaction to the loss of a loved one. Compassion is often nothing but an obligatory attitude. A dead person is alive. To witness the joy of these dancers, the person who was being honoured that night had been unusually dynamic. One of the names by which Jews designate a cemetery is *beit el hayim*, 'the house of the living'. They also know that the dead regenerate the living as long as they are treated properly. *Let the survivors bury the dead* . . . so that they can reap the benefit of the power of those who are born at death. Let the dead bless the living!

My mother died in 1999. When I returned with my father to spend the night in that same apartment in Garges-lès-Gonesses where they'd lived for more than three decades, it was the first time

I heard him eulogizing her. 'She was a remarkable woman, with exceptional intelligence, an intelligence that does not exist in anyone else,' he declared.

Surprised, I didn't know what to say. During these last years after my father retired, they had remained alone, in an interminable face-to-face, that sometimes became a psychodrama. He would tease her, criticize her, make fun of her family. They argued a great deal. In truth, they were bored. My mother would sometimes call me to describe the suffering he was causing her. I would listen for a long time without saying a word, then conclude by suggesting, 'If you can no longer bear it, you can always get a divorce.' This usually calmed her down. And here was my father enumerating her virtues, glorifying her, honouring her, lamenting her. 'And the poor thing, she suffered so much during these last years. The damp had penetrated her bones. She could hardly walk.' It was too much. A tear began to trickle down my cheek. I dissolved into sobs. It was the first time I'd wept since our departure from Egypt—I mean, the first time I'd wept with grief. It did not last long. My father's surprised look was enough to interrupt the abandon I'd allowed myself for this brief instant. He was not crying. We do not cry. By his invocations, he'd incited tears the way the old women did at home in Egypt, enumerating the virtues of the departed. Her name was Rena, to sound Italian, a contraction of Regina, 'the queen'. Her real name should have been Malka in Hebrew, or Malika in Arabic. And then she was called Rena, which later slipped towards Renée when the family became infatuated with Frenchness. That's what her cousins called her, and the friends she'd made in France. Now that she was gone, about to be reborn elsewhere, my father called her by her nickname, Ranou. And that night, he repeated it endlessly. His sister-in-law, Eva, his brother's wife, had departed a little before my mother, leaving my mother as the last woman in the family, at least in France. This griot, able to recite the genealogies for a dozen generations, was buried without a single old woman, without any professional mourner. Once again, my father compensated for the lack, the absence of mourners during the *shiva*, the 'seven'. Jews evoke the dead for seven days, praying, welcoming anyone who'd known them, tirelessly evoking the memory of the deceased. During these seven days, sorrow is acceptable, the excess permitted only to the closest. Afterwards, they accompany the dead person with daily prayers for one year, generally the time of their journey into the world of the dead. Some arrive more quickly, some more slowly. The wisest know how to read the progression of the dead by the modifications of the objects remaining among the living—the *mezuzah*s, for example, those scrolls affixed to the doorjambs of entryways. During this year, sorrow is unwelcome, the evocation of the dead is perceived as suspect, sometimes perverse. Among Jews, death is impure and can contaminate the living, especially the most vulnerable. One avoids speaking of the dead in front of children, or before someone recently bereaved, for fear that they will be sullied. But the Jews of Egypt, even while respecting the prohibitions, maintained a close relationship with their dead. At least once a year, they would go as a family to the Bassatine cemetery to eat with them. They would set themselves up in the concessions, in the cellars, sometimes even on the mortuary stones, to spend the day. They bring with them a picnic meal of favas and bread, which they would eat on top of the graves. They were careful not to pick up the crumbs that escaped from their meal. They thought of them as food for the dead. After all, we lived in Egypt, a land that since a long time ago, well before the pharaohs, knew how to honour the dead. My mother would certainly have welcomed such a treatment; she deserved it. For how long would the Jews of Egypt be able to continue to exist without Egypt?

She was a tiny woman, as delicate as a twelve-year-old child. Most of the time she spoke out of obligation, because you very well had to say something in front of people, because it wasn't right to keep silent. But she suffered from it, she contracted beneath the effort and forced herself to find an intellectual interest. She raised me poorly, having passed down to me the habit of always looking for the person with whom it was worthwhile to spend time. Even when I did not see her, *kanet be allini*, an Arabic expression *salli*— difficult to translate. Under duress, one could render it by the verb 'to distract' or, more precisely, those persons with whom one does not regret spending time. Perhaps one could translate it as 'keeping company'? That's it: she kept me company. Those endless discussions about our family, about Egypt where we were all born and where none of us would be buried, these moments of fulfilment, of serenity, that's what I miss the most . . .

Once my mother was dead, I changed. The dead are nothing like the living persons they had been. My mother also changed! When she was alive, I would never have imagined leaving the country where she was, not even the city. The distress I saw in her eyes nailed me to the spot. In 1977, after I had completed the third cycle of my thesis, Devereux had arranged with Georges Devos, from the Department of Anthropology at the University of California, Berkeley, for me to go there as a postdoc student. I found a thousand reasons to decline the proposal. But once my mother entered the world of the dead, she was different. Alive, she would hold me back; dead, she was pushing me forward. Africa, where I'd gone on numerous occasions—to Mali, to Benin, to Togo, to Burkina Faso, to Senegal—for short stays in quest of healers of madmen was beckoning. I made my decision. In 2000, I was a tenured professor in my university, the dean of my faculty, the director of the institute of distance teaching, with more than 5,000 students, vice-president of the university and the head of an innovative ethnopsychiatry lab. As soon as the opportunity presented itself, I accepted a position in the diplomatic service without hesitation. From one day to the next, I found myself in Bujumbura, in Burundi, where I discovered an Africa I did not know, as poor as the poorest in West Africa. Nevertheless, I did not find there the multitude of languages, nor the proliferation of fetishes. The people were sad,* wandering like ghosts through the mists on the hills. Ten years earlier, in 1993, a year before the massacre in Rwanda, there had been a terrible massacre there, which had left more than three hundred thousand dead, often without burial, without rites, almost without memory, except for that dark miasma hanging over the city. A little more than a year before my arrival, one November night, Dr Kassy Manlan, a representative from the World Health Organization, had been assassinated after publicly denouncing the disappearance of funds designated for the purchase of anti-malarial drugs. His corpse, bound and weighted down with stones, thrown into Lake Tanganyika, strangely spared by the crocodiles, had risen to the surface, God knows how, pointing a finger at the highest authorities of the state. Three months after my arrival, in July 2003, Agathon Rwasa's rebels were attacking the city. One night I heard them coming down from the hills to cries of '*Vive Jesus*! We will take Jerusalem.' They were children, twelve to fifteen years old, barely able to hold their Kalashnikovs, too heavy for their small, emaciated arms. They'd been rendered insane by crude drugs, inhaled glue, petrol infused in their ears. I could hear bullets crackling against the wall of the house. Anxious, thinking there must be something that could be done, I telephoned the French ambassador, my superior in the hierarchy. He burst out laughing: 'If you're afraid, take refuge in your bathtub. They're usually made of cast iron. It seems they're good protection against bullets.' Welcome to the Ministry of Foreign Affairs! The next day, a Sunday, a heavy silence had descended upon the city. Wanting to see the outcome of the night's fighting. I went out. The corpses were literally nailed to the wall, riddled by large-calibre bullets. The government had sent the army to arrest the rebels. The machine guns and the ancient Panhard EBR tanks had been sprayed with Canon 75 field guns. It was carnage. That day, they counted close to three hundred dead—barely a paragraph in the French press. When I was able to watch the evening news televised by France 2, the transmission lasted thirty seconds and was not repeated during the following days. It seemed that no one was interested in the Burundian disorder. But unlike the living, the dead are not fazed by political cynicism. They would express their demands in an unexpected manner.

His name was Gustave. He was a gigantic crocodile some 6 to 7 metres long—a monster! One day, when I'd ventured into the

Ruzizi valley, I saw him from afar, dozing on a bank, with two females at his side. He was so big, they in contrast looked like lizards. I stood there, fascinated by this creature that seemed to have emerged from a science-fiction flick. Gustave was a maneater. He'd begun to develop the taste after the massacre of the Tutsis, who were thrown by the Hutus into the river by the hundreds. Later, after the disappearance of the corpses, he continued to seek human flesh. He watched for fishermen who ventured into the water to cast their lines, snatching them to devour them in the depths. Several hundred victims were attributed to him—five hundred, it was said. They'd tried everything to eradicate Gustave. He'd been chased, fired at with rifles and even machine guns—but the bullets ricocheted off his armour. And he was cunning. In 2004, a team of journalists led by a renowned naturalist, a specialist in large reptiles, had tried to capture him. They'd built a gigantic trap made of aluminium rings that the team had larded with pieces of flesh cut from human backs. The trap was laid, the bait replenished every night, sometimes with a goat, sometimes a bull. Armed with their cameras, they spied on Gustave. For one month, he did not reappear. Tired of struggling, they packed their bags. They recounted their adventure in a documentary entitled *Capturing the Killer Croc*, later rebroadcast on a French network. But they had not so much as turned their backs before Gustave devoured a new victim. After that, the crocodile became a true myth. Everyone, without saying so, thought of him as the incarnation of remorse, a sort of giant Erinye sprung from unjustly spilt blood, the earth's anger turned against its inhabitants.

He was photographed again in 2007.

It is dangerous to neglect the dead. It's not a question of turning it into a mystique, all the same! What is this world in which one is interested only in the well-being of the survivors and never in the fate of the dead?

12

Amokrane in Parliament

Migrants wander around naively. Not having mastered the implicit codes, they accept the natives' words at face value. I heard 'thought', I heard 'research', I heard 'writing', and I latched onto them. I'm still glued to them, right up until this text taking shape before my eyes, ultimately a new exercise in sincerity. I continue to believe that you cannot convince through reason what you have learnt from experience. People have listened to me, it's true, people have read me, imitated me, plagiarized me, criticized me, slandered me, attacked me . . . I know that some did not like the originality I expressed. I, who never knew how to participate in the life of the chapel, I never learnt that sometimes you should keep your mouth shut.

The ethnopsychiatry clinic I developed during the last decades of the century was in keeping with the metamorphoses of French society. I was among the first to draw attention to the impact of new populations, on the unprecedented dynamism engendered by their presence, on the specifics of the beings, the invisible ones who'd followed them here. Having myself undergone the journey of migration before them, I knew its twists and turns; I thought about it with sympathy, without fear of complexity. A few thinkers, true ones, who feared neither diversity nor sidelong glances, agreed to engage with me. They were not many, and they did not come from my discipline. Isabelle Stengers, the first, offered to share long afternoons of discussion with me. Astonished by the tender blue of her eyes, her lovely hands, their fingers stained by the hand-rolled cigarettes that never stopped burning, I remain fascinated by the form of her intelligence, sharp as a scalpel. She does not speak *about* philosophy, she *creates* it. Uninhibited, she falls asleep as soon as you recite before her the commonplaces of the history of philosophy. I loved her—I love her still, she who knows how to tell me what I am unaware of. During the eighties, Isabelle was interested in atypical individuals, those who were barely tolerated within their own disciplines. She'd written a book with Prigogine. She'd just completed a book on Leon Chertok—the doctor, prince of therapists—who'd come straight from pre-war Russia, with his lordly manners. I'd known Chertok years before, during my apprenticeship. He always made me change my views. He taught me the technique of hypnosis, although he himself had no need for any technique. It was easy for him to make the patient's arm numb, to put a coin on it and to suggest that it was burning. When he removed the coin, the student would see a circle of burnt flesh before their eyes. When questioned, he replied that there was a mystery in hypnosis that had nothing to do with suggestion, transference, or any other known factor. He would repeat that when it came to hypnosis, you had to accept that you knew nothing. We who listened to him would think that he was deploying the tricks of a magician. What followed justified him. I admired Chertok. He was one of those rare psychoanalysts endowed with courage. He'd demonstrated it during the Occupation, as a young Russian emigré, an active member of the 'red orchestra', a spy network. He went through the war in the midst of occupied Paris by passing himself off as a French aristocrat. How did he manage, with his Russian accent so thick you could cut it with a knife? He'd taken some real risks in the fight against the Nazis, most likely laughing off the difficulties, as he still did. That's what Chertok was like. And so afterwards, he never let himself be affected by his colleagues who gave him the cold shoulder, thinking of him as a common juggler and deliberately treating him as a hysteric. I, for one, knew he was a real *mensch*, as they say in Yiddish.

In 1995, I wrote a book with Isabelle Stengers, *Medicins et sorciers* (*Doctors and Healers*), a simple, clear book, presenting the richness of the therapeutic thoughts carried by migrants—possession by spirits, the vengeance of the dead, attacks of sorcery. My colleagues, the psychoanalysts, wondered how to shut me up. After reading it, a well-known ethnologist, wild with rage, threw it to the ground and literally trampled on it. Isabelle laughed. I was afraid. I had good reason to be. Common thought, recited everywhere, can prove to be deadly. Once again, I'd behaved as I had during my early school days. I'd said who I was and proclaimed it at the top of my lungs. Through Isabelle, I met Bruno Latour whose erudition had not clouded his imagination. An immense gentleman, something like De Gaulle, a little stooped, with bushy eyebrows, a notebook in hand, he seemed to be constantly bent over the poor world.

Bruno is a painter whose brush is made of words and colours. We came together around his interest in what we both called 'beings', the non-humans, and our common passion for their ecology. As for me, I flushed them out, meeting them in the fire of my consultations; sometimes I invoked them. As for him, he tirelessly constructed systems to always welcome them. A sort of Einstein of anthropology, he expanded our universe.

Our meetings were orchestrated by Philippe Pignarre, a demiurge of electric subtlety. He had maintained his militant practice of bringing an audience to its feet. He'd even succeeded in clarifying the pronouncements of a pharmaceutical lab. For this feat alone, a statue should be erected in his honour. From the heart of this laboratory, with Isabelle's help, he launched a publishing imprint, the aptly named Les empecheurs de penser en rond—'the preventers of circular reasoning'. Soon, we named our little group, 'Recalcitrance', this 'band of four' that had decided to resist commonplace thought. We would discuss writers who were delivering the social sciences from the platitudes in which they were already mired, which has only gotten worse since then. Philippe published Richard Pollak, Mikkel Borch-Jacobsen, Bertrand Meheust, Robert Garrett, Ian Hacking, Sue Estroff, Vinciane Despret, and many others. Later, still others joined us, thinkers who saw themselves in our refusal to submit to conventional thinking, to accept formulae that invariably become persecutory facts.

Catherine Clement also approached me. There are only a few people with whom friendship ripens over time, to the point where their presence becomes a given, as if they had always been there, as a part of your family, so to speak. Catherine Clement became for me the big sister I never had. I never saw anything like her, a gifted child who remained that way. Her mind still sparkles with the curiosity she had at the age of four. She is passionately interested in human beings. Like Freud, I've never understood the biblical injunction to 'love thy neighbour as thyself'. How can you love the whole world, or rather, each one? I love my family, my friends, my lovers; I love authors in whom I've found thoughts that seduced me; I love people whose actions seem courageous to me, decisive or even simply important. But my love is always the result of a selection. How can one love one's neighbour? No matter who? She can do it! She does it! When she read my work, she didn't know me. She took the first step, she invited me to think with her, the way a child invites another child to play marbles. You can't say no! We talked, for a long time. Today, we still talk just as much. We sometimes argued. We wrote a book together, laying out our conflicts. We disagree on many unimportant issues: on God, on psychoanalysis, on the way to conduct political battles. But we are united on the essential—to do everything to make life more intense.

There was also the subtle Frédéric Pagès, intelligent and facetious, who grew up in the same northern suburbs of Paris, a man with a fiery pen and gentle tongue. He's the one who hides behind the insolent Botul, who treats philosophy and philosophers as we should never have stopped doing, with humour. He assailed me with questions, smilingly caught me in my contradictions, wanted to look with his eyes and his hands into every detail of the objects I'd fashioned. Both of us knew that we shared the same love for a developing, modern consensus which recognizes the power of thought among the poor.

I was too timid, also too proud, to take the smallest step. They all came to me, as did several others as well. They have each, at one time or another, participated in the ethnopsychiatry consultations, joining our group of therapists, each introducing their own investigations, their own ways of understanding and acting. It is fitting that the therapeutic space be made up of numerous intelligences, that it be as rich, as full, as the world itself.

Saint Denis, 1997

2 p.m. The setting for the creation of the world: a large room, able to hold some thirty chairs arranged in a circle. Each person sits where they choose. In the centre, a low table, covered with African fabrics, and a note of warmth—coffee, tea, cakes. There are rules of hospitality when one receives strangers. When Abraham the patriarch perceived two unknown individuals coming towards him from afar, he hastened to prepare a meal and threw himself to the ground to wash their feet. For him, the visit of strangers was an opportunity to seize, and not, as has been claimed, because he loved his neighbour, but because he knew that the one whose face you've never seen before, whose name or country or father you don't know, could be revealed to be God in person, God in the guise of a human. And so, since then, whoever receives strangers about whom he knows nothing, owes them everything. That was our philosophy.

Amokrane entered the consultation room with some apprehension. He was a stiff little man, hardened by mountain labours and guerilla winds. He soberly considered the faces of those who, not wanting to make him uneasy, kept their heads down, as if taking notes. He looked questioningly, hesitating, from one chair to the next. His wife, a young woman, her face tortured with anxiety, was making every effort to disappear—but how to do so in a circle? I like that moment of tumult that precedes the beginning of consultations, that hubbub that imitates the banality of the everyday, underlining that here it's about life and without ceremony. Once everyone was settled, conversation ceased and attention was directed at the sufferer, Amokrane. Abdelhamid was there, breathing innocence, with the limpid look he claimed to have inherited from the Greeks of *The Iliad*. He too, like Amokrane, had a fist as hard as wood. When he shook your hand, you didn't know whether you were holding a human or a fetish. Abdelhamid had completed part of his apprenticeship in Kabylia in the sixties under the direction of teachers from Egypt. I liked to trade Arab proverbs with him, like stamp collectors who trade stamps. He straddled languages, letting his thoughts roam in search of unexpected etymologies. Abdelhamid, the subtle one, who would one day discover the truth in a tiny detail of the analysis of a word.

In orderly worlds, introductions never begin with a person's name. One does not say, 'Who are you? What is your name?' But 'What village are you from? Which is your family? Who is your father? Who is sending you to me?' One knows that every stranger is a messenger. In anticipation of this consultation, Abdelhamid had gone to meet Amokrane at his home, a kind of courtesy visit. They'd first introduced themselves according to the rules, exchanging information about the origins of their names, the lives of their ancestors, the Marabout brotherhoods to which they'd been attached in Kabylia. Amokrane continued to speak with Abdelhamid in Kabyle, to dispel his boredom and also to reduce the apprehension that was putting his stomach in knots, which he would not acknowledge. It is not right for a man to fear encounters with others. When I returned from lunch, I surprised them both still pursuing continuing their endless discussion about origins. Mariam was also there, a young woman from Senegal, proud, her neck erect, her head like that of a dogon figurine. With every movement, she was crumpling the colours of her bazins. Her long fingers played with the reflections of her gold, the gold on her hands brushing the gold on her face. She kept her eyelids half-shut, as if to hide the dazzling visions passing through her. In the waiting room, she poured the mint tea, offered the pastries, her eyes lowered, miming humility—with a dash of mockery—like a well-bred African woman. Mariam, with a timeless beauty, who transformed the trivial into ontological questions. She knew women's secrets, hidden since the beginning in the distribution of shells on the sand. Every now and then, she hinted at this knowledge.

Also, Viviane, a tender creole, her head filled with political strategies, and her heart with love songs. Beneath the mask of her huge, ingenuous eyes, you could find, depending on the day, the rigour of a computer or the wild passion of the islands. And then there was Alhassane, tall Peule from Manding, who moved to the rhythm of a chameleon's crawl. To show that he was listening, he was resting his chin in the hollow of his hands opened like a chalice. I never knew what he was really thinking, Alhassane, who above all liked to exchange greetings for hours. Perhaps he knew how to decipher, by hearing one detail, such a sign of an ancestor, such a constraint of a devil. Perhaps he wanted to reproduce his days in Kankan, sitting cross-legged at the foot of the cheesemaker, lost in contemplation of sand. Or he was listening in the depth of his memory to the music of the griots singing the epic of Soumaoro. I introduced each of them to Amokrane, specifying their place of origin and the languages they knew, slipping in a word about each. At the sound of his name, Alhassane respectfully bowed his head, bringing his hand to his heart. I noted Amokrane's reaction, clucking at this excess of Muslim politeness.

Also present was Genevieve, the *rouée* who'd traversed Congo, Zaïre and Central Africa to end up here, in this Paris of multiple charismatic churches that reminded her of her native Brazzaville, or Kine-la-belle, Kine-sur-Seine. She knew the languages from there, Munukutuba, Lingala, Szngo, Swahili. Her dark skin vividly highlighted the petulance of her clear eyes. Despite having raised six living children, she knew better than anyone how to sketch out a Michael Jackson dance step. Geneviève was life, towards and against everything. She said she had a spider in her belly that let her know the malevolent intentions secretly nourished by her interlocutors. And the spider did not hesitate to throw itself on the hypocrite in the secret of his nights. And so, the person fell ill or else went through a period of bad luck and Geneviève would nod her head knowingly.

Facing a clinical situation that left us puzzled, Geneviève always had the simple idea that no one had yet thought of. By the look on her face, Amokrane did not inspire her with confidence.

Peter was also there, Peter who regularly deserted his parasitology laboratory to participate in this republic of simple people that we'd invented. Never wearing the same suit, dressed with refined elegance, he did violence to himself, swallowing the rational critiques that came to him in the presence of the beings we invoked. A high-level researcher, he'd decided, God knows why, to explore other forms of reason. He'd just bought an old Rolls, to me the most beautiful of all, a Silver Cloud II. We chuckled when we observed the astonished looks of our colleagues, the university folks from Paris 8, their eyes wide open at the sight of the capitalist vehicle gliding like a breeze into our far-left parking lot. Peter seemed genuinely concerned for Amokrane, whose fundamental anguish he perceived.

I don't recall if Fang Ling was with us that day. She didn't come very often; though she always accompanied our Chinese patients. She had a laughing intelligence and knew how to deliver the most acerbic remarks with a radiant smile. She explained so many things to us about the ecology of spirits in China, which ones you invoke, which ones you take to court. But Souren, the Armenian with the crude tongue, was there, I'm sure. With his hair and his thick curly beard, he was living proof of the realism of Assyrian bas-reliefs. And Henriette, the Berliner, always trying to reconcile the complexities of life's beings with the world of her youth composed of psychoanalysis and good intentions.

Amokrane greeted each, learning about their family, their mother tongue—sometimes saying a word about what he knew of these distant lands. Then he turned to me: 'I have to warn you,' he said firmly, 'I will not under any circumstances agree to talk with you, unless you begin by answering one question—just one question.'

I immediately suspected then that this consultation would be a very long one. 'Ask me your question.'

And so he asked: 'What was there at the beginning?'

At first, I did not grasp his meaning. He was asking what was there at the beginning. What beginning? So, I turned to Abdelhamid: 'He wants you to tell him about the creation of the world.'

'Really? The creation of the world?'

The Big Bang or Genesis? What does he want to know that he doesn't already know? At the beginning, the earth was *Tohû wâ bohû*, as the biblical text puts it. How to translate? 'At the beginning, the earth was deserted and disorganized' . . . without structure, without plan, without coherence . . . 'Without God', that's what's implied. That's what the word *bohû* means. Does he want to talk about a time without witness? Does he want to talk about the origin of his suffering? 'At the beginning.' But what beginning?

It was a Tuesday. I looked at each of those around me. I turned towards Saliha, a Kabyle woman, queen of the unconquered; the folds underlining her eyes had retained the imprint of the wind. Deep within myself, I identified her with the Kahina, warrior priestess, 'the Kabyle Joan of Arc', who for the longest time resisted the seventh-century Arab invasion until she was beheaded. Wild Saliha, the irreducible. Precious Saliha, who had not renounced the spirits that make one dance, nor the plants that bring one ease. She lowered her head, not knowing how to respond to Amokrane's question. I turned then towards Loubaba, of the honeyed words, Loubaba who knew how to speak of misfortune with a stream of polished words. Sweetness has always frightened me; it often announces violence. Sweet Loubaba, indispensible for the violence of healing!

'It seems to me that he's asking this question of *you*,' she said. 'It's you he wants to hear.'

Lucien, with whom we had so often discussed questions of origins, must have been absent that day, leaving me alone, without a placenta to seek, without the dead to feed, without a fontanelle to incise. Usually, we embodied two complementary roles, like the good cop–bad cop of American thrillers. He the night, I the day; to him the words that escape, to me those that arrive. The only thing that came to me were certain expressions that must have come from his grandfather: 'Break your head', 'Search through the multitude . . .', 'Don't be overcome by fog.'

The psychologist accompanying Amokrane diverted our attention a bit by offering some fragments of his history. She explained that, at the beginning, he had had a problem concerning marriage. Born to a Marabout family in which he was supposed to choose a paternal cousin, a young woman with the same name, that of his tutelary ancestor, he'd married a stranger. And on his wedding day, he'd been unable to deflower her. The *taleb*, the 'healer', had burnt incense; another questioned the sacred book and concluded that it was a *s'hur*, a sorcery attack. In the end, Amokrane could only approach Tassadit, his intended, after an animal sacrifice in the sanctuary of the saint. They were barely twenty years old. They decided to emigrate to France. For a time, Amokrane worked courageously, in the harmony of the four children born to him in France, and all was well with the world. Three years ago, he'd let himself be seduced by a neighbour, a Moroccan. There had been screams and arguments. The woman's husband had burst into Amokrane's home, accusing him, insulting him. They came to blows. Six months later, after he'd given up this adulterous relationship, one night, the 'phenomenon' descended onto him. He couldn't really identify it, most likely a supernatural being.

I turned towards Amokrane.

'How to know?' he replied to my unspoken question. 'The voice is sometimes feminine, sometimes masculine. No, it's not the Moroccan woman. Nor is it a *djinn,* I'm certain, because I don't believe in *djinn*s. No, it's a "phenomenon", a phe-nom-e-non.'

Since that night, the 'phenomenon' spoke to him unceasingly, sometimes in his head but also in his ears. What was it saying? It was questioning him, but in an irritating manner. For example: Why was he going a certain way? Why was he leaving the house? Why was he staying in bed? Or it was criticizing him, apostrophizing him, even sometimes insulting him. But it was also instructing him, urging him to doubt his religion. Amokrane supplied me with a host of improper questions that were filling his mind.

'Why be a Muslim? Why not Christian, Jewish or Buddhist? And why not no religion at all? What was there before the Prophet? What were Muslims before the Prophet? And before Allah? And before the dinosaurs? Before the sun? 'Which is why I asked you this when I entered,' he repeated. 'What was there at the beginning?'

With Lucien, during our visits to Benin, I'd learnt the stories of the Yorubas. In the beginning, Olodumaré was bored. What could he do, he who was both matter and space, object and will? He extended indefinitely, in a dense, undifferentiated totality. To introduce life, he offered the first sacrifice. What could he cut, he who was everything, the all? There was nothing at hand. He cut himself. Of the two halves, one remained him; from the other, seven gods emerged. He cut some more and divided the group of gods into two: on one side the first six, and on the other the one people call Legba. The divinities, who did not know what to do in this infinite world, took refuge on a palm tree that had sprung up in the middle of the ocean, surrounded by waves. And the gods settled according to the separation, the first six on one branch, and the seventh, Legba, on another.

Here then was the beginning, in the time before time. Olodumare, the creator god, gave different elements to each of the divinities to differentiate them: to Shango, lightning; to Ogun, iron weapons; and to Omolu, also called Sakpata, smallpox. But to the last one, the seventh, the youngest, he gave a simple stone. This stone, which in Yoruba is called 'black the eyes open', the farther one throws it, the more it falls at your feet. This stone is the origin of the earth. It is to Legba, the unconquerable, that he conferred the capacity to create.

I said none of all this to Amokrane; I only thought of it while wondering how to answer his initial question. Amokrane questioned me again: 'I'm going to ask you another question. I need to know. Have you practised some magic on me? Perhaps you worked from a distance? The phenomenon informed me about you before I entered this room. It told me, "Don't believe him!" But with the phenomenon, I never know what to think. Perhaps it means that in fact I should believe you. Who can know?'

I turned towards Alhassane and asked him to recount the origin story of the Manding people. I knew the stories; we'd often discussed them—with him, with Malamine, with Youssouf Cissé as well.

At the beginning were the twins. A first pair of twins, a boy and a girl, who gave birth to another pair, who engendered in turn a pair of twins, and so on and so forth. It was perfect; it was orderly, constructed for eternity. But such a world, the world of the beginning, has no history. And so, God split them; the twins were separated. The human's twin became the *djinn*; or perhaps it was the oppposite . . . the *djinn*'s twin was the human. They departed, going its own way. The human chose the village, the *djinn* preferred the bush; the human chose the predictable, the djinn the excesses. And so, since that time, the *djinns* enjoy creativity and humans preserve the memory of it.

But then, how to make the world continue? Humans cannot reproduce without the help of the *djinns*; their organizations, their structures, would soon suffocate life in its seed, reinstating the uniformity of the initial time. That is why, whenever it is a matter of founding a village, for example, or a family, or even only to give birth, humans renegotiate their alliance with their founding twins.

Poor Amokrane. He'd thought he'd founded a family in France. He too had the naivety of migrants. He saw his son, Mohand, looking at him with commiseration. Before us, the sixteen-year-old adolescent was sadly shaking his head. He was ashamed of this father who was spilling such senseless words. Amokrane had thought that in order to be a man it was enough to live according to man's law, but his twin had caught him, thrown him to the ground, reminding him of the initial contract.

The Yorubas, the Mandingos, all know that, in each generation, the same danger presents itself, threatening to halt the flow of life. Creation is not an act accomplished for eternity. No, creation begins anew each day. Olodumare separated the first gods into two groups, the first six on one side, and Legba, the seventh, the divine producer of disorder, on the other. In Benin, I had seen dozens of representations of Legba, set up on the thresholds of houses, in order to protect them from boredom and death. The Jewish people's most beautiful invention is their calendar. In order to establish life, they separated the week into two, on one side the first six days, on the other, Shabbat, the Sabbath. Among the Jews, the days are a kind of divinities, six on one side, the seventh on the other, like the gods of the Yorubas. For Jews, it is sufficient to separate, scrupulously to observe the Sabbath, to establish life and joy in one's home. For the Jews, creation is accomplished every week.

I now understand Amokrane's question; it is also mine. As a migrant, you can certainly survive. But one day the question of creation arises, and so you wonder, how was it at the beginning? And everything collapses, like a house of cards. It's clear that in the beginning there was division. But each creator god initiated a different type of division. Olodumaré, the Yoruba, at first divided himself, then he divided the gods into two groups—six and one. As for the Jewish God, He 'withdrew' it is said, to leave room for the world. Then He separated day from night, the waters above from the waters below, and to conclude, He separated the days into two groups, six on one side and, on the other, the Sabbath.

Youssouf Cissé, researcher and hunter, who also knew the origin stories, one day reported that for the Bambaras, life was born from the original break. Matter, compacted from the beginning was crossed by a sort of lightning, a fracture. From there the first sign appeared and it was the spinning, in a spiral that descended from the highest heaven, the first created, which the Bambaras recognized as the characteristic of the *djinn*s. It's true that you can sometimes seek them out, in the bush, take hold of a leaf to raise it in a whirlwind. The creator god of the Bambaras next created other movements, the rising, the falling, the flowing, like that of a river's waters. And to conclude he created harmony in the unfurling of time.

Each creator god can be known by his way of fracturing, then dividing the compact core of the origins. Who was there at the beginning? Your god! It's your god who was there at the beginning, Amokrane! Because it's truly the gods who created men and not the inverse! Feuerbach was wrong, Marx too, and Freud as well. The gods created humans, and as one travels the globe, it's easy to see that different gods created different men.

A moment of relaxation after the tension of the discussion.

Cups of coffee begin to circulate, tongues to loosen.

Amokrane turns towards Abdelhamid, whispering secrets into his ear. His wife relaxes a bit, hearing Saliha's advice. Beside me, Catherine is silent. She is giving me sidelong glances, dumbfounded. Her eyes question me. I know what she's asking. What then to make of those whose father was created by one god, and the mother by another. Catherine, the rock with a diffuse sensuality, who harvested words and thoughts, who had the gift of finding an object, a date, a book, a citation. Catherine, engaged in putting the world back in order—and she would do so, beyond all expectation! Her father was Christian, her mother Jewish. She was no more double than any of us; she was not divided, not afraid. She had retained only a sort of hesitation, as if her thought could never be certain. It is not modernity that invented mixtures; it has only accelerated them. But the gods perhaps have not reacted as quickly. If religions are the sciences of the gods, concerned with learning their natures and demands, politics should be that of their pedagogy.

Through my remarks during this consultation, I sent each person back to the source of their vitality, Mariam to the red men, her Peule ancestors, of whom it is said in West Africa that they are hybrids of Blacks and Whites, and Viviane to the unspeakable horror of her ancestor, a slave, violated by a White man. Humans mingle out of pleasure or from force, but their gods remain of the same substance, of the same metal, always imposing the same restrictions on their faithful. It is the gods we must from now on educate, to whom we must impart our multiplicity. I looked around at this astonishing assemblage of educated individuals conscious of their attachments—my friends, Abdelhamid, Saliha, Viviane, Catherine. They were the prefiguration of that organization indispensable to our modernity, from which will emerge one day, I am confident, a true parliament of the gods.

When fertile females are born in a hive, the old queen flies off, with a part of the swarm, to establish a new hive elsewhere. I found myself dreaming of Yom-Tov, the grandfather of my maternal grandfather, the Grand Rabbi of Egypt, who decided to abandon the community for which he was responsible, departing one day on a white donkey headed for Jerusalem.